# What Your Colleagues Are Saying . . .

This resource is for all your students. It will guide your instruction and invention such that your students are making progress and you will have evidence to support their next steps learning. It's an amazing collection of ideas that you can implement tomorrow to impact the reading skills of your students.

—**Douglas Fisher**
Professor, San Diego State University

Wiley Blevins provides teachers new to the science of reading with the missing manual for making any literacy program's phonics instruction more effective. This book will help build their instructional decision-making skill and capacity for more effective lessons. A must-have for those serious about equitable outcomes for all students.

—**Zaretta Hammond**
Author of *Culturally Responsive Teaching and The Brain*

Wiley Blevins's new book, *Differentiating Phonics Instruction for Maximum Impact*, is a must-read for all educators. When it comes to word learning, one-size-fits-all is not a viable option. But, with Wiley's book in hand, teachers become prepared to implement a systematic, responsive, and joyful approach to building and using word knowledge. This easy-to-navigate resource includes plentiful research-supported routines, lessons, and tools that are sure to enhance existing classroom instruction. Teachers—get ready to confidently support the success of ALL classroom learners!

—**Pam Koutrakos**
Instructional coach, consultant, and author
*Mentor Texts That Multitask* and the *Word Study That Sticks* books

Wiley Blevins's book is essential for teachers. He cuts through the clutter surrounding phonics, providing his readers with a clear understanding of what should be taught and why it is important. He also provides effective, research-based practices designed to meet the needs of every student in the classroom. An indispensable resource.

—**Melanie R. Kuhn**
Jean Adamson Stanley Faculty Chair in Literacy at
Purdue University and Moderator of thereadingforum.com

Wiley Blevins dispels the myth that differentiation is something that occurs only after a whole class lesson fails to meet individuals' needs. Through concrete examples, he shows us simple ways to bake differentiation into all instructional plans, programs, and resources. He also shares ways to modify instruction on the spot to support both student enrichment and acceleration. I can't wait to use this book in my day-to-day work with teachers.

—**Leah Mermelstein**
Consultant and author of *"We-Do" Writing*

In his inimitable way, Wiley Blevins once again advances phonics instruction with practical, fresh routines straight from the classroom. His guidance is specific and actionable—so much so that I could often "see" phonics lessons playing out. And, the book supports lasting instructional change with guidance for instructional leaders with "look-fors." What a gift this book is to educators everywhere.

—**Heidi Anne Mesmer**
Professor, Literacy Education, Virginia Tech

# Differentiating Phonics Instruction for Maximum Impact

# Differentiating Phonics Instruction for Maximum Impact

## How to Scaffold Whole-Group Instruction So All Students Can Access Grade-Level Content

### Wiley Blevins

Differentiation is *not just* what happens in small groups after a lesson has failed to meet individual needs. It is *not just* what should be happening during whole-group lessons. Differentiation needs to happen before, during, and after a lesson. It must be baked into the DNA of your instructional plan, program, and resources in order to meet the needs of all your students every minute of the day.

CORWIN Literacy

FOR INFORMATION:

Corwin

A SAGE Company

2455 Teller Road

Thousand Oaks, California 91320

(800) 233-9936

www.corwin.com

SAGE Publications Ltd.

1 Oliver's Yard

55 City Road

London EC1Y 1SP

United Kingdom

SAGE Publications India Pvt. Ltd.

Unit No 323-333, Third Floor, F-Block

International Trade Tower Nehru Place

New Delhi 110 019

India

SAGE Publications Asia-Pacific Pte. Ltd.

18 Cross Street #10-10/11/12

China Square Central

Singapore 048423

Vice President and
  Editorial Director:  Monica Eckman

Executive Editor:  Tori Mello Bachman

Associate Content
  Development Editor:  Sarah Ross

Editorial Assistant:  Zachary Vann

Project Editor:  Amy Schroller

Copy Editor:  Karen E. Taylor

Typesetter:  C&M Digitals (P) Ltd.

Proofreader:  Dennis Webb

Indexer:  Integra

Cover Designer:  Scott Van Atta

Marketing Manager:  Margaret O'Connor

Printed in the United States of America

*Library of Congress Cataloging-in-Publication Data*

Names: Blevins, Wiley, author.

Title: Differentiating phonics instruction for maximum impact : how to scaffold whole-group instruction so all students can access grade-level content / Wiley Blevins.

Description: Thousand Oaks, California : Corwin, 2024. | Series: Corwin literacy | Includes bibliographical references and index.

Identifiers: LCCN 2023039083 | ISBN 9781071894279 (paperback) | ISBN 9781071931493 (epub) | ISBN 9781071931509 (epub) | ISBN 9781071931516 (pdf)

Subjects: LCSH: Reading—Phonetic method. | Reading—Remedial teaching.

Classification: LCC LB1050.34 .B539 2024 | DDC 372.46/5—dc23/eng/20231012
LC record available at https://lccn.loc.gov/2023039083

This book is printed on acid-free paper.

24 25 26 27 10 9 8 7 6 5 4 3

# Contents

# PART II: HIGH-IMPACT ROUTINES

# PART III: TOOLS TO USE

# CHAPTER FOURTEEN

Visit the companion website for downloadable
items at **resources.corwin.com/differentiatingphonics.**

# About the Author

**Wiley Blevins, EdD**, studied at the Harvard Graduate School of Education and Bowling Green State University. He is an author, educational consultant, and researcher, and has taught both in the United States and South America. Wiley has written over 17 books for teachers, including *A Fresh Look at Phonics, Phonics From A to Z, Differentiating Phonics Instruction for Maximum Impact,* and *Choosing and Using Decodable Texts*. He has authored several phonics and reading programs and wrote the phonics brief by the International Literacy Association (Meeting the Challenges of Early Literacy Phonics Instruction). Wiley's current focus is on adaptive technology, differentiated professional development, and children's literature. Wiley has written over 100 children's books and is SVP and Associate Publisher at Reycraft Books, a new imprint focused on publishing books by authors and illustrators from under-represented groups.

# PART I

# Responsive Phonics Instruction

Photo source: iStock.com/monkeybusinessimages

# CHAPTER ONE

# Why Introducing All Students to Grade-Level Content Is Key

## And Common Misconceptions About Tiered Instruction

Walk into any classroom and the range of student needs will be wide. In a Grade 1 classroom you might have students who are just learning English as a second or third language. You might have some students who can't read simple CVC words (consonant-vowel-consonant words) like *cat* and *run* and others who are already reading multisyllabic words like *funny* and *kitten*. You might have students who learn new high-frequency words like *they* and *said* after only a few exposures and others who need dozens or more exposures and more intensive instruction and practice. The responsibility of all of us working in classrooms is to meet the needs of *all* our students. We must provide instruction, especially whole-group instruction, that doesn't just "teach to the middle" in which students below grade-level expectations are lost and students above grade-level expectations are bored because they already know it. Instead, we need to provide instruction that meets the widest range of student needs. This instruction scaffolds, front-loads, modifies, and enriches at key points of the lesson to offer access and value in that instruction.

> We must provide instruction, especially whole-group instruction, that doesn't just "teach to the middle."

Take a look at this simple five-word spelling test (Figure 1.1) I gave the first week of school to some Grade 1 students in New York City. What does it tell us about each student's phonics instructional needs? What does it tell us about phonics instruction in general?

Figure I-I • Simple Five-Word Spelling Test

| DICTATED WORDS | STUDENT I | STUDENT 2 |
|---|---|---|
| 1. **sad** | 1. sad | 1. sad |
| 2. **big** | 2. big | 2. bag |
| 3. **rake** | 3. rakce | 3. rak |
| 4. **coat** | 4. cote | 4. kot |
| 5. **flower** | 5. flowre | 5. flar |
| **STUDENT 3** | **STUDENT 4** | **STUDENT 5** |
| 1. sd | 1. Seivrne | 1. ePraH |
| 2. bg | 2. Bog | 2. PEBL |
| 3. lk | 3. Rigvet | 3. eHPLn |
| 4. kt | 4. Tetvai | 4. sieHgt |
| 5. fw | 5. Levneia | 5. cSeph |

**Notice that Student 1** has mastered spelling words with short vowel CVC spellings and is starting to apply (and overgeneralize) final-*e* spellings. Since this skill will not be focused on for a couple of months in Grade 1, this student is starting the year above grade-level expectations. The whole-group lessons currently planned will cover skills the student has already mastered and will not accelerate his growth unless enrichment opportunities are provided during those lessons. This student can also benefit from small-group instruction on skills further along in the phonics scope and sequence to challenge him and accelerate his growth in reading and spelling.

**Notice that Student 2** has a good grasp of consonants and short vowel spellings and is meeting grade-level expectations. This student is spelling words with more sounds using more letters, so she has strong phonemic awareness skills as well. The whole-group lessons planned will address this student's needs.

**Notice that Student 3** is a vowel avoider. She has some grasp of consonants but did not master short vowel spellings in kindergarten. While the early lessons planned in Grade 1, which review the skills from kindergarten, will be beneficial, this student needs additional work segmenting sounds and attaching a spelling to each sound. Increased focus on reading short vowel CVC words will be helpful. Using sound boxes and counters, so the student can physically mark each sound and then replace each counter with a spelling, will be beneficial during whole-group lessons (already planned), but additional work with these tools needs to be offered during small-group instruction. In addition, reading and building word chains using minimal contrast short vowel words (e.g., *hat, hit, hot*) will also be extremely helpful.

**Notice that Student 4** has some grasp of beginning sound-spellings but lacks the ability to segment words and attach learned spellings to each sound. While the student understands that words have letters, there are a lot of kindergarten skills this student has not mastered. The whole-group lessons will be quite challenging for this student. The incorporation of some alphabet review and simpler words in activities will be helpful, but other scaffolds and supports will need to be provided. In addition, intensive small-group work on phonemic awareness (at the phoneme/sound level) and alphabet recognition (basic letter-sounds) will be needed.

**Notice that Student 5** knows that words are comprised of letters but lacks necessary phonemic awareness and alphabet recognition skills. The student, whose name is Stephanie, does have some awareness of the letters in her name. This student needs intensive supports during whole-group and small-group instruction and is severely behind grade-level expectations.

What do these data on Grade 1 students reveal? The realities that most teachers in elementary schools face—a wide range of student needs. This is what makes teaching phonics so challenging and why differentiation is such an important consideration when planning instruction.

The range we see in just these five students also speaks to the reality that we *do* have tools to lean on as we differentiate instruction. First and foremost—a strong scope and sequence. In fact, when we know the scope and sequence *for each grade*, we can be nimble and responsive with our students. By knowing the scope and sequence for the grade I am teaching, I can quickly determine which words in a text students can fully sound out and, if they struggle, I can provide phonics-based corrective feedback (e.g., highlighting the missed sound-spelling and guiding the students to sound out the word again using that reviewed information) to reinforce skills with which they lack fluency. Further, knowing the scope and sequence of the grade I am teaching, as well as the scope and sequence of the previous grade and next grade, allows me to place students along a learning continuum during small-group time to meet them where they are in terms of their decoding needs. As you read this book, think of your scope and sequence as the spine of your instruction.

## DIFFERENTIATION: IT'S NOT TEACHING TO THE MIDDLE

Current understandings of differentiation: engaging and challenging every student at every skill level during whole-group lessons

*Photo source:* iStock.com/SolStock

Differentiation isn't a new concept, but it's certainly one that teachers have strong feelings about. *Can't be done! Too difficult and not realistic! A myth!* These are all statements I've heard and read in books, articles, and on social media. Yet the progress of every child in our classrooms is our responsibility. Most instructional programs are targeted for those "in-the-middle" on-grade-level students. The instruction is too easy for some of the students and too difficult for others. We all know that bored and/or frustrated students don't sit quietly smiling during these lessons. And the reading growth of these students can and should be targeted as well during the entire instructional day, not just after the lesson failed to meet their specific needs.

In the mid-1980s, I was preparing for my student teaching, arguably the most exciting semester for any college of education student. I couldn't wait! I was assigned the cooperating teacher everyone feared—the one whose student teachers were often seen crying. Undaunted, I was convinced I would win her over. For the first several weeks of student teaching, she asked me to sit in the back of the room and observe her. While my other student teaching friends were slowly taking over the teaching of different subjects—reading, math, science—I was still sitting in the back of the room watching.

So, one day I asked my cooperating teacher when the "teaching" part of student teaching was going to begin. She sighed and said I could introduce the spelling words and concept on Monday at the end of the day. I raced back to my dorm room and spent the weekend planning a spelling lesson that would knock her socks off!

The moment arrived. I stood in front of the classroom as a hushed silence swept over the room. Both the students and I could feel the excitement in the air. My cooperating teacher sat in the back of the room (my usual perch) with her notebook and a pen in hand. As I worked my way through the lesson, it felt so good. It was like fireworks were exploding in the background. In the back of the room my cooperating teacher wrote feverishly. At one point, I actually wondered if she was a walking thesaurus. I mean, how many ways can you write "great job!"

When the lesson ended, I strutted to the back of the room to receive my praise. My cooperating teacher announced we would debrief after the children left for the day. So the moment of my triumph arrived. We sat at a table as I eagerly

> She looked at me, then her notes, then back at me, and said, "Wiley, I don't know what you were doing in front of my class, but it wasn't teaching."

awaited her positive feedback. She looked at me, then her notes, then back at me, and said, "Wiley, I don't know what you were doing in front of my class, but it wasn't teaching." I sat in stunned silence remembering all her previous student teachers in a puddle of tears back at the dorm.

She went on. "I have five students (she listed them) who are above level. They got nothing out of that lesson. You wasted their time. How can I have you in front of my class if that is what you are going to do?" Then she listed four students who were quite a bit below grade level. She said, "My job is to get these students on grade level. They got nothing out of that lesson. They were completely lost. How can I let you stand in front of my class if you are going to ignore their needs?" Then she mentioned the one student in our class who had recently moved to the United States from China. Her father was a professor at the nearby college. "Now there's Liz. She could have been in Beijing and gotten more out of that lesson," she announced.

I was crushed.

But she didn't stop there.

"I simply can't have you doing whatever you called what you were doing in my class. From now on, I need you to write me detailed lesson plans to review before the lesson. I need to know *when* and *how* you are going to address the needs of my above-level and below-level students as well as Liz, our English learner. You cannot waste a minute of their instructional time. If you need to do things before the lesson to get them ready, tell me what that is. And if you need to do some follow-up things after the lesson, tell me what those things will be. But you better be giving them what they need DURING the lesson."

I scraped back to the dorm repeating in my head: "There's no crying in student teaching. There's no crying in student teaching!"

Although what my cooperating teacher did felt brutal at the time, it was brilliant. She taught me how to think in the most global sense every time I stood in front of a group of students.

She taught me the realities of what good teaching requires and the realities of the range of needs my future students would have. She taught me how to teach—to really teach each and every child.

I thank her.

It's not easy, but it can and must be done.

And that's the purpose of this book—to help you succeed. The activities in this book will help you adjust and modify whole-group instruction. The activities will, over time, give you a nimble, global sense of all your learners. These activities will become habits. My hope is that these adjustments will also give you ideas about how to better meet the needs of all your students before, during, and after whole-group lessons and will serve as springboards to other things you might do for your students. The best teachers I've worked with over the years are never satisfied; they are constantly looking for ways to refine and elevate their teaching. It's what makes teaching so much fun. We keep learning and improving!

> She taught me how to think in the most global sense every time I stood in front of a group of students.

## COMBINING DIFFERENTIATED INSTRUCTION AND ADAPTIVE INSTRUCTION

While differentiated instruction is defined differently by different educators, what I'm addressing is actually a combination of **differentiated instruction** and **adaptive instruction**. Differentiated instruction is carefully planned activities and supports decided prior to a lesson. Adaptive instruction is on-the-spot modifications made to meet student needs that arise during instruction. For example, I was recently modeling a dictation lesson in a kindergarten classroom I had never been in before. The teacher had told me she was working with the students on tapping the sounds in short vowel CVC words and had done some spelling of these words. As we started the lesson, it became clear to me that several students could not easily orally segment the sounds in CVC words. So I made an on-the-spot decision to draw sound boxes on the board. I guided students to stretch the sounds in words. Then we marked the sounds on the sound boxes. Finally, I guided students as we identified each sound and replaced the mark with the letter for that sound. We did several of these together. I continued dictating words and, for students who needed to continue using the sound boxes, I gave them a sound box template and counters. For students who didn't need that support, they tapped the sounds and wrote the words. These modifications are often necessary during lessons as issues arise, and it's helpful to have these potential scaffolds planned and the necessary resources (e.g., sound boxes and counters) readily available.

# TEACHING PHONICS BASED ON RESEARCH

Before we dig into the specifics of differentiating and adapting phonics instruction, let's take a quick look at where phonics instruction fits into all that we know we must do to help our students become skilled, proficient readers who enjoy exploring the world of books.

Differentiated instruction is carefully planned activities and supports decided prior to a lesson. Adaptive instruction is on-the-spot modifications made to meet student needs that arise during instruction.

English is an **alphabetic language**. We have 26 letters in our alphabet. Alone and in combinations, these letters and spellings stand for the 44 sounds in English. Phonics instruction is the teaching of these spelling-sound correspondences. Learning the basic phonics skills we typically teach in kindergarten, Grade 1, and Grade 2 gives students a tool to access, or sound out, approximately 84 percent of the words in English text. Students have enough skills to figure out all or nearly all of the word. That's a powerful tool!

Strong phonics instruction starts with a **defined scope and sequence** that serves as the spine for the instruction and all associated activities. This scope and sequence must be developed to progress from easier to more complex, separate the teaching of confusing letters and sounds, and contain a **built-in review and repetition cycle to ensure mastery** of taught skills so students can cumulatively transfer these skills to all reading and writing demands. The **application of the phonics skills to reading and writing** is essential because it is through this application that the learning "sticks." This application begins with the reading of **controlled, decodable texts** and dictation, or guided spelling, wherein the teacher models how to transfer a student's growing phonics skills to writing, as well as to writing about the decodable texts read to deepen comprehension. As students learn increasing numbers of phonics skills, they can begin to tackle bridging texts, which are a bit less controlled, and finally more authentic trade books.

The two words most closely associated with this strong phonics instruction are *explicit* and *systematic*. **Explicit** means that sound-spelling correspondences are initially taught directly to students, rather than through a discovery, or implicit, method. That is, students are taught, for example, that the /s/ sound can be spelled with the letter *s*. A discovery method is less effective for initial teaching because it relies on students having prerequisite skills that some do not have (e.g., sophisticated phonemic awareness skills). As a result, the implicit method can leave some students behind—either not learning the new content or having difficulties and confusion (Adams, 1990).

**Systematic** means that the instruction builds from easy to more complex skills with built-in review and repetition to ensure mastery. Two critical aspect of systematic phonics is that the instruction has a clearly defined scope and sequence (rather than being random) and that it builds from the known to the new in easy steps that make the new learning more obvious and easier to grasp. **For example, systematic does NOT mean that all children receive the same phonics instruction on the same day at the same time and ONLY that instruction.** Students need to receive both grade-level instruction during whole-group lessons (with differentiation and modifications for some students), and targeted small-group instruction that addresses a lack of mastery of previously taught skills (for below-level students), reinforcement of current skills (for on-level students), or acceleration along the phonics scope and sequence (for above-level students) if the students have already mastered the week's focus skills. That is, this small-group instruction meets students where they are and rapidly moves them forward.

The best phonics instruction is also **active, engaging, and thought provoking**. Students are playing with letters and

> Strong phonics instruction starts with a **defined scope and sequence** that serves as the spine for the instruction and all associated activities.

sounds and discussing what they observe about how words work to deepen their understanding of our alphabetic system so they can read and write. Phonics instruction involves talk. It involves observation. And it involves tons of application to authentic reading and writing experiences.

## WHAT THE SCIENCES OF READING BRING TO THE PARTY

At the time I'm writing this book, educators are engaged in a national conversation about what has been labeled the **sciences of reading.** This conversation clarifies the important role of phonics in early reading development. While the sciences of reading conversation is *not* solely about phonics, early efforts have been focused on improving the phonics instruction provided to students. The big shift in the sciences of reading is going beyond the research conducted by teachers and educational researchers and incorporating research by other fields of science, such as that of cognitive scientists who conduct brain research, linguists, speech language pathologists, and so on. This inclusion has led to a broadening and deepening of our understanding of what comprises the most effective early reading instruction. Unfortunately, national surveys in English-speaking countries have revealed that this knowledge base is largely unknown by classrooms teachers because it is not being taught in many colleges of education. In addition, some of the most popular, widely used reading instructional resources do not incorporate this research into their materials. These circumstances have led to local and state boards of education funding additional training for teachers in this knowledge base. That knowledge base is now making its way into classrooms.

This new emphasis on the sciences of reading has led to some important changes in phonics instruction that are greatly benefiting students, but this whirlwind of information has also resulted in some serious misconceptions and overgeneralizations as surface knowledge of the research has led to preference over data, and even legislation based on limited research support.

> The big shift in the sciences of reading is going beyond the research conducted by teachers and educational researchers and incorporating research by other fields of science, such as that of cognitive scientists who conduct brain research.

It should be stated that the sciences of reading is *not* a program and is *not* a philosophy. It is just a body of evidence about how to teach children to read. We know a lot, but there are still unanswered questions. This growing body of knowledge enables teachers to fine-tune their instruction to maximize student learning. That's exciting! But we should also proceed with caution and work to understand more deeply the research and its limitations for classroom application.

> It should be stated that the sciences of reading is *not* a program and is *not* a philosophy. It is just a body of evidence about how to teach children to read.

## THREE MODELS OF READING TO CONSIDER

One of the most interesting outcomes of the national sciences of reading conversation is that two older models of reading have been reintroduced to teachers to clarify what is needed in order for students to learn to read: The simple view of reading (SVR) by Gough and Tunmer (1986) and Scarborough's Reading Rope (2001). These older models of reading help to situate phonics instruction in its proper place (Gough et al., 1996). Recent models, such as the active view of reading (AVR; Duke & Cartwright, 2021), have also emerged. This model includes the connections across the learning strands (e.g., bridging skills like vocabulary, morphology, and fluency) and the importance of things like executive functioning (self-regulating) skills.

**The simple view of reading** (Figure 1.2) explains that reading comprehension is a product of decoding (all the work readers do with phonics) and language comprehension (e.g., vocabulary and background knowledge learned primarily through listening to complex read-alouds in the early years of instruction). One without the other does *not* lead to skilled readers who can readily understand the texts they need to tackle at each grade level. For example, if we overemphasize phonics instruction in the early grades and don't simultaneously and equally build students' content knowledge and vocabulary, students won't have all the necessary skills to tackle more complex texts as they move up the grades. Likewise, if we don't do a good enough job with phonics in the early grades, students will enter later grades without the ability to decode words effortlessly with these basic skills. This lack of facility will lead to fluency issues, which have a negative impact on comprehension as students aren't able to get through enough words quickly enough to form meaningful units as they read. When I work with schools in developing a systematic approach to phonics instruction, one of the first questions I ask is, *What is your structured plan for building knowledge and vocabulary? Are you using your read-alouds in the primary grades to do this?* Every school should have a plan in place.

Figure I-2 • The Simple View of Reading

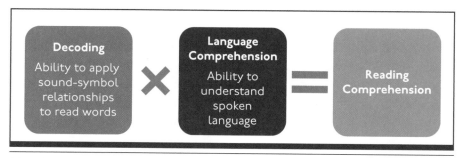

SOURCE: Adapted from Gough and Tunmer (1986) and Hoover and Gough (1990).

While the SVR model explains a lot, it does not provide specifics on what, when, and how to teach word recognition and language comprehension—necessary details for planning effective instruction.

**Scarborough's Reading Rope** (Figure 1.3) clarified the SVR model and illustrated how, as one becomes more fluent in word recognition skills (e.g., through phonics) and more strategic in using language comprehension skills, these skills begin to intertwine—creating skilled, fluent readers capable of comprehending more complex texts. This model identifies key areas in each "bucket" (e.g., word recognition, language comprehension) on which we need to focus our instructional efforts. It gives us more information about the *what*, but doesn't define *when* or *to what degree* each skill needs to be emphasized as students move through the grades.

Both models of reading highlight the critical role phonics plays and emphasize that phonics alone is not enough. In addition, the phonics instruction we deliver must be aware

Figure I-3 ♦ Scarborough's Reading Rope (2001)

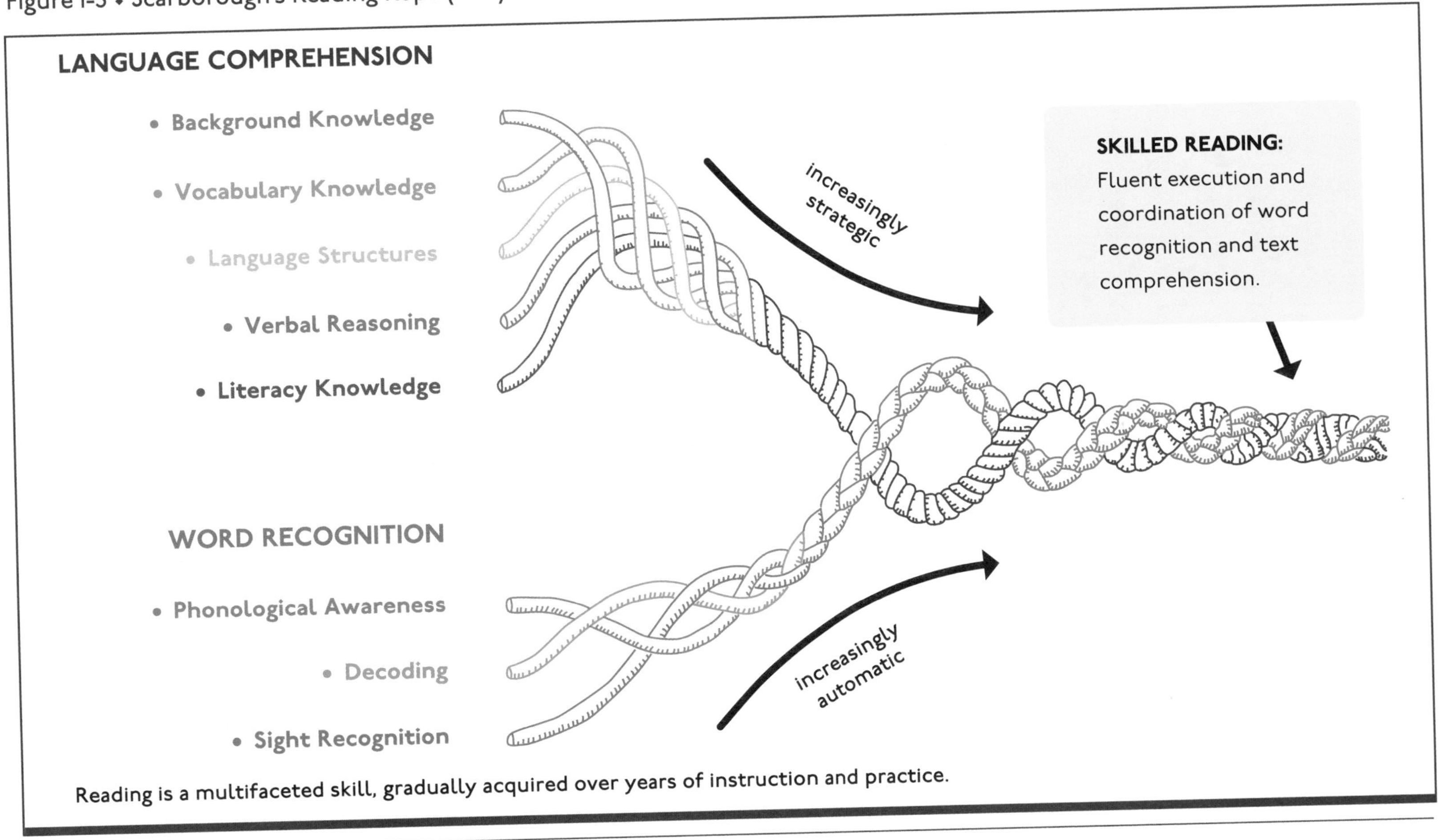

**LANGUAGE COMPREHENSION**

- Background Knowledge
- Vocabulary Knowledge
- Language Structures
- Verbal Reasoning
- Literacy Knowledge

**WORD RECOGNITION**

- Phonological Awareness
- Decoding
- Sight Recognition

*increasingly strategic*

*increasingly automatic*

**SKILLED READING:** Fluent execution and coordination of word recognition and text comprehension.

Reading is a multifaceted skill, gradually acquired over years of instruction and practice.

SOURCE: Adapted with permission from Scarborough (2001).

The phonics instruction we deliver must be aware of grade-level reading demands while simultaneously meeting students where they are.

of grade-level reading demands while simultaneously meeting students where they are.

**The active view of reading model** (Figure 1.4) is a newer model of reading by Duke and Cartwright and high-lights important aspects of reading development that overlap and serve as bridges between the word recognition and language comprehension "buckets," such as vocabulary, morphological awareness, and fluency. We often hear fluency being described as the "bridge to comprehension," and this model shows its importance and the research-based impacts that focusing on these aspects has on student development. Research shows that many of the bridging aspects of reading instruction have a significant impact on student growth (see effect sizes).

Fluency is and should be a focus from the beginning of phonics instruction (hence the need for cumulative and spaced practice during which students continue to work on a skill for an extended period and then are asked to use the skill in purposeful ways at spaced intervals to ensure mastery). Fluency is a key reason students struggle as they encounter more complex texts throughout the grades and is an oft overlooked aspect of reading instruction.

Also, as fluency increases, teaching switches from focusing on decoding words using individual spellings to focusing on morphology (a morpheme is the smallest unit of meaning in a word, such as the base word, suffix, prefix, or Greek or Latin root), which helps readers use word parts to both decode words and determine meaning. Morphology increases in importance and instructional emphasis as students move through the grades. Phonics does not end in Grade 1 or 2 after the basic skills are introduced. It transforms into word study, which involves syllabication strategies, the teaching of syllable types, morphology work using roots and affixes, looking at spelling consistencies across related words (e.g., sign/signal/signature), and the understanding of how authors use context clues (e.g., restatements, definitions, synonyms) to assist readers in sounding out words and determining word meanings. There is so much we can and should teach our students about how English words work that will benefit them in both reading and spelling, well past kindergarten and Grade 1.

Figure I-4 ◆ The Active View of Reading Model

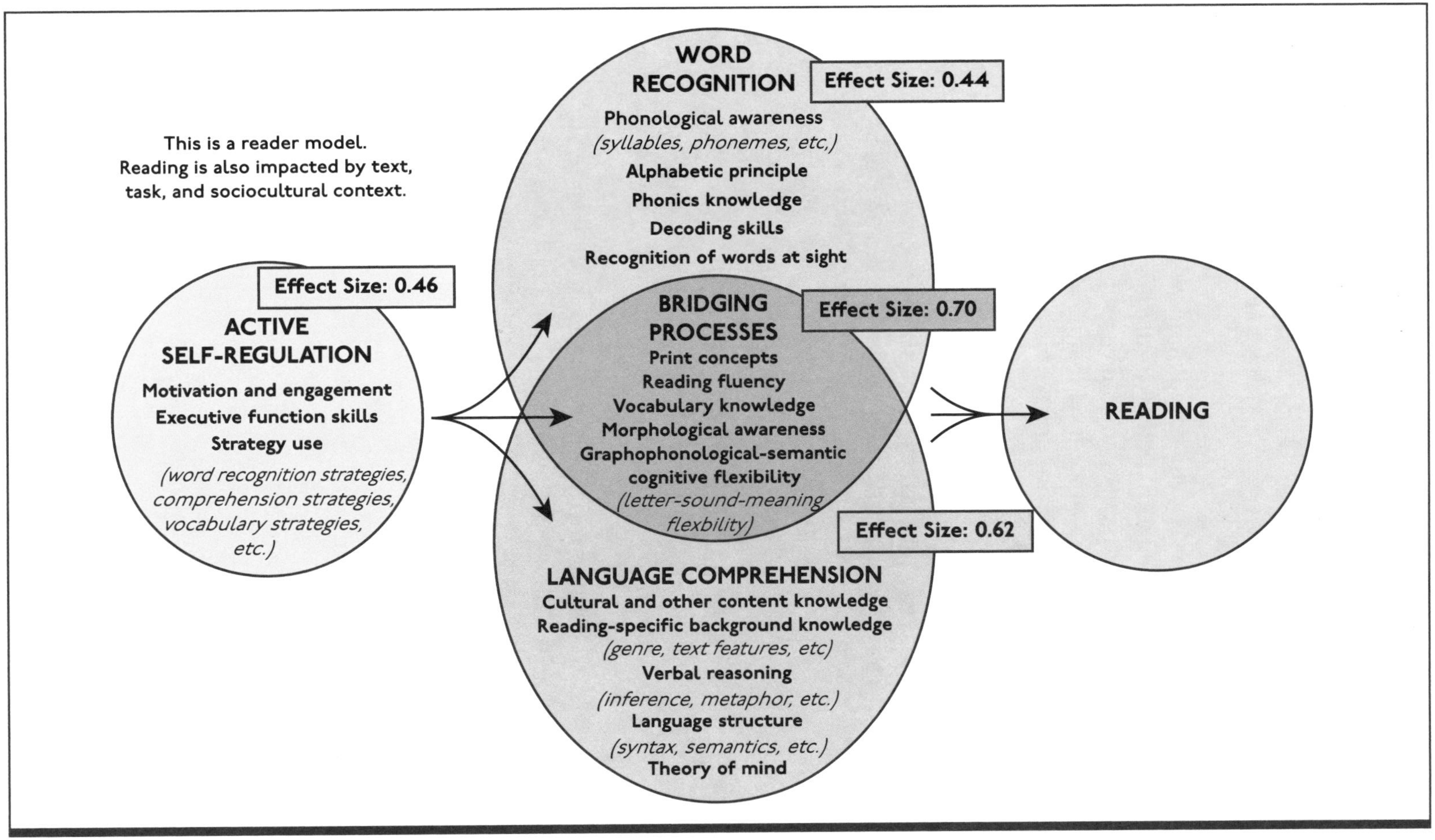

**WORD RECOGNITION**  Effect Size: 0.44
Phonological awareness
*(syllables, phonemes, etc.)*
Alphabetic principle
Phonics knowledge
Decoding skills
Recognition of words at sight

**BRIDGING PROCESSES**  Effect Size: 0.70
Print concepts
Reading fluency
Vocabulary knowledge
Morphological awareness
Graphophonological-semantic
cognitive flexibility
*(letter-sound-meaning flexibility)*

**LANGUAGE COMPREHENSION**  Effect Size: 0.62
Cultural and other content knowledge
Reading-specific background knowledge
*(genre, text features, etc)*
Verbal reasoning
*(inference, metaphor, etc.)*
Language structure
*(syntax, semantics, etc.)*
Theory of mind

**ACTIVE SELF-REGULATION**  Effect Size: 0.46
Motivation and engagement
Executive function skills
Strategy use
*(word recognition strategies, comprehension strategies, vocabulary strategies, etc.)*

This is a reader model.
Reading is also impacted by text, task, and sociocultural context.

READING

**SOURCE:** Used with permission of the International Reading Association, from "The Active View of Reading," Duke, Nell K. and Cartwright, Kelly B., Vol. 56, 2021; permission conveyed through Copyright Clearance Center, Inc.

## WHY IT ALL COMES DOWN TO THIS: DIFFERENTIATED PHONICS INSTRUCTION

All three models of reading show that phonics instruction is critical, and that's why in the last several years we've seen a dramatic increase in whole-group phonics instruction—every child needs grade-level instruction, and whole-group time is the surest way to provide that access. Students get more time with and feedback from the teacher, as opposed to working independently for large chunks of the literacy block. But this is where misconceptions arise, and vexing problems of practice flare, with teachers understandably asking, *How do I teach a vast range of students in a single whole-group lesson?* This entire book is devoted to answering that question. Because, while small-group instruction is critical, and tiered instruction is forever, it is my strong belief that excellent Tier 1 whole-group instruction reduces the number of students who will need Tier 2 and Tier 3 support. Excellent, *differentiated* whole-group instruction, that is. It also significantly increases the amount of time every student gets direct instruction from the teacher.

> It is my strong belief that excellent Tier 1 whole-group instruction reduces the number of students who will need Tier 2 and Tier 3 support.

With the increase in whole-group as opposed to small-group teaching dominating the delivery of phonics instruction, in large part due to a lack of teaching and paraprofessional personnel, it is imperative that teachers differentiate instruction for students below grade-level expectations, for those above grade-level expectations, and for those who are multilingual learners. No instructional time should be wasted for any students, and phonics lessons can and should be modified to support the wide range of students' needs found in most classrooms. In addition, phonics instruction needs to occur in both whole-group and small-group settings to meet these needs more fully. The graphic in Figure 1.5 shows the big picture of where differentiated phonics instruction resides.

### Tier 1 Whole-Group Instruction

All students must be introduced to grade-level content, including each grade's key phonics skills. Too often students who haven't mastered previous grades' phonics skills are stuck in grade-level

Figure I-5 • Where Phonics Instruction Resides

| Tier 3 Intensive Intervention | Pull-Out/ Resource Room | | Flexible Skills-Based Lessons |
| Intensive Support in Small Groups or One-on-One | | | |

| Tier 2 Intervention, Maintenance, and Acceleration | AFTER Whole-Group Lesson | Above Grade-Level Expectations | Acceleration in Scope and Sequence |
| | | On Grade-Level Expectations | Maintain Skills to Stay On Track |
| Additional Differentiated Support in Small Groups | | Below Grade-Level Expectations | Remediate Previous Skills Not Yet Mastered |
| | | Multilingual Learners | Language Support |

| Tier I Grade-Level Content | DURING Whole-Group Lesson | Above Grade-Level Expectations | Enrichment Support |
| | | On Grade-Level Expectations | Planned Lessons |
| Grade-Level Instruction That Meets All Students' Needs | | Below Grade-Level Expectations | Scaffolds and Modifications Embedded |
| | | Multilingual Learners | Scaffolds and Modifications Embedded |

| FrontLoad Content Prepare Scaffolds | BEFORE Whole-Group Lesson | Below Grade Level Preread Decodable Build Vocabulary | Multilingual Learners Preread Decodable Build Vocabulary |

19

instruction that is not differentiated and unnecessarily frustrating for them, or they are placed along a phonics continuum based on their instructional needs and only receive that instruction. This lower-level phonics instruction is often provided at a slow rate, resulting in students not gaining access to all their grade-level skills. This pace condemns these students to continuing to the next grade behind, and further so. While it is essential that we address students' learning holes in their foundational skills, we must also expose them to grade-level skills. But how do we do this when these students are so far behind? We differentiate the instruction and modify our expectations of their learning outcomes during the whole-group lessons, such as focusing on a smaller set of grade-level words to read or spell during the lesson. These differentiations to whole-group lessons not only ensure that students are introduced to grade-level skills but also appropriately modify their learning expectations and decrease their cognitive load and frustration. Modifying expectations does *not* mean lowering expectations.

Modifying expectations does *not* mean lowering expectations.

## Tier 2 Small-Group, Skills-Based Instruction

Small-group time is when you reinforce the week's target phonics skill to make sure on-level students stay on track, provide targeted instruction for below-level students to address deficits in previously taught skills, and accelerate learning for students who have already mastered the week's focus skill.

Comprehensive phonics and spelling assessments and a phonemic awareness assessment will be needed to help you determine each student's specific skill needs (also an alphabet assessment for kindergarten students). The "Comprehensive Phonics Surveys" and the "Comprehensive Spelling Surveys," especially the "Quick Assessment for Placement," which are all provided in the appendix (pages 232 and 243), are organized around skill categories (e.g., short vowels, long vowels, consonant blends and digraphs) to give you an instructional starting point with students.

Comprehensive phonics and spelling assessments and a phonemic awareness assessment will be needed to help you determine each student's specific skill needs.

**For below-level students**, be careful to adjust the pace of this instruction based on how students are reading and writing words with the skills. It will be unnecessary to spend an entire week on some of the skills if students are showing competence with the skills. Other skills might require more than a week.

**For above-level students**, use the "Comprehensive Phonics Surveys" and the "Spelling Survey—Quick" in the appendix to place them farther in the scope and sequence and begin instruction there during small-group time. During whole-group lessons, you can provide enrichment activities.

**For on-level students**, small-group time offers you an opportunity to keep them on track for grade-level reading success. For example, some students progress at an expected rate until they hit a wall when the complexity increases too quickly, such as when multiple spellings for long or complex vowels are introduced. This extra instruction and practice can assist in keeping them on track.

## Tier 3 Small-Group or Individual Instruction

Contrary to common practice, learners in Tier 3 need loads of reading and writing practice with target words and meaningful books instead of isolated skill work.

*Photo Source:* iStock.com/Halfpoint

Some students will require even more intensive intervention support than Tier 2 instruction can provide. A well-designed, research-based intervention resource is required to meet these students' needs, as it will take some time to get them back on track and able to be successful in Tier 1 and Tier 2 classroom instruction.

It's all about intensity, intentionality, and the dosage of instruction and practice students need to master the basic phonics skills and beyond. Each tier of instruction increases that dosage. My one main concern with Tier 3 instruction is

My one main concern with Tier 3 instruction is that it too often involves increased amounts of isolated skill work and focuses *only* on phonics. What these students need is the opposite. They must get increased amounts of the *application* of phonics skills *to* reading and writing.

that it too often involves increased amounts of isolated skill work and focuses *only* on phonics. What these students need is the opposite. They must get increased amounts of the *application* of phonics skills *to* reading and writing. So a little instruction should be followed by loads of reading and writing words with the target skills.

In addition, vocabulary and background knowledge must be added to this Tier 3 work. It can be a separate stream of knowledge-building support or tightly connected to the simpler decodable texts that students are reading. For example, if students are reading a simple, decodable text on frogs, the teacher can read aloud a more complex text on animal habitats. The language and information learned in this read-aloud can be carried over to the discussion of the simple, decodable text to elevate the language used and build more of the skills these students need. If students struggle in reading, they read very little. It is through reading that vocabulary and background knowledge are built for our older students. So we need to fill in those gaps through our complex read-alouds, the rich conversations we have about those read-alouds, and the ways we connect them to conversations and writings about other texts students read.

FIVE KEY TAKE-AWAYS

1. When whole-class, Tier I phonics instruction is high quality and effective, fewer students will need Tier 2 and Tier 3.

2. Differentiating phonics instruction in whole-group lessons is the most efficient way to keep the most students engaged in—and succeeding with—grade-level skill acquisition.

3. Plan small-group instruction to target the needs of students who are above grade level, on grade level, and below grade level. Students in *each* group need sufficient challenge to be engaged and grow their skills.

4. Below-grade-level students need the opposite of what they are often given—they need MORE access and opportunities for meaningful reading and writing practice and MORE vocabulary and content-knowledge building.

5. The sciences of reading is a body of research, not a program. In addition, a scientific base to instruction does not mean that there is a fixed, inflexible way of doing things. The most effective teachers teach systematically and explicitly while also differentiating and adapting plans based on current student data.

# CHAPTER TWO

# What Is Differentiated Phonics Instruction?

## And Why It Lifts Even Students Who Are Above Grade Level

So what does differentiated phonics instruction *really* look like, for whom, and when? Throughout the book, I will provide detailed examples and sample lessons, but let me start with a quick overview. What follows are differentiated supports for a Grade 1 phonics lesson. When taken as a whole, these can feel overwhelming—so many adjustments to each part of a daily phonics lesson are needed. My recommendation is to observe these in their entirety, and then start slowly when applying them. For example, start with one instructional routine, such as blending. Incorporate the differentiated supports for several weeks to a month until they become habit. Then move on to another key phonics instructional routine. Over time, you will build your capacity to meet the needs of all your students throughout the entire phonics lesson in ways that will be immediately impactful and habit forming.

## DIFFERENTIATION: ABOVE-LEVEL STUDENT SUPPORTS

Students who are reading and spelling words above grade-level expectations for phonics need both **acceleration** and **enrichment** to maximize their learning during each week's instruction. These supports can be used during whole-group lessons to differentiate the instruction and practice or during small-group lessons. These are the students whose needs are most frequently ignored during whole-group lessons (and who rarely get much small-group support). However, we can do much to help them fully realize their learning potential through some simple lesson modifications.

## Acceleration

The most effective and impactful thing you can do for above-level students is to place them along the phonics continuum at a point that best meets their instructional needs. This will maximize their learning growth potential.

- **Administer the "Comprehensive Phonics Survey" and the "Comprehensive Spelling Survey—Quick"** (see the appendix) to determine student mastery of grade-level phonics skills. Use these results to determine a starting point for one or more small groups of above-level students. Just a word of caution: Some students who are reading above grade-level expectations are not consistently and accurately spelling words with *phonics* skills that are at grade level. The results of these assessments will often show students at different points along the phonics continuum (e.g., higher in decoding/reading than encoding/ spelling). These students will benefit from the grade-level encoding work done with each whole-group lesson.

- **Use the weekly lessons in your program or resource during small-group time** to teach and practice these advanced skills. Since you probably won't have time to meet every day with above-level students, focus on key parts of the lesson such as blending, reading and writing about decodable texts, word building, and dictation.

- **Assign other portions of the lesson for independent or partner work**. Generally speaking, providing above-level students with independent, enriching reading and writing experiences linked to this small-group support is a powerful way to meet their needs.

## Enrichment

So that above-level students benefit from whole-group lessons on the on-level skills you have determined they have mastered, do the following:

- **During whole-group lessons**, include additional above-level student supports provided in the samples that follow to offer enrichment for key activities (e.g., word building, dictation, reading decodable text, and writing extension, including a word bank with more complex words).

- **During small-group time**, you can also use these enrichment activities for students who are only slightly above level and can benefit from this stretching of their skills. However, acceleration (by placing students further in the scope and sequence) is the best way to maximize their learning potential.

Following are some possible ways to differentiate key components of a phonics lesson for students who are above grade-level expectations. Since most phonics curricula do not provide these supports during whole-group lessons (only during small-group lessons), you can fold these into your weekly instructional routines.

# SAMPLE ABOVE-LEVEL SUPPORTS

| PHONICS FOCUS: LONG *A* SPELLED *AI* AND *AY* | | |
|---|---|---|
| **PHONICS ROUTINE** | **SUPPORTS** | **EXAMPLES** |
| **Blending** | Connect the target skill with words containing that skill and with more complex skills. For example, if the skill is short *o* and you have students blend CVC words like *hop* and *hot*, add words at the end that include consonant blends and digraphs like *stop* and *chop*. This skill is found later in the scope and sequence. For other skills, add multisyllabic words, such as compound words or words with suffixes and prefixes, that you want to continue working with students on during small-group time (e.g., *read/reread, hope/hopeful, ball/football*). | Add challenge words at the end of the activity, such as multisyllabic words like *raining* and *playing*.<br><br>**See Chapter 5: Blending Routine** |
| **Dictation** | Add more complex words as you did for blending. You might choose to use some of those "challenge" blending words during dictation. Dictate these words for students to spell *while* the other students are self-correcting their on-level dictation (that you have displayed on the board for students to check). | Add the following words and sentence after students spell the simpler words for that lesson: *rainbow, playing, My birthday is in May.*<br><br>**See Chapter 9: Dictation Routine** |
| **Word Building** | When the word-building activity is completed, have on-level students practice reading to partners the words that you have written on the board as they are built, or provide time for students to build their own words using the letter cards. Use this time to guide above-level students to build the more complex words. | Add the following word sequence to the activity after students build the simpler words: *brain, train, training, retraining.* |
| **Word Sort** | Add more complex words to the word sort or replace some of the existing words with more complex ones. You might choose to use some of the words from the blending and dictation activities. | Add these longer, more complex words to the word sort, or replace some of the existing words with these: *raining, rained, playing, played.*<br><br>**See Chapter 11: Word Sort Routine** |

| PHONICS FOCUS: LONG *A* SPELLED *AI* AND *AY* | | |
|---|---|---|
| **PHONICS ROUTINE** | **SUPPORTS** | **EXAMPLES** |
| **Word Ladder** | This can become an independent or partner activity. Students can move to another part of the room to complete it. | Have students complete the word ladder independently or with a partner. |
| **High-Frequency Words** | Include the new high-frequency words from the stories you read with students during small-group lessons. | Have students write sentences in their writer's notebooks for the high-frequency words from their phonics lesson. Include additional words for these students that are further in the scope and sequence or that are generally more difficult for students (e.g., words that begin with *th* and *wh* like *there/where* or *that/what* and irregular words like *they* and *does*). Each week, have students read their sentences from the beginning of the year to a partner. |
| **Read Decodable Text** | When rereading the week's decodable text with on-level students to build students' fluency, have above-level students reread their text from the small-group lesson or another more complex text during that same time. It's just a book switch—no need to move to a different part of the room or disrupt the flow of the lesson. | Have students read the decodable text during the initial whole-class lesson to confirm mastery of the week's phonics skill in context. When students are rereading the decodable text during subsequent whole-group lessons, have above-level students read or reread a decodable text from their accelerated phonics lesson further in the scope and sequence or read a self-selected book during this time. |
| **Writing About Decodable Texts** | Add more sophisticated vocabulary words for students to include in their writing and review the writings to work on more complex skills, such as sentence construction and variety. | Challenge students to include these two words in their writing about the decodable story: *explore, discover*.<br><br>Put these words in a word bank on the board. Model for students how to combine sentences and select more precise vocabulary. |

# DIFFERENTIATION: BELOW-LEVEL STUDENT SUPPORTS

It is estimated that about 95 percent of elementary students, regardless of background, are cognitively capable of learning to read when they receive direct instruction on the foundational skills of reading.

*Photo Source:* iStock.com/BartCo

Students who are reading and spelling words below grade-level expectations for phonics must have access to grade-level content, but that content needs to be differentiated and scaffolded. In addition, modified expectations are needed. These supports can be used during whole-group lessons to differentiate the instruction and practice, or during small-group lessons. **Modified expectations do NOT mean lower expectations.** Modification generally relates to the amount of content students are expected to cover in a specific time or to the supports provided for their reading and writing tasks (e.g., smaller chunk of text in the time given, sentence frames and a word bank for writing support). Although phonics instruction needs to have a clearly defined scope and sequence (with built-in review and repetition to achieve mastery), that does not mean students learn phonics skills in that predetermined sequence. We can work on learning new skills while also working on fluency with previously taught skills yet to be fully mastered.

## Frontload Content

The students who are reading and spelling below grade level will need supports before, during, and after a lesson to access the content properly and solidify their learning. Keep in mind that small-group work is not something we do only after students have struggled in a lesson. As a teacher, you know which students might struggle with a specific activity or reading during a whole-group lesson. A brief small-group lesson *prior* to the whole-group lesson might be the necessary scaffold or support. Here are some examples:

- **If students are reading a decodable text in a whole-group lesson, have them listen to an audio recording** of the story during small-group time and follow along with the text prior to the whole-class reading. This will enable them to participate more fully in the lesson when reading, talking about, and writing about the story.

- **In addition, guide students through an echo read of all or a portion of the text prior to the whole-group lesson** to further prepare students for the whole-class reading. This echo reading should include a focus on the big ideas and key vocabulary in that text.

## Modify Expectations

So that below-level students benefit from whole-group lessons on skills that are further in the scope and sequence from where they are in terms of mastery and to minimize their frustration with the new content, do the following:

- **Hold students accountable for only a portion of the content**. For example, during blending work, have students practice only a subset of the words to get to mastery with them. During word sorts or word building, have them sort or build only a subset of the words. This ensures work with the new skill, but in a way that is not overwhelming.

- **Revisit the skill during small-group lessons.** Because you have given these students access during the whole-group lesson, they have a solid introduction to grade-level skills to build on when they get to that skill during small-group lessons (once they have worked on previous skills they haven't yet mastered).

- **Design instruction with the awareness that students don't learn phonics skills in a lockstep manner.** Once they understand how the system works (i.e., we have letters that, by themselves and in different combinations, can be used to stand for the sounds of English), it's a matter of us introducing them to these specific sound-spellings and giving them ample practice to master them and easily transfer them to all reading and writing situations. If we create a classroom environment in which we model and promote active observations of words, some students begin learning sound-spellings through these observations before we formally introduce them.

## Address Previous Skill Needs During Small-Group Time

So that students who are below grade level benefit from phonics instruction, focus during small-group time on skills you have determined they have not mastered.

- **Make sure the pacing is robust during these lessons** (e.g., not too slow that students can't catch up), and you focus on high-impact activities like blending, word building, dictation, and reading and writing about decodable texts.

# SAMPLE BELOW-LEVEL SUPPORTS

| PHONICS FOCUS: LONG A SPELLED AI AND AY | | |
|---|---|---|
| PHONICS ROUTINE | SUPPORTS | EXAMPLE |
| **Blending** | Modify expectations by reducing the number of words you hold students accountable for. In this way, they learn a subset of the words with the new skill, and you minimize their frustration (cognitive load). | Have students focus on only some of the words in the blending exercise. Hold them accountable for only a small set of words (e.g., the first two rows of words or the first two words in each row plus the review words).<br><br>**See Chapter 5: Blending Routines** |
| **Dictation** | Include words with review skills in the dictation. If you can provide minimal contrasts, such as dictating *ran* (lower level) and then dictating *rain* (on level), this contrasting will help make the new learning easier to grasp and will allow students to connect it to known (or previously taught but perhaps not yet mastered) skills. | Make sure words that can be decoded with previously taught skills are also included in the dictation activity. In addition, do more dictation focusing on these previously taught skills during small-group time. |
| **Word Building** | Modify expectations by reducing the number of words you have students build with the new skill. Make sure simpler words are at the beginning of the word-building activity. Then have students read, build, and write simpler words on their own that you write on the board while you continue the activity with the rest of the students. | Guide students to build only the first two to three words, and then write a list of words on the board using previous skills for them to build and read with partners using letter cards while you continue the whole-class activity.<br><br>You can also involve students in the entire whole-group lesson, but circulate and offer support for harder words (e.g., write words or difficult spellings for students to trace), and then do word building during small-group time using simpler skills yet to be mastered. |
| **Word Sort** | Modify expectations by reducing the number or complexity of words you hold students accountable for sorting. Select a few high-utility words. In this way, students learn a subset of the words with the new skill, and you minimize their frustration. | Select a subset of the words from the word sort (e.g., four to five words for students to sort). Holding students accountable for only some of the on-level words will reduce the cognitive load.<br><br>As an alternative, have students sort half of the on-level words in the word sort and replace the other half with simpler words (e.g., contrasting long *a* and short *a* spellings).<br><br>**See Chapter 11: Word Sort Routine** |

*(Continued)*

(Continued)

| PHONICS FOCUS: LONG *A* SPELLED *AI* AND *AY* | | |
|---|---|---|
| **PHONICS ROUTINE** | **SUPPORTS** | **EXAMPLE** |
| **Word Ladder** | Frontload the activity by completing it in small groups and then repeating it during the whole-group lesson. You might wish to complete only a portion of the ladder during small-group time. | Guide students to complete the word ladder during small-group time, with support from you, prior to the whole-group lesson (a revisit of the activity). This provides a preview of the word meanings (vocabulary support) and another opportunity to practice spelling the words. |
| **High-Frequency Words** | Provide word banks, sentence frames, and sentence starters for support. | Have students write sentences in their writer's notebooks using the high-frequency words from their phonics lesson. Provide sentence frames or starters as needed. Each week, have them read their sentences from the beginning of the year to a partner. Include words from previous lessons they are still working on. |
| **Read Decodable Text** | Frontload the reading of the decodable text during independent time (listening to an e-version) and small-group time (echo reading and discussing all or a portion of the book). So when students read the book during whole-group time, it will be their second or third exposure to the book. When students reread the book on subsequent days, have them reread only a portion of the text to minimize frustration. | Have students follow along while listening to an e-book version of the decodable text (if available) before reading it with the whole class. Also, meet with students during small-group time to echo read and discuss all or a portion of the text prior to reading it with the whole class. Focus on vocabulary and key ideas. |
| **Writing About Decodable Texts** | Provide sentence stems and frames (including summary paragraph frames for reluctant writers) to scaffold the writing. | Provide sentence stems and frames (including summary paragraph frames) to scaffold the writing. Prompt students to complete the stems or frames, and THEN have them continue writing beyond that scaffold. In addition, provide a few words in a word bank for students to include, such as a couple of decodable words and one or two target high-frequency words. |

- **Level up where possible during small-group lessons**. For example, if students are still working on short vowel CVC words (e.g., *top, sell*), include those words in the blending, dictation, and word-building exercises but also include a few words with skills later in the sequence that you have introduced during whole-group time, such as a consonant blend (e.g., go from *top* to *stop* and *sell* to *smell*). The focus of the lesson is on the earlier skills, but the connection to newer skills is also made and reinforced in a simple and scaffolded manner.

## DIFFERENTIATION: MULTILINGUAL LEARNER SUPPORTS

Today's phonics instruction for multilingual learners takes an asset-based approach.

*Photo Source:* iStock.com/Courtney Hale

What should be the focus during phonics for English learners? This question is one I encounter often in my work in schools around the country. Many supports can and should be provided for multilingual learners during the literacy block and beyond. When it comes to phonics instruction, however, there are three main areas of support that have the biggest impact on student learning.

1. **Sound Transfer and Articulation:** Provide information on which sounds do and do not transfer in

various languages, such as Spanish and multiple Asian languages. This is important for several reasons:

- It can alert you to the need for articulation support in which you model and help the student focus on the position of the mouth (tongue, lips) and whether or not the sound is voiced (throat vibration) or unvoiced (no throat vibration) to help students feel and say the sound.

- In addition, if students have some literacy learning in their primary language, knowing the sounds and (especially) the spellings that transfer can accelerate English learning.

- If you are teaching in a dual-language setting, knowing which sounds and spellings transfer can help you better focus your instructional time (e.g., not repeating transferrable skills and focusing on the nontransferable skills).

2. **Vocabulary:** Even though most of the words in early phonics instruction are Tier 1 words commonly used or understood by students when speaking or listening, for English learners, some of these words might be unfamiliar. In addition, the words get progressively more difficult as students move up the scope and sequence. The goal of phonics instruction must be both the decoding of words with the newly taught phonics skill *and* knowing the meanings of these words. The activities are not word-calling endeavors; we are building foundational skills in multiple areas of language. This requires you to pull out words from the week's instruction and do additional vocabulary work during small-group lessons to support these students. These words need to be

- addressed in concrete ways (e.g., showing a picture, acting out, demonstrating),

- connected to a student's prior knowledge (e.g., saying the word in the student's primary language), and

- connected to other known words (e.g., through a webbing of related words, discussing synonyms and antonyms, and so on).

You can reinforce these word meanings while reading.

3. **Build on Students' Primary Language:** The best instruction for multilingual learners takes an additive, asset-based approach and values what these learners bring from their primary language to the learning of English. This might be vocabulary (e.g., Spanish-English cognates), knowledge of a writing system (e.g., sharing some or most of the same printed letters), and so on. Simple modifications, such as allowing students to discuss their understanding of a story in their primary language before guiding them to express these ideas in English, can go a long way to honoring their existing language skills.

## SAMPLE MULTILINGUAL LEARNER SUPPORTS

| PHONICS FOCUS: LONG *A* SPELLED *AI* AND *AY* | | |
| --- | --- | --- |
| **PHONICS ROUTINE** | **SUPPORTS** | **EXAMPLES** |
| **Introduce Sound-Spelling**<br><br>Sound Transfer and Articulation Support | Focus on the articulation of sounds that do not transfer from English to the students' primary languages.<br><br>If articulation videos and sound wall cards are available, use these resources. | In Cantonese, Vietnamese, and Hmong, there is only an approximate transfer for the long a sound. Focus on articulation. Model correct mouth position. Contrast /a/ and /ā/. Have children make each sound to feel the difference. If handheld mirrors are available, use them for support. |
| **Vocabulary Focus**<br><br>Blending Lines and Decodable Texts | Introduce words for all pictured items. Also, select a set of words from the decodable texts, blending activities, and other words to preteach. You might need to focus on a few each day during a small-group lesson.<br><br>Even though the words in decodable texts are often basic, Tier I words, some words in these books might be unknown to our multilingual learners who are learning | Preteach the name of each pictured items on all activity pages. Also, identify key objects, places, and people in the decodable text illustrations. |

*(Continued)*

(Continued)

| PHONICS FOCUS: LONG *A* SPELLED *AI* AND *AY* | | |
|---|---|---|
| **PHONICS ROUTINE** | **SUPPORTS** | **EXAMPLES** |
| Blending Lines and Decodable Texts *(continued)* | English as an additional language; they might also be unknown to our native English-speaking students with limited literacy backgrounds. For example, words like *log, tad, sip, cap, vet, zap*, and others might be unknown to some students.<br><br>Select a set of these words each week and teach them during small-group time. The goal is for students to be able to both read and define them by the end of the week.<br><br>To really know a word, we need to focus on its meaning, sounds and spelling, and the context in which it is used. For example, for the word *bat*, we would discuss the word's multiple meanings (a flying animal and something used in a baseball game to hit the ball). For the word *rain*, we might discuss what it is, what we wear on a rainy day, and what time of year it usually rains. So during these targeted vocabulary lessons, do the following **vocabulary routine**:<br><br>• Read aloud the word in English and in the student's primary language. You can use a translation app on your phone for students to hear the word in their primary language. Have students say the word, and address any pronunciation or articulation needs.<br><br>• Provide a brief definition using simple, kid-friendly language. Demonstrate, act out, or pantomime the word.<br><br>• Connect the word to known words. Start with synonyms and antonyms. For example, connect the word *cap* to the more familiar word *hat*. Or connect the word *sad* to its opposite—*happy*. | Preteach other words students will encounter in the weekly texts and activities: *plain, stray, sail, brain, raise, trip, train, museum.*<br><br><br><br>*Image Source:* iStock.com/Yayasya |

| PHONICS FOCUS: LONG *A* SPELLED *AI* AND *AY* | | |
|---|---|---|
| **PHONICS ROUTINE** | **SUPPORTS** | **EXAMPLES** |
| | • Display a photo or create a simple drawing to illustrate the word. For example, words like *bug, log,* and *hut* can be easily shown. However, illustrations are sometimes not available.<br><br>• Have students say the word three times at the end of the lesson to increase the number of times they have said and heard the word. | |
| **Read Decodable Text**<br><br>Preview the Text | Frontload the reading of the book prior to the whole-group lesson so students can participate successfully in that lesson. | Use the following **preview routine** for any decodable books or passages in your reading program or set of materials.<br><br>**Introduction:** Introduce the story by reading aloud the title and explaining that students will be reading this story to (1) practice their skill in sounding out words and (2) check their understanding of what they read. Remind them that we also read stories for fun and to learn new things. Praise students for their efforts and remind them that you are there to help with any challenges.<br><br>**First Read:** Have students follow along while listening to the audio recording (e-book version, if available) during independent work time prior to the whole-class reading.<br><br>**Second Read:** Guide students through an echo reading during small-group time before the whole-group lesson. Focus on vocabulary and general understanding.<br><br>**Third Read:** Have students read the book during the whole-group lesson with their peers. This careful scaffolding should enable them to have a more successful whole-group reading experience. |

*(Continued)*

(Continued)

| PHONICS FOCUS: LONG *A* SPELLED *AI* AND *AY* | | |
|---|---|---|
| **PHONICS ROUTINE** | **SUPPORTS** | **EXAMPLES** |
| **Writing About Decodable Texts** | Provide sentence frames and sentence starters at various levels of language acquisition to aid students in writing. Create frames and starters for each week of instruction. | Provide sentence frames and sentence starters to scaffold the writing. Then prompt students to write more (not simply stopping when the frames are completed).<br><br>Examples:<br><br>Spain is ____.<br><br>Spain has ____ and ____.<br><br>In Spain, _____. |
| **High-Frequency Words** | Include activities during small-group instruction to frontload (or review) the key words, such as the Read, Build, Write routine or activities with two-sided flashcards. | **Read, Build, Write Routine**<br><br>Select the target high-frequency words from the decodable text and any others that students struggle with and engage them in the **Read, Build, Write** activity.<br><br>• **Read** Write the word. Have students read it aloud.<br><br>• **Build** Have students build the word with letter cards.<br><br>• **Write** Have students write the word on paper or a dry-erase board. Prompt them to say each letter name as they write the word.<br><br>When these tasks are completed, guide students to orally segment the sounds in the word. Then review the written parts of the word students already know (e.g., in the word *said* students might know the /s/ sound spelled *s* and the /d/ sound spelled *d*). |

| PHONICS FOCUS: LONG *A* SPELLED *AI* AND *AY* | | |
|---|---|---|
| PHONICS ROUTINE | SUPPORTS | EXAMPLES |
| **High-Frequency Words** *(continued)* | | Guide students to draw a circle or box around the part(s) of the word that are irregular (e.g., *ai* in the word *said*) or unknown based on the phonics skills previously taught. They can also put a heart above these irregular spellings because this is the part they have to remember "by heart." |
| | | Students can write sentences during independent work for each of these words. To scaffold the exercise, offer sentence starters (e.g., *We have* _____). Prompt students to write sentences about a specific topic or story they recently read to make the exercise more impactful. |
| | | **Two-Sided Flashcards** |
| | | Have students write the words on one side of an index card, one word per card. You can do this during the "Write" portion of the Read, Build, Write, Extend routine. Then co-construct a simple sentence that students can write on the back of each card, using the word. You can write the sentence for students to copy. Students then practice reading the words in isolation and in context using the flash cards. These two-sided cards offer students additional exposures to these words both in isolation and in context. |

*(Continued)*

(Continued)

| PHONICS FOCUS: LONG *A* SPELLED *AI* AND *AY* | | |
|---|---|---|
| **PHONICS ROUTINE** | **SUPPORTS** | **EXAMPLES** |
| **Additive, Asset-Based Approach** | Use students' home language for support. | Allow students time to discuss stories and answers to questions in their primary language before sharing answers in English, so they can process their understanding fully as you build their oral English skills. For Spanish speakers, highlight cognates where appropriate. For students speaking an English variant or dialect, allow them to use the speech patterns in their variation of mainstream English and then, when appropriate, engage them in translation drills to go back and forth between mainstream English and their variation of English (e.g., African American English, Chicano English). |
| **Other** <br> General Support | Frontload vocabulary and reinforce it during and after lessons. | Throughout most phonics programs, there are student activity pages with many pictured items. Preview the names of these items for students before they complete the activities. |

# FIVE KEY TAKE-AWAYS

1. Students above grade-level expectations need both enrichment during whole-group lessons and challenge lessons and activities during small-group lessons.

2. Students below grade-level expectations need scaffolds and supports before and during whole-group lessons, as well as content-load modifications to minimize frustrations.

3. Students below grade-level expectations need small-group lessons to address previous skills not yet mastered while also receiving grade-level whole-group lessons.

4. Students meeting grade-level expectations might need small-group support at different points in the phonics scope and sequence based on increased challenges.

5. Students who are multilingual learners can benefit from support with articulation, a focus on sounds and spellings that do not transfer from their language into English, additional vocabulary support, and use of their primary language in an asset-based way.

# CHAPTER THREE

# High-Impact Routines

## And How They Put the Seven Components of Strong Phonics Instruction Into Action

Instructional routines allow for the most efficient teaching. They are critical to phonics instructional success. They bring a beneficial predictability to daily learning, which allows students to focus on the content rather than the task. As you master the instructional routines described in the rest of this book, you can increase the pace of lessons, and modify them to better meet the needs of your students.

We have learned a lot over the years about the most common routines used during phonics instruction. Many of the routines featured in this book have been fine-tuned over decades of research and classroom practice. All of them are considered "high-impact routines," meaning these routines focus on the skills known to develop students' literacy the best. And they all relate to the seven characteristics of strong phonics instruction, which I describe further on the next page.

In the chapters that follow, you will find high-impact instructional routines for

- Chapter 4: Progress Monitoring

- Chapter 5: Blending

- Chapter 6: High-Frequency Words

- Chapter 7: Reading Decodable Text

## For Further Support

Please note the following:

- **Differentiated application** of these routines for students below grade-level expectations, for those above grade-level expectations, and for multilingual learners are provided.

- **Creative and joyful alternatives** to many of these routines—activities that can be used occasionally to add variety and fun to your instruction—are also provided (e.g., word spinners, spinning cubes).

- **Professional development videos** by author Wiley Blevins are available on YouTube as well: https://www.youtube.com/watch?v=mdLldfB9pQM&t=4ls.

- Chapter 8: Writing About Decodable Text
- Chapter 9: Dictation
- Chapter 10: Word Building
- Chapter 11: Word Sort
- Chapter 12: Phonological and Phonemic Awareness (rhyme, oral blending, oral segmentation, phonemic substitution, phonemic addition, phonemic deletion)

In addition, important **Teacher Alerts** and **Principal/Coach Look-Fors** are provided. These are designed to target key aspects of routine application that can increase their impact on student achievement. With high-quality instructional materials that contain research-based and evidence-based routines, you can maximize your instructional time for the benefit of *all* your students.

## SEVEN CHARACTERISTICS OF STRONG PHONICS INSTRUCTION: A CHECKLIST

These high-impact phonics instructional routines are centered on the seven characteristics of strong phonics instruction. Based on my work with teachers, school districts, and publishers, these seven are characteristics that all strong phonics programs or instructional resource systems must have in place. Absence or weakness in any one or more of these characteristics can have negative effects on student learning gains. Let's briefly review them to frontload foundational knowledge for these upcoming chapters.

### I. Readiness Skills

*The two best predictors of early reading success are phonemic awareness and alphabet recognition.*

- Phonemic awareness is the understanding that words are made up of discrete sounds. A range of subskills is taught to develop phonemic awareness, with oral blending and oral segmentation having the most positive impact on reading and writing development. I refer to these skills as the *power skills.*

- Alphabet recognition involves learning the names, shapes, and sounds of the letters of the alphabet with fluency.

- Phonemic awareness and alphabet recognition are focused on primarily in kindergarten and Grade 1.

- If students cannot orally blend sounds, then they will not be able to sound out a word in print. Likewise, if students cannot orally segment a word into its constituent sounds, they will struggle writing the word because early writing involves attaching a letter or spelling to each sound we hear in a word.

- Students MUST be attending to words at the phoneme, or sound, level very early in kindergarten for the phonics instruction to make sense to them. Therefore, the phonemic awareness skills taught and practiced must be connected to these early reading and writing skills. Too often, the phonemic awareness and phonics work is siloed. That is, students are clapping syllables and producing rhymes during phonemic awareness but are expected to read and spell CVC words during phonics instruction. This disconnect is not helpful. Students need to be working on words at the phoneme level in both parts of the lesson—phonemic awareness and phonics for maximum learning benefit.

## 2. Scope and Sequence

*A strong scope and sequence that builds from the simple to the complex in a way that works best for student learning is critical to student achievement at all stages of learning.*

- While there is no one "right" scope and sequence, programs that strive to connect concepts and move through a series of skills in a small stair-step way offer the best chance of student success.

- A scope and sequence is NOT just a list of skills, and students do not master a skill in both reading and writing in the week that skill is introduced. A good scope and sequence provides information on when a skill will be introduced—when the work on that skill begins. Then, baked into the DNA of the instructional materials, must be multiple weeks of review and repetition of that skill (for most students it takes four to six weeks of intensive and intentional work to master a skill in both reading and writing). Documenting that on a scope and sequence chart can be helpful (e.g., focus/new skill and review skills included purposefully in the week's activities).

- Conceptual leaps must be considered when creating and using a scope and sequence. For example, reading CVC and CCVC words, such as *top* and *stop*, require students to connect one letter to one sound—the simplest skill conceptually. Reading words with consonant digraphs (e.g., *shop*, *chip*) requires students to understand that two letters together can be used to represent a new sound (a bit more difficult conceptually). Reading words with long and complex vowels requires students to understand that one sound can be represented by multiple vowel team spellings (e.g., *rain*, *ray*) and that the position of the spelling in the word often matters. This is conceptually even more complex. Then there are the final-*e* words with vowel teams that work together but the letters aren't together in a word (e.g., *make*, *ride*). This is very complex conceptually. A scope and sequence that bounces around "conceptually" can be challenging for students. Using minimal contrasts (e.g., going from the known to the new as in *hop/hope* and *ran/rain*) can help students better understand these conceptual leaps. Ask: *What do you see that's different? What do you hear that's different? Why?*

## 3. Blending

*This is the main strategy for teaching students how to sound out words and must be frequently modeled and applied.*

- It is the focus of early phonics instruction, but still plays a role when transitioning students from reading one-syllable words to multisyllabic words.

- Blending lines (see Chapter 5) offer one way to provide ample blending models and practice and focuses on students learning a core set of words with a new skill (e.g., eight to twelve words) that can be built on in later weeks.

- Blending work should be differentiated for the widest range of students' needs and can offer leveling up of skills, such as transitioning from one-syllable to multisyllabic words in a simpler way.

## 4. Dictation

*To best transition students' growing reading skills to writing, dictation (guided spelling) is critical and should begin as early as kindergarten.*

- While not a spelling test, this activity can accelerate both students' spelling abilities and their understanding of common English spelling patterns.

- Dictation should be done multiple times a week and can be done in both whole-group and small-group sessions, depending on time constraints and learning needs.

- Dictation should be differentiated to provide maximum benefit.

- Dictation is only one of several important encoding (spelling) activities that should be a part of the weekly instructional cycle. Others include word building, word sorts with rich conversations about spelling patterns, writing about decodable texts, and so on. The important thing is that some encoding work is done in each phonics lesson each day.

## 5. Word Awareness

*Students need opportunities to play with words and experiment with how word parts combine to solidify and consolidate their understanding of how English words work.*

- Word sorts  and word building are two key activities to increase students' word awareness.

- Word sorts are only effective if they are followed up by conversations about what students notice about spelling patterns that will help them as they write words (e.g., for long *a* the spelling *ai* only appears in the middle of a word or syllable whereas the *ay* spelling appears at the end). Formally teaching these generalizations is key.

- Word building, or word chains, include phonemic awareness (sound manipulations), decoding, and encoding work. They assist students in becoming flexible in their use of taught sound-spellings.

## 6. High-Frequency Words

*Those high-utility words that are irregular (do not follow common sound-spelling patterns) or that need to be taught before students have all the phonics skills to access them through sounding out must be addressed instructionally in a different way.*

- Typically the top 200 to 300 words are taught in Grades K–2. Past Grade 2, when the majority of the key high-frequency words have been introduced, students need to be assessed continually on their mastery of these words, as a lack of fluency can impede comprehension.

- Irregular words should not be taught as whole units to be memorized. In order for students to orthographically map these words into memory so they can be automatically retrieved and easily distinguished from other similar words, the reader must attend to the individual sounds and spellings of the word—just like they do with decodable words.

- Routines such as Read, Spell, Write, Extend and Heart Words are effective ways to help students focus on the individual sounds and spellings in these irregular high-frequency words.

- High-frequency words that become decodable at different places in the phonics scope and sequence should be included in the lessons (e.g., blending lines, dictation, decodable texts), but do not need to be taught using a routine like Read, Spell, Write, Extend because students have the skills to sound them out fully and simply need lots of opportunities to do so.

## 7. Reading Connected Text

*The type of text we use in early reading instruction has a powerful effect on the word reading strategies students develop (Juel & Roper-Schneider, 1985) and can affect student motivation to read (Blevins, 2000).*

- Controlled, decodable text at the beginning level of reading instruction helps students develop a sense of comfort in and control over their reading growth and should be a key learning tool in early phonics instruction.

- Decodable, or accountable, texts are important practice tools in kindergarten and Grade 1 to help students gain mastery in using their growing phonics skills to read words.

- Seeing the concentrated number of decodable words in these passages can also benefit students' spelling as they become statistically aware of the most common spelling patterns used in English writing.

- Bridging texts that are slightly less decodable become important practice tools as students have enough phonics skills mastered and are ready to transition to reading less-controlled texts, like picture books. Some students are ready to begin this transition near the middle of Grade 1—but still benefit from the decodable text readings for new skills because they offer intentional practice with a high concentration of words with the new phonics skill.

- For decodable texts to be highly impactful, they must be used for more than decoding and fluency-building practice. They can also be used to develop early reading behaviors, comprehension, vocabulary, writing, and syntax skills. (See Chapter 7 and 8.)

## PLUS You, the Teacher

*The power and impact of the above characteristics depend on them being implemented by a skilled, informed teacher.*

Teachers with stronger backgrounds in linguistics and research-based phonics instructional routines are better equipped at noticing and addressing student errors, have improved language of instruction, and can more easily differentiate their teaching to meet student needs. Differentiated professional development can assist schools and districts in building teacher capacity when it comes to phonics instruction.

## Professional Learning

Professional development can also be powerful when its focus is on common ways phonics instruction falters, and even fails. I have worked with schools that courageously look at their current instruction through this lens and have been amazed at the way admitting missteps galvanized change. In the next section, let's explore all this. And as I tell teachers, coaches, paraprofessionals, leaders, and all involved—being aware of these "red flags" is not about assigning blame to anyone. We each work within a system at a grade level, a school, or a district; when students aren't well served, it's the system that didn't come through, not the teacher. And it's usually the system—be it an entire staff or a district—that must work together in new, transparent, accountable ways to improve things. Everyone needs to be well-trained in effective literacy instruction. As you will discover in the next section, nine times out of ten, teachers struggle because they are using programs and resources that are flawed.

# TEN REASONS PHONICS INSTRUCTION SOMETIMES FALLS SHORT OF EXPECTATIONS

The reality is that the hard work of teaching phonics begins *after* all these characteristics are in place. Why? Common obstacles related to instruction and instructional materials often stand in the way of maximizing students' learning of basic phonics skills. These range from a lack of application to daily reading and writing experiences (where the learning "sticks") to a lack of review and repetition, resulting in decayed learning. The following are the 10 most common phonics instructional obstacles or pitfalls, all of which you have some degree of control over. Your phonics instructional materials must be analyzed for these common issues. These obstacles need to be addressed and removed to maximize student learning with the materials you are using. Even highly rated phonics materials can possess one or more of these obstacles.

## 1. Inadequate or Nonexistent Review and Repetition Cycle

We underestimate the amount of time it takes young learners to master phonics skills in both reading and spelling. When a new skill is introduced, it should be reviewed systematically and purposefully for at least the next four to six weeks. The goal must be to teach to mastery rather than just exposure. Only then can students transfer the skill to all reading and writing situations (and it takes much longer to master these skills in spelling than in reading for most students). With the fast pacing of most curricula, a more substantial review and repetition cycle often must be added. This can be achieved by increasing opportunities to practice previous skills in blending work or dictation and by the repeated readings of previously read accountable texts. The instruction must include a fluency strand that involves intentionality with daily and weekly increased practice of the skill and quick assessments to monitor both fluency (automaticity) and transfer (the ability to apply the skill to new words with ease).

## 2. Lack of Application to Daily Reading and Writing Experiences

Students progress at a much faster rate in phonics when the bulk of instructional time is spent on applying the skills to authentic reading and writing experiences rather than on isolated skill-and-drill work. At least half of a phonics lesson should be devoted to application exercises. For students who are below level, the amount of reading during phonics instruction must be even greater. You cannot achieve fluency at the rate needed unless students are picking up a book and a pencil during the bulk of a phonics lesson. Isolated skill work doesn't get students to achieve mastery at the expected rates necessary to maintain grade-level skills.

## 3. Inappropriate Reading Materials to Practice Skills

The connection between what we teach and what we have young learners read has a powerful effect on their word reading strategies and their phonics and spelling skills. It also affects students' motivation to read. Having decodable, accountable, controlled texts as part of the daily phonics lessons provides more substantial decoding practice and helps to scaffold the leap from most phonics lessons to the reading of less-controlled texts. These are critical practice tools designed to build phonics fluency. The amount of control (e.g., decodability) and the amount of time needed in this type of text varies on the basis of student needs, but generally they are key practice tools used during kindergarten and Grade 1 when new phonics skills are introduced. Adherence to a specific percentage of decodability is problematic, and no current research supports a specific percentage.

## 4. Ineffective Use of the Gradual Release Model

Some teachers of struggling readers spend too much instructional time doing the "heavy lifting," such as over-modeling and having students simply repeat (e.g., "parrot" activities). Whoever does the thinking in a lesson does the learning. Students might struggle, but they must do the work and the teacher's role is to provide timely corrective feedback and support. Lessons should involve increased amounts of student talk, interaction, and response opportunities. Active, engaging, and thought-provoking instruction is needed.

## 5. Too Much Time Lost During Transitions

Phonics lessons often require a lot of manipulatives and materials. Transitional times when materials are distributed or collected should be viewed as valuable instructional moments in which review skills can be addressed (e.g., sing the ABC song, do a phonemic awareness task, review letter-sound action rhymes to focus students' attention on an instructional goal). Every minute of a phonics lesson must be instructive. Planning these transitions is critical for their effectiveness.

## 6. Limited Teacher Knowledge of Research-Based Phonics Routines and Linguistics

Teachers with a background in phonics or linguistics are better equipped to make meaningful instructional decisions, analyze student errors, and improve the language and delivery of instruction. Also, teacher attitudes toward phonics instructional materials (e.g., decodable text) and routines (e.g., sorts, word building, blending) matter.

## 7. Inappropriate Pacing of Lessons

Some teachers spend too much time on either activities they enjoy or ones that are easier for students and less time on the more challenging or substantive activities that increase learning. Lessons should be fast paced and rigorous. They should focus on those activities that more quickly move the needle in terms of student learning, such as blending practice, dictation, word awareness activities, and reading and writing about accountable texts.

## 8. No Comprehensive or Cumulative Mastery Assessment Tools

Assessment of phonics skills must be done over an extended period of time to ensure mastery. Weekly assessments focusing on one skill often give "false positives." That is, they show movement toward learning but not mastery. If the skill is not worked on for subsequent weeks, learning can decay. Cumulative assessments help teachers determine which skills truly have been mastered. They are a critical phonics instructional tool. Assessments should evaluate accuracy and automaticity in both decoding (reading) and encoding (spelling). They can involve more formal weekly fluency checks (e.g., reading cumulative words lists and engaging in the dictation of cumulative spelling sentences) and less formal assessments such as listening to students read and assessing errors and evaluating their recent writings through a phonics lens to determine spelling skills in need of more instructional focus. These assessments can be used to adjust the pacing of the instruction as well as to form skills-based small groups.

## 9. Transitioning to Multisyllabic Words Too Late

Most curricula focus on monosyllabic words in large portions of Grade 2, yet the stories students read at that grade are filled with more challenging, multisyllabic words. More emphasis needs to be given to transitioning to longer words at this grade (e.g., going from known to new words like *can/candle* and teaching the six major syllable types). This work can begin at the end of Grade 1 to provide a closer alignment between phonics instruction and reading demands. Introducing multisyllabic words also helps students move into the consolidated alphabetic phase of word learning, where they begin to attend to larger word parts to more effectively access words for both decoding and meaning (e.g., morphology and vocabulary).

## 10. Overdoing It (Especially Isolated Skill Work)

Some curricula overemphasize phonics (especially the isolated skill-and-drill type of work) while ignoring other key aspects of early reading needs (e.g., vocabulary and content knowledge building) that are essential to long-term reading progress. Modifying reading time to provide a better balance is important because all these skills plant the seeds of comprehension as students encounter increasingly more complex texts.

Phonics instruction is an essential part of early reading and writing instruction. Students need to learn how to decode words efficiently to increase their word recognition skills. The more words students recognize automatically, the better their reading fluency, which has a powerful effect on their comprehension of text. And that's the point. Phonics instruction is designed to increase students' ability to read and make meaning from text. Students who can read texts with ease, generally read more and find pleasure in it. However, it needs to be done in a way that is most effective and efficient. It is paramount that teachers and creators of curriculum materials take an objective and thorough look at how we improve that instruction to maximize student learning.

FIVE KEY TAKE-AWAYS

1. High-impact routines are critical to phonics instructional success.

2. There are seven foundations of strong phonics: readiness skills, scope and sequence, blending, dictation, word awareness, high-frequency words, reading connected text.

3. It's important to analyze current teaching materials keeping in mind the 10 common reasons phonics fails. Most programs need augmenting and adapting.

4. Think of this book as a hub airport that can take you to further professional development destinations. See the appendix, the book's companion website (http://resources.corwin.com/blevinsphonics), Blevins's YouTube videos, and other resources recommended throughout.

5. Think of YOU as the greatest asset of all. Whether you are a teacher or another type of educator, all students' success as readers, writers, and thinkers is brighter because you are here, with this book in hand.

# CHAPTER FOUR

# Progress Monitoring

## And an Assessment Decision Tree to Keep It Simple

Effective differentiated and adaptive instruction relies on assessment—both formal and informal. Throughout each section of the book, I have included some of the assessment tools I use to monitor students' phonics mastery in both reading and writing, check for decayed learning so I can provide timely course corrections to avoid learning holes in a student's foundation, and create skills-based small groups for more intensive work—whether the students are below, on, or above grade-level expectations. What follows is the "Assessment Decision Tree" I use to assist me.

## ASSESSMENT DECISION TREE

**Step 1: Determine which students are below or above grade-level expectations.**

- Most districts have assessments in place to determine which students are not meeting grade-level expectations. These assessments, such as DIBELS® or Acadience, are often administered at the beginning, middle, and end of the year. They provide a starting point for digging in deeper to determine specific skill needs. They are often not granular enough to plan instructional groups and modifications but give vital information on who is on track and who is not as well as areas of instruction requiring additional attention.

- An alternative that some districts use is a fluency assessment in which students read grade-level passages (usually two or three passages for one minute each) and get a wcpm (words correct per minute) score. These scores are compared to grade-level norms, such as those provided by Hasbrouck and Tindal. Students above the 50th percentile are deemed capable of tackling grade-level texts. For students below the 50th percentile, additional assessments will need to be given to determine specific areas of need, such as phonics, phonemic awareness, or vocabulary. These quick fluency assessments are a time saver as they reduce the number of students that teachers need to evaluate, often with a large battery of assessments at the beginning of the year.

- Students need to be reading in Grade 1 and, if not, intensive support needs to be given. We cannot wait until Grade 3 to begin addressing foundational skill needs. (We actually have the tools to determine which students are at risk by mid-kindergarten and should begin intensive support by then). In the United Kingdom and Australia, a phonics screening check is administered in the third term of Grade 1 (Year 1). This assessment requires students to read a series of real and nonsense words reflective of the phonics skills taught. The percentage of students who pass this check is reported by class and school. The purpose of the assessment is NOT punitive. It is to determine which teachers and schools need additional support, such as training, stronger resource materials, and so on. The goal is for classrooms and schools to increase the percentage of students passing this assessment each year as they fine-tune their instruction. These improvements are reported and celebrated, and this assessment is affecting change in these countries. This is the type of assessment I think U.S. schools should consider implementing. It is easy to administer, specific, and provides immediate granular results that, combined with an action plan, improves students' foundational skills learning.

Figure 4-1 • Oral Reading Fluency Data

| GRADE | PERCENTILE | FALL WCPM* | WINTER WCPM* | SPRING WCPM* | AVG, WEEKLY IMPROVEMENT** |
|---|---|---|---|---|---|
| **1** | 90 | | 97 | 116 | 1.2 |
| | 75 | | 59 | 91 | 2.0 |
| | 50 | | 29 | 60 | 1.9 |
| | 25 | | 16 | 34 | 1.1 |
| | 10 | | 9 | 18 | 0.5 |
| **2** | 90 | 111 | 131 | 148 | 1.2 |
| | 75 | 84 | 109 | 124 | 1.3 |
| | 50 | 50 | 84 | 100 | 1.6 |
| | 25 | 36 | 59 | 72 | 1.1 |
| | 10 | 23 | 35 | 43 | 0.6 |
| **3** | 90 | 134 | 161 | 166 | 1.0 |
| | 75 | 104 | 137 | 139 | 1.1 |
| | 50 | 83 | 97 | 112 | 0.9 |
| | 25 | 59 | 79 | 91 | 1.0 |
| | 10 | 40 | 62 | 63 | 0.7 |
| **4** | 90 | 153 | 168 | 184 | 1.0 |
| | 75 | 125 | 143 | 160 | 1.1 |
| | 50 | 94 | 120 | 133 | 1.2 |
| | 25 | 75 | 95 | 105 | 0.9 |
| | 10 | 60 | 71 | 83 | 0.7 |
| **5** | 90 | 179 | 183 | 195 | 0.5 |
| | 75 | 153 | 160 | 169 | 0.5 |
| | 50 | 121 | 133 | 146 | 0.8 |
| | 25 | 87 | 109 | 119 | 1.0 |
| | 10 | 64 | 84 | 102 | 1.9 |
| **6** | 90 | 185 | 195 | 204 | 0.6 |
| | 75 | 159 | 166 | 173 | 0.4 |
| | 50 | 132 | 145 | 146 | 0.3 |
| | 25 | 112 | 116 | 122 | 0.3 |
| | 10 | 89 | 91 | 91 | 0.1 |

*WCPM = Words Correct Per Minute          **Average words per week growth

SOURCE: Hasbrouck & Tindal (2017).

**Step 2: Determine specific skill needs to adjust whole-group instruction and form skills-based small groups. Most of these assessments are only administered to a sub-set of students based on the assessment results in Step 1.**

- Administer a **comprehensive phonics survey** to determine specific skill needs for students below or above grade-level expectations. These surveys require students to read a series of words organized in related groupings, such as words with short vowel spellings, words with consonant digraphs, words with long vowel spellings, and so on. Several commercial assessments can be used, such as Hasbrouck's Quick Phonics Assessment (QPA), or you can use those provided by me. I have a Comprehensive Phonics Survey for use in kindergarten and the beginning of Grade 1, and another for use beginning in mid-year Grade 1 and beyond (Grades 2–6). See the appendix or download these from the companion website (resources.corwin.com/differentiatingphonics)

- Administer a **comprehensive spelling survey** to determine specific skill needs for all students. Note that even students on level for reading might have skill deficits in their spelling of words using previously taught skills. These surveys require students to spell a series of words organized in related groupings, such as words with short vowel spellings, words with consonant digraphs, words with long vowel spellings, and so on. Several commercial assessments can be used, such as Hasbrouck's Quick Spelling Assessment (QSA), or you can use those provided by me. I have included a Comprehensive Spelling Survey for use in kindergarten and the beginning of Grade 1, and another for use beginning in mid-year Grade 1 and beyond (Grades 2–6). See the appendix or download these from the companion website (resources.corwin.com/differentiatingphonics).For students below grade-level expectations for decoding, it will also be necessary to administer both a **phonological awareness assessment**, to determine if there are any needs in blending and segmenting sounds, and an alphabet recognition assessment for students who perform poorly on the lowest level of a cumulative phonics survey (i.e., reading short vowel CVC words). Several strong commercially available phonological awareness assessments are available, such as the PAST (Phonological Awareness Screening Test), which you can download from https://thepasttest.com/. For alphabet recognition, you can use the assessments provided in this book. The **letter and sound assessments** here are organized by a research-based sequence of most likely to least likely known letters and sounds. See the appendix or download these from the companion website (resources.corwin.com/differentiatingphonics).

**Step 3: Monitor progress by providing timely, on-the-spot formative assessments weekly and monthly to stay on top of specific student needs. These quick, informal assessments offer additional information on student progress and can be used to prevent decayed learning.**

- Administer weekly fluency checks. These assessments require students to read a set of words that reflect the current skill and taught skills from the previous four to six weeks. The assessment takes about a minute per student. Because the assessment is cumulative, skills can be tracked over time to determine when mastery (automaticity) and transfer occur, so these checks can alert you if decayed learning is occurring (the skill is slipping away). It is unnecessary to test every student every week, and most teachers do not have the time. Rather, select a subset of students to assess at the end of the week for about 10–15 minutes. Look at the assessments for each student over time to track a skill from one assessment to the next. Is automaticity improving? If not, continue work with fluency. Are skills slipping away? If so, provide more intensive work on that skill during whole-group and small-group lessons. See Appendix G: Fluency Check Examples, or download these from the companion website (resources.corwin.com/differentiatingphonics).

- Dictate **cumulative spelling sentences** at the end of each week. These sentences contain both words with the current skill and words requiring the use of skills taught during the previous four to six weeks. Mark words misspelled and code them by skill (e.g., digraph *ch*, long *a* spelling *ai*). Look at the coded errors. If a lot of students are struggling applying a skill to writing, add more work with that skill during whole-group dictation and word-building lessons. If only a few students are struggling with the skill, form a skills-based small group for intensive work on that skill. See Appendix H: Cumulative Spelling Sentences, or download these from the companion website (resources.corwin.com/differentiatingphonics).

- Listen to students read decodable texts that are reflective of the cumulative skills they have learned. Use the **reading observation forms** I have provided in Appendix I to code errors. This evaluation can serve as a valuable and more skills-focused assessment of student reading than a running record with a leveled text, which might not have many words that students need to decode using previously taught phonics skills. You can do this observation more formally once a month, or select students each week to observe and cycle through all the students each month. See Appendix I: Reading Observation Forms, or download these from the companion website (resources.corwin.com/differentiatingphonics).

- Place a **phonics skills checklist** in students' **writer's notebooks**. When a skill is introduced, have students circle the skill on the checklist. This indicates that you will now hold them accountable for correctly writing words using this skill. Once a month, evaluate students' writings using a phonics lens. Look at the circled (previously taught) skills. If you see evidence of consistent and accurate use of the skill in writing, place a check mark in the "Mastery" column to indicate students are moving toward mastery, and, when conferencing with students, record some sample words correctly spelled to celebrate their success. Examine skills that are circled, but not yet mastered. If many students are struggling with specific skills, add more work with these skills during whole-group dictation and word building. If only a few students are struggling with specific skills, skills-based small groups can provide more intensive support. This process, along with the cumulative spelling assessment, is an easier way to stay on top of students' spelling needs, which can be quite diverse in any given classroom; and it better assists you in differentiating support. See Appendix J: Phonics Skills Checklists for Writer's Notebooks, or download these from the companion website (resources.corwin.com/differentiatingphonics).

FIVE KEY TAKE-AWAYS

1. Comprehensive phonics and spelling assessments are needed to provide you with big-picture information about students' phonics skills as compared to grade-level expectations.

2. Quick assessments, such as fluency reads, at the beginning of the year can help you determine the subset of students for which you need to conduct additional assessments to determine areas of need.

3. Frequent progress monitoring tools—often cumulative in nature—are needed to stay on top of students' phonics and spelling progress and to address potential decays in learning.

4. Assessments are only valuable if they are linked to the next steps in your instruction—both whole-group modifications and the formation of skills-based small groups.

5. Once next steps are determined, use the high-impact routines in the following chapters to deliver the needed instruction, including the differentiated supports.

# PART II

# High-Impact Routines

*Photo Source: iStock.com/Weedezign*

# CHAPTER FIVE

# Blending Routine

## And How to Differentiate

## WHAT IS IT?

Blending is the main strategy we teach students so they can decode, or sound out, words (Resnick & Beck, 1976). It is simply the stringing together of letter sounds to read a word. For example, if a student sees the word *sat*, he will say the sound for each letter or spelling (*/s/, /a/, /t/*) and string or sing together the sounds (*/sat/*).

## RESEARCH HIGHLIGHTS

- Blending is a strategy that must be frequently modeled and applied in phonics instruction to have the maximum benefit for students (Resnick & Beck, 1976).

- Research shows that teachers who spend larger than average amounts of time on blending—modeling blending and providing loads of practice blending words in isolation and in context (e.g., daily in early reading instruction and practice)—achieve greater student gains (Haddock, 1978; Rosenshine & Stevens, 1984).

- Recent research by Gonzalez-Frey and Ehri (2021) found that connected phonation—stringing together the sounds as you blend them together—is more effective than segmented phonation for teaching beginning readers to decode unfamiliar words. It is easier to hold onto the sounds in working memory when they are strung together. (In segmented phonation, students are asked to tap each sound before blending them together.)

## IMPLICATIONS FOR YOUR INSTRUCTION

- When you begin to teach students how to blend words, it is best to use words that start with continuous sounds. These are sounds that can be stretched without distortion. These sounds include the vowel sounds and several of the consonant sounds (/f/, /l/, /m/, /n/, /r/, /s/, /v/, /z/). In this way, you can more easily model how to move from one sound to the next, blending them to form a word, as in /sssaaat/ to make /sat/. As a result, words such as *am*, *sad*, and *fan* are great words for beginning blending models.

- Why is this an important consideration for your teaching? If, for example, you chose the word *bat* instead to introduce how to blend words, there is a great likelihood you would add a vocalization to the end of the /b/ sound since it is a stop sound and very difficult to pronounce purely in isolation. What would result would sound like /buh/ to your students. Now imagine you ask students to string together the sounds in *bat* that you just pronounced individually (/buh/, /a/, /tuh/). The resulting word would be /buh-a-tuh/, instead of /bat/.

- Once students understand the principle of blending, you don't need to worry about this as much. And, when sounding out words beginning with stop sounds like /b/, /k/, and /d/, you can move quickly from the first to the second sound in the word with no or minimal pause between them to avoid the vocalized "*uh*."

### Where can you find words for creating blending lines?

To save time in creating blending lines, use one or more of the following resources:

- *Phonics from A to Z*, 4th edition, by Wiley Blevins (2023a)
- *Teaching Phonics and Word Study*, 3rd edition, by Wiley Blevins (2023b)
- *Week-by-Week Phonics and Word Study*, by Wiley Blevins (2011c)
- Phinder at devinkearns.com/phinder
- Spelfabet at spelfabet.com/au/spelling-lists
- Internet search by spelling pattern (e.g., words with *ai*)

- Keep in mind that two types of blending are commonly used in classrooms, and each has a different purpose during phonics instruction: *final blending (additive)* and *successive* or *continuous blending (whole word)*.

## ROUTINE 1A: BLENDING WORDS (FINAL/ADDITIVE)

| ROUTINE STEPS | SAMPLE TEACHER TALK |
|---|---|
| Write the letter (or display a letter card), point to it, and say the sound. | [Write or display the letter *s*.] <br><br> /s/ |
| Write the next letter (or display a letter card), point to it, and say the sound. | [Write or display the letter *a* after the letter *s* to form *sa*.] <br><br> /a/ |
| Slowly slide your finger under the two letters as you blend the sounds. | /sssaaa/ |
| Repeat, but this time slide your finger under the letters and blend more quickly. | /sa/ |
| Write the next letter, point to it, and say the sound. | [Write or display the letter *t* after the letter *a* to form *sat*.] <br><br> /t/ |
| Slowly slide your finger under all three letters as you blend the sounds. | /sssaaat/ |
| Repeat at a faster pace and say, *The word is _____ .* | /sat/ <br><br> *The word is* **sat**. |

**NOTE:** This is the type of blending I recommend when first introducing the principle of blending to your students. It allows you to work slowly through the process of sounding out a word while reinforcing each letter sound. *However, this is not the most efficient form of blending, and I wouldn't continue it past the first few weeks*—after students understand the principle behind blending and have had some practice doing it on their own. The only time I recommend going back to final blending is when working with readers during small-group differentiation time. It is helpful to work through the word sound by sound to identify if a specific sound-spelling (e.g., the vowel letter sound) is standing in the way of them successfully reading words. If your student does know each letter and sound in the word but cannot blend the sounds, then the issue might be related to phonemic awareness or working memory. That is, the student might struggle with oral blending or retaining the sounds long enough in working memory to blend them together.

## ROUTINE 1B: BLENDING WORDS (SUCCESSIVE/ CUMULATIVE/WHOLE WORD)

| ROUTINE STEPS | SAMPLE TEACHER TALK |
|---|---|
| Write the word on the board (or display it using letter cards). | [Write or display the word *sat*.] |
| Put your finger at the beginning of the word. Slowly run your finger under the letters in order as you string together the sounds. Do not pause between sounds. Each sound must "melt" into the next sound. | /sssaaat/ |
| Slowly compress the word. Therefore, go from stretching the sounds at a slow pace to a bit faster and finally to a normal speed. Tell students that the word is _____. | /ssaat/ /sat/ The word is **sat**. |

**NOTE:** This is a more efficient form of blending that you will use for the bulk of your phonics instruction.

## BLENDING LINES

*Photo Source:* iStock.com/SerhiiBobyk

Blending lines are rows of words you use to model for students how to read words that can be decoded using the new target phonics skill and for students to practice sounding out words that require using both this new skill and previously taught skills.

- **Blending lines should be used every day during whole-group instruction.** Students will also read the words and interact with them during independent work time. In addition, you will use the words to provide extra support during skills-based small-group lessons.

- **The number of words and rows in these blending lines can vary.** However, *there should be at least eight to twelve words containing the new target skill* that students will gain fluency with by the end of the initial introductory week.

- **Select words (and sometimes spellings) containing the target skill** for the top portion of the blending lines.

- **The middle portion of the blending lines contains review words** to extend the learning. *Once students learn a new phonics skill, many need four to six weeks of intentional practice and application to achieve mastery in both reading and spelling words containing that skill.* They can then transfer the skill to other reading and writing needs. As a result, some of the words in this portion can be familiar (e.g., words they have seen in stories read) to check on retention, and others should be new (e.g., words they haven't seen in stories read) to check on the ease with which they can transfer these skills. That's the true test of mastery.

- **The bottom portion contains challenge words** to offer an enrichment for students needing this leveling-up work during whole-group lessons.

- **For additional enrichment,** you can also add a sentence or two as time permits.

- **Blending lines are designed to take no more than five minutes of an instructional block.** The goal is to get some practice reading words in isolation before reading them in context through the use of decodable connected texts. The speed with which you move through the blending lines will increase throughout the week, and you might not get through all of them the first day or so.

# SAMPLE BLENDING LINES

| Kindergarten | **New Skill: Short *i*** | | | | | |
|---|---|---|---|---|---|---|
| | **1** *i* | *a* | *n* | *p* | | (new letter-sound and some review letter-sounds) |
| | **2** *it* | *sit* | *in* | *pin* | | (minimal contrast words) |
| | **3** *is* | *tip* | *pit* | *pat* | | (other words, including some from story) |
| | **Review** | | | | | |
| | **4** *man* | *tap* | *sat* | *am* | | (known and new words reviewing previous skills) |
| | **Challenge** | | | | | |
| | **5** *sits* | *taps* | *pats* | *naps* | | (uses skill from later in the sequence) |
| | **In Context** | | | | | |
| | **6** *It can sit.* | | | | | |
| | **7** *It is a map.* | | | | | |
| Grade 1 | **New Skill: Long *a* spelled *ai, ay*** | | | | | |
| | **1** *ran* | *rain* | *plan* | *plain* | *sad*   *say* | (minimal contrast words) |
| | **2** *may* | *pay* | *play* | *say* | *stay*   *stray* | (minimal contrast words) |
| | **3** *pail* | *sail* | *tail* | *trail* | *train*   *brain* | (other words, including some from story) |
| | **4** *chain* | *tray* | *faint* | *nail* | *paint*   *raise* | (hardest words, some from story to frontload) |
| | **Review** | | | | | |
| | **5** *go* | *she* | *hope* | *cute* | *ride*   *same* | (easier known words) |
| | **6** *bring* | *ranch* | *chop* | *sink* | *pitch*   *when* | (harder known and new words) |
| | **Challenge** | | | | | |
| | **5** *rain   rainbow day birthday* | | | | | (uses skill from later in the sequence) |
| | **In Context** | | | | | |
| | **6** *"Rain, rain, go away," yelled Gail.* | | | | | |
| | **7** *I had to wait all day for the train to come.* | | | | | |

| Grade 2 | **Check Foundational Skills: *r*-Controlled Vowel *ar*** | | | | | | |
|---|---|---|---|---|---|---|---|
| | **1** *cat* | *car* | *cart* | *pat* | *part* | *park* | (minimal contrast words) |
| | **2** *bark* | *scar* | *star* | *start* | *spark* | *shark* | (other words, including some from story) |
| | **3** *yard* | *yarn* | *barn* | *chart* | *smart* | *chart* | (other words) |
| | **Transition to Longer Words** | | | | | | |
| | **4** *hard* | *harder* | *hardest* | *large* | *larger* | *largest* | (add a word part such as a prefix or suffix, or create a compound word) |
| | **5** *farm* | *farmer* | *start* | *starting* | *arm* | *armful* | |
| | **Challenge** | | | | | | |
| | **6** *streetcar* | *backyard* | *postcard* | *ballpark* | *bookmark* | *landmark* | |
| | **7** *departing* | *restarting* | *recharge* | *lifeguard* | *harmful* | *guitar* | |
| | **In Context** | | | | | | |
| | **8** *There's a big red barn on Farmer Bob's wheat farm.* | | | | | | |
| | **9** *Mark went to the market to get a large bag of apples.* | | | | | | |

## Tips on Creating Blending Lines

For details on creating blending lines, see *A Fresh Look at Phonics* by Blevins (2016). Note that blending lines can be used for students in Grade 3 and up who have not mastered or gained fluency with essential skills taught in K–2. Use the Grade 2 sample blending lines as your model, as these provide that leveling up (transition to multisyllabic words) critical for these students. We don't want them stuck in one-syllable word work. We want to start there in a lesson and level up to words closer to grade-level expectations.

## ROUTINE 1C: BLENDING LINES

| ROUTINE STEPS | SAMPLE TEACHER TALK |
|---|---|
| **Days 1–2** | • Model the first two words and discuss students' observations. Ask: *What do you see that's different? What do you hear that's different?* |
| | • Then guide students in a choral blending of the remaining words. Tap and pause on a word for students to whisper-blend; then tap again for students to chorally blend. (E.g., Tap on the word and say *"whisper-read."* Then tap on the word again and say *"all together."*) |
| | • Continue through the blending lines. Stop when all have been completed or the activity has lasted about five minutes. |
| | • Students will practice reading these words independently, and you can pick up any missed words on subsequent days. |
| **Days 3–5** | • Guide students in a choral blending of the words. Tap on each word for students to chorally blend. Slowly increase the speed each day. |
| | • Make sure students are completing daily practice activities during independent work time. Select activities that require students to reread the blending lines and complete an activity with some or all the words. For example, students might underline the target spelling as they say the sound, circle words with a specific spelling pattern, select five words to dictate to a classmate to spell, select three words to use in a story about the week's topic, and reread the blending lines on their own or with classmates. |
| **Corrective Feedback** | • When students make an error say, *My turn.* Make the sound that students missed. Have them repeat the sound. Tap under the letter and say, *What's the sound?* Students chorally respond. Return to the beginning of the word. Say, *Let's start over.* Blend the word with students again. |

### Alternate Pacing (for students needing more initial support)

| ROUTINE STEPS | SAMPLE TEACHER TALK |
|---|---|
| **Day 1** | • Model the first two words and discuss students' observations. Ask: *What do you see that's different? What do you hear that's different?* |
| | • For the remaining words, run your finger under each letter as you slowly string together the sounds with students. Then have students chorally blend the sounds again. Keep your voice soft so that you can hear the students. |
| | (Do NOT blend by yourself and then have students repeat. That is just a repeated, parroting activity requiring minimal student effort and diminished learning opportunities.) |

| ROUTINE STEPS | SAMPLE TEACHER TALK |
|---|---|
| **Day 2** | • Guide students in a choral blending of the remaining words. Tap and pause on a word for students to whisper-blend, and then tap again for students to chorally blend.<br><br>• Continue through the blending lines. Stop when all the blending lines are completed, or the activity has lasted about five minutes.<br><br>• Students will practice reading these words independently, and you can pick up any missed words on subsequent days. |
| **Days 3–5** | • Guide students in a choral blending of the words. Tap on each word for students to chorally blend. Slowly increase the speed each day.<br><br>• Make sure students are completing daily practice activities during independent work time. Select activities that require students to both reread the blending lines and complete an activity with some or all of the words. |

# ROUTINE 1: BLENDING—TEACHER ALERTS AND PRINCIPAL/COACH LOOK-FORS

| TEACHER ALERTS<br>Things to consider | PRINCIPAL/COACH<br>LOOK-FORS |
|---|---|
| [ ] Spend more time decoding words presented in connected text rather than in isolation.<br><br>[ ] Make sure words in blending lines are high utility, i.e., words students are likely to encounter in reading or use in writing.<br><br>[ ] Don't overdo the modeling. Model one to two words, and then have students do the work. Provide quick corrective feedback, as needed. | [ ] Quick-paced activities are being used.<br><br>[ ] The teacher models only one to two words, and then has students chorally do the rest the first time.<br><br>[ ] Blending lines are quickly revisited, calling on individual students, pairs, tables or rows, or other groupings.<br><br>[ ] Blending lines are revisited multiple times throughout the week (e.g., used in a quick review or lesson warm-up, reviewed in small-group work).<br><br>Copies of blending lines can be used for independent and at-home work. |

# DIFFERENTIATE IT!

| WHO? | HOW? |
|---|---|
| **Students Above Grade-Level Expectations** | The blending lines, by their basic construction, already have built-in enrichment in the "Challenge" line of words. Select words to focus on requiring a skill further in the scope and sequence, preferably words you will reinforce with these students during small-group work. For example, if you are teaching short vowel CVC words, a "Challenge" line could include words that begin with consonant blends or consonant digraphs. For some of your on-level students, this brief conversation about the advanced skill can rapidly level up their skill progress as well. |
| | Create a separate set of blending lines for your students' use during small-group time, focusing on the new advanced skill—word sets they can use to practice with partners during independent work. To save time, you can use the blending lines for that skill for the on-level students (which you will get to later in the year). Then, when you get to that skill in your curriculum, the above-level students will know the words and can work with students needing support during partner work. |
| **Students Below Grade-Level Expectations** | Two key aspects of the blending lines are already built in to support your below-level students. The first row of the blending lines begins with two words that go from the known to the new, and this line is the easiest of the lines because you are providing additional modeling and conversation around the phonics concept. |
| | In addition, the "Review" rows of the blending lines address skills taught in the previous four to six weeks, skills for which these students will need support. |
| | If you have students working on even earlier skills, and many teachers do, modify the expectations and amount of work during class, partner, and independent work. For example, when students practice rereading the blending lines during independent/partner time assign them only some of the lines, such as "Line I" and the "Review" rows. You can also create a separate set of blending lines for these students to use during small-group time, focusing on the earlier skills they have yet to master—word sets they can use to practice with partners during independent work. |

| WHO? | HOW? |
|---|---|
| **Multilingual Learners** | In addition to articulation support while sounding out the words in the blending lines, many students will need vocabulary support. For example, words like *log, tad, sip, cap, vet, zap,* and others might be unknown to some students—whether they are learning English as an additional language or are native English speakers.<br><br>Select a set of these words each week and teach them during small-group time. The goal is for students to be able to both read and define these words by the end of the week. To really know a word, we need to focus on its meaning, sounds and spelling, and the context in which it is used.<br><br>For example, for the word *bat,* we would discuss the word's multiple meanings (a flying animal and something used in a baseball game to hit the ball). For the word *rain,* we might discuss what it is, what we wear on a rainy day, and what time of year it usually rains.<br><br>During these targeted vocabulary lessons do the following **vocabulary routine**:<br><br>• Read aloud the word in English and in the student's primary language. You can use a translation app on your phone for students to hear the word in their primary language.<br><br>• Provide a brief definition. Demonstrate, act out, or pantomime the word.<br><br>• Connect the word to known words. Start with synonyms and antonyms. For example, connect the word *cap* to the more familiar word *hat*. Or connect *sad* to its opposite— *happy.*<br><br>• Display a photo or create a simple drawing to illustrate the word. Some words, e.g., *bug, log,* and *hut,* can be easily shown. However, illustrations are sometimes not available.<br><br>When activity pages contain illustrations of words both with and without the targeted phonics skill (e.g., both /s/ and a letter-sound not targeted), write the targeted letter (s) under each picture whose name begins with that letter-sound (/s/), and review these picture names before students complete the activity. Most students can benefit from this support. |

## JOYFUL LEARNING VARIATIONS

While instructional routines are important for the efficiency of our teaching and for aiding in student learning, sometimes I like to mix it up and do an alternate activity with the same instructional focus and goal. Here are some possibilities for blending words.

### Spin It!

Create spinners from construction paper or use one of the several premade electronic spinners. On the first and third spinner write consonants, consonant blends, and/or consonant digraphs (based on the skills you are teaching and reviewing). On the second (middle) spinner, write the vowel spellings. Students spin the spinners and sound out the word formed. They then must decide if it is a real word or a nonsense word. (Note: This helps students get ready for nonsense word reading tests, which can be challenging conceptually for some.) If it is a real word, record the word on the board or paper. When the activity is completed, read the list of real words formed.

Short Vowel Review: Spin It!

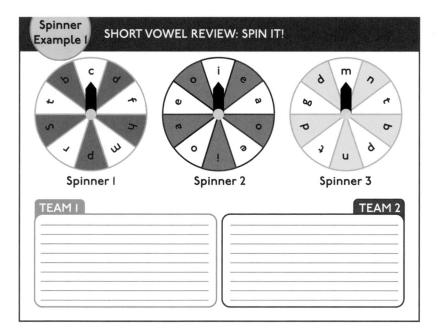

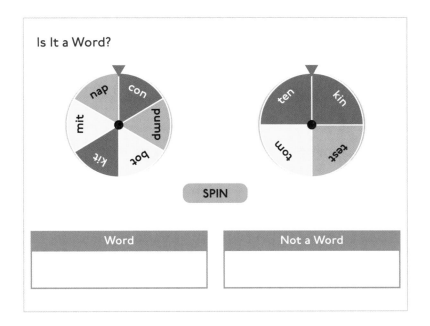

**Is It a Word?**

SPIN

| Word | Not a Word |
|------|------------|
|      |            |

You can have students sort the word list by spelling pattern as an activity during independent work time. You can also divide the class into teams and make this a game-like activity, as you see which team can form five (or ten) real words first. For older students, replace the spellings on the spinners with larger word chunks, such as prefixes, suffixes, and common syllables.

## Letter Cubes

Create simple paper cubes/dice or use the widely available whiteboard cubes (on which you can write spellings on each side of the cube but erase them for later use). Use consonants, consonant blends, and consonant digraphs that your students are working on. Then write on the board spelling patterns with your target skill (e.g., *-ear, -air, -are*). Have students work with partners or in small teams to roll the cubes/dice, seeing how many real words they can create using the letters shown and the spelling patterns.

## Automaticity/Speed Drills

These drills provide a set of words (generally 10–25) that are repeated multiple times on a grid. Students practice reading these words over and over and try to improve their scores.

That is, they try to increase the number of words they can read in a predetermined time, usually one minute. This activity is NOT about speed or speed reading. It is about repetition and automaticity. The increasing score throughout the week is physical evidence of student progress and highly motivating for many students.

**To create an automaticity/speed drill**

1. Select skills students need to develop automaticity on (phonics, high-frequency words).

2. Select a 100-word (or 50 if for kindergarten and early Grade 1) drill grid.

3. Select 10–25 words and write repeatedly in grid in random/mixed order. Make copies for students.

4. Differentiate for all student needs (e.g., put simpler words on the top half of the grid and more complex words on the bottom half).

5. Allow students time to practice independently, with partners at school, and at home prior to each testing.

**What do the students do?**

1. Distribute copies of the speed drill.

   Have students underline the focus pattern quickly as they say the sound or sounds.

2. Read the words on the drill with students to check decoding. That is, read the first couple of rows with the new words. You don't need to read the entire grid.

3. Have students practice independently.

4. Time students throughout the week and record their scores (a teacher or partner can do the timing and recording).

## Sample Drills

Note: Drill 1 is on a 50-word grid. It contains 10 words (in the first two rows) repeated. Drill 2 is a differentiated drill. The top half contains one-syllable words, and the bottom half contains multisyllabic words; both sets of words contain the target skill. Assign all or only portions of the drill as appropriate to meet specific student needs.

## BUILD FLUENCY

**Speed Drill**

**Directions:**

1. Underline the letter *e* in each word as you say the sound.
2. Say each word in the first two rows with your teacher.
3. Practice reading the words on your own.
4. Have a partner time you reading the words for one minute. Keep practicing to improve your speed.

| | | | | | |
|---|---|---|---|---|---|
| 1. | men | pen | get | let | leg |
| 2. | well | tell | red | bed | yes |
| 3. | let | men | leg | pen | red |
| 4. | bed | get | well | yes | tell |
| 5. | pen | leg | men | red | get |
| 6. | well | let | tell | yes | bed |
| 7. | leg | red | get | men | yes |
| 8. | let | pen | well | yes | bed |
| 9. | tell | get | leg | bed | men |
| 10. | red | tell | pen | well | let |

| | Words Per Minute | Date | Partner |
|---|---|---|---|
| Timed Reading 1 | _____ | ____ | _____ |
| Timed Reading 2 | _____ | ____ | _____ |
| Timed Reading 3 | _____ | ____ | _____ |

## FOUNDATION SKILL FLUENCY

### Speed Drill

**Directions:**

1. Underline the long o spelling pattern in each word.
2. Pronounce each word with your teacher.
3. Practice reading the words on your own.
4. When you are ready, have a partner time you reading the words for one minute. Keep practicing to improve your speed.

| | | | | |
|---|---|---|---|---|
| cold | joke | pro | grown | hose |
| wrote | thrown | broke | bolt | Joe |
| toe | loaf | groan | goes | quote |
| throat | smoke | ghost | colt | toad |
| go | video | soak | zone | globe |
| coach | hello | most | goes | stone |
| shown | told | so | stove | soak |
| glow | drove | jolt | road | stroll |
| foam | hold | no | post | goats |
| known | toast | Joe's | boat | smoke |
| unroll | rainbow | Mexico | tadpole | ago |
| headphone | outgrow | folding | follow | truckload |
| rolling | elbow | windblown | shadow | snowman |
| window | explode | buffalo | video | untold |
| below | sideshow | approach | snowing | awoke |
| ago | awoke | tadpole | truckload | approach |
| rainbow | outgrow | follow | window | unroll |
| sideshow | Mexico | rolling | headphone | windblown |
| snowman | elbow | snowing | folding | video |
| explode | below | shadow | buffalo | untold |

| | Words Per Minute | Date | Partner |
|---|---|---|---|
| Timed Reading 1 | _____ | _____ | _____ |
| Timed Reading 2 | _____ | _____ | _____ |
| Timed Reading 3 | _____ | _____ | _____ |

# EARLY KINDERGARTEN CHALLENGES

A handful of engaging practices help students catch up in kindergarten.

*Photo Source:* iStock.com/monkeybusinessimages

With increasing numbers of students attending preschool programs, larger numbers of students enter kindergarten ready to begin sounding out and spelling words earlier than ever before. Now most programs have students blending words a couple of months into the school year. However, this poses an enormous challenge for students who didn't have access to those early literacy experiences before entering school, and the aggressive pace of the instruction makes it challenging for them to keep up. We must better support these students in their first year of school. Most programs race through the alphabet. It's much too fast for these students. So, an extended and differentiated alphabet and phonemic awareness strand needs to be layered onto your existing curriculum.

# ADDING A DIFFERENTIATED ALPHABET AND PHONEMIC AWARENESS STRAND

If you teach kindergarten and some students enter without sufficient prior literacy instruction, integrate these practices to help them catch up:

## Tips for Sound Box Practice

You can begin by having students listen for the position of a sound in a word. Here is an example. Say: *Where do you hear the /s/ sound—at the beginning or the end of sun? If you hear it at the beginning, drag your counter to the first box; if you hear it at the end, drag your counter to the last box.* Say words like *sat, sun, bus, miss,* and so on. Guide students to drag the counter to the appropriate box. Then repeat the activity, but this time guide students to place the *s* letter card (or magnetic letter) in the box where they hear the /s/ sound to reinforce the letter-sound connection. Slowly build from this activity using *one* letter-sound to the full-on activity using *three* letter-sounds. This helps to move students from the partial alphabetic phase of word learning, in which they use only parts of the word to figure it out, to the full alphabetic phase of word learning, in which they can fully sound out words. (See the description of Ehri's phases of word learning on page 190 for more details.)

- Add more letter-sound work to your blending lines for several months into the school year.

- Provide additional reading of alphabet books during read-aloud time for several months into the school year.

- Review the alphabet as part of your daily warm-up and transitions (e.g., tap on a letter and have students chant the name, sound, and perform an action—it will take time for them to master these things, but the daily repetition is critical).

- Conduct daily small-group work on these prerequisite skills. These can be daily short bursts, such as five to ten minutes of alphabet work with an intentionality and intensity that will help these students catch up. I recommend focusing on two to three letter-sounds per week.

- Get students to attend to words at the phoneme level as soon as possible. This means skipping over some of those phonological sensitivity skills (e.g., rhyme, onset-rime) and working at the sound level. An ideal activity to do daily is the one on page 151 of Chapter 9 (on dictation) that uses sound boxes: model for students how to stretch the sounds, mark each sound on the sound boxes, and then replace a letter with each sound.

## ASSESSMENT TOOLS

To stay on top of students' mastery of blending words with the taught phonics skills, I rely on two tools.

1.  **Cumulative Fluency Checks:** These weekly checks require students to read a series of words containing the current skill and the previous five weeks of skills. Students are evaluated on their accuracy and automaticity in reading the words. This information is tracked over time. That is, when a skill is introduced, it will appear on the assessments for the following five weeks. If, over time, the students are less accurate reading the words (they often do well that first week because the skill is fresh in their thinking), then the learning is decaying. We can provide immediate course corrections to increase the intensity and intentionality of the work with the skill so that it doesn't become a learning issue. This is critical ongoing differentiation. If students are accurate with the skill for all six weeks (the initial week and the five weeks after) but aren't automatic, we can provide additional fluency-building work such as repeated readings of decodable texts and so on. Below is an example of how a skill is tracked over time.

2.  **Reading Observation Checklist:** It is essential that we listen to students read and use those observations to evaluate the skills with which they need additional support. I created a two-sided reading observation checklist for this purpose. On the first side, I record observations about a student's ability to self-correct, general fluency, and overall comprehension of the text. On the second side, I jot down words the student struggled to read. I record any fully decodable words (based on what I've taught) that were misread, fully decodable words that the student self-corrected or read slowly, and irregular high-frequency words the student struggled with. At the bottom of this page is the scope and sequence for the year. I examine the student's mistakes and circle any skills that seem to be especially challenging. I use this information to adjust whole-group work, form skills-based small groups for the upcoming week, and when conferencing with the student. Below is an example of a Grade 1 "Reading Observation Form," which you can download from the companion website.

Figure 5-1 • Cumulative Fluency Checks

**CUMULATIVE ASSESSMENT**

| Lesson | Word | |
|--------|------|---|
| I | at | ☐ |
| | map | ☐ |
| | had | ☐ |
| | rags | ☐ |

Number Correct (accuracy): _/4

Number Automatic (fluency): _/4

**CUMULATIVE ASSESSMENT**

| Lesson | Word | | Lesson | Word | |
|--------|------|---|--------|------|---|
| 3 | mop | ☐ | 2 | bit | ☐ |
| | box | ☐ | | lick | ☐ |
| | dot | ☐ | | him | ☐ |
| | log | ☐ | | kits | ☐ |
| | | | I | at | ☐ |
| | | | | map | ☐ |
| | | | | had | ☐ |
| | | | | rags | ☐ |

Number Correct (accuracy): _/12

Number Automatic (fluency): _/12

**CUMULATIVE ASSESSMENT**

| Lesson | Word | | Lesson | Word | |
|--------|------|---|--------|------|---|
| 5 | eggs | ☐ | 2 | bit | ☐ |
| | pens | ☐ | | lick | ☐ |
| | beg | ☐ | | him | ☐ |
| | let | ☐ | | kits | ☐ |
| 4 | hug | ☐ | I | at | ☐ |
| | buns | ☐ | | map | ☐ |
| | fuzz | ☐ | | had | ☐ |
| | nut | ☐ | | rags | ☐ |
| 3 | mop | ☐ | | | |
| | box | ☐ | | | |
| | dot | ☐ | | | |
| | log | ☐ | | | |

Number Correct (accuracy): _/20

Number Automatic (fluency): _/20

86

## Reading Observation Form

**Student** _____ **Date** _____

Observe students while reading aloud. Use the Reading Behavior Look-Fors and Prompts to respond to student errors. Record your observations in the General Notes section.

| READING BEHAVIOUR LOOK-FORS | PROMPTS |
|---|---|
| Student self-monitors and self-corrects using known sound-spelling correspondences. <br><br> 1    2    3 | *Run your finger under each letter or spelling as you say the sound. Blend the sounds together.* <br><br> Point to and state any missed letter-sound or sound-spelling, then guide the students to blend the word again. |
| Student understands what is read. <br><br> 1    2    3 | Fiction: *Tell me in your own words what the story is about so far* <br><br> Informational: *Tell what you have learned about so far.* <br><br> Ask questions periodically throughout the reading to check on students' comprehension. Focus on both literal and higher-order questions. Have students support their answers using evidence from the text, such as reading the sentence that answers the question. |
| Student reads with appropriate grade-level phrasing and speed. <br><br> 1    2    3 | *Read this sentence again. Make it sound like you are talking to me.* <br><br> *Look at the punctuation and end mark. How does that change how you will read this sentence?* <br><br> Select sentences to model aspects of fluency, such as proper phrasing/chunking and changes in intonation based on end punctuation. Model, and have students repeat. |

KEY:   1 = not observed        2 = developing        3 = observed

**General Notes**

---

## Reading Observation Form continued . . .
### Focus on skills

Note specific words students struggled reading (both decodable words and irregular high-frequency words) and comment on overall fluency.

| DECODABLE WORDS | HIGH-FREQUENCY WORDS | FLUENCY |
|---|---|---|
|  |  |  |

Circle any phonics skills students struggled applying when decoding words. Use this information to provide additional phonics instruction and practice during Small Groups.

| | | |
|---|---|---|
| Short Vowels  a    e    i    o    u | Long vowels  a    e    i    o    u |
| i-blends | r-controlled Vowels   ar    er/ir/ur   or |
| s-blends | Short and Long oo |
| r-blends | Diphthongs   ou/ow    oi/oy |
| Digraphs  sh  th  ch/tch  wh  ng/nk | Complex Vowel /ô/(au, aw, ai) |
| Final e | r-controlled Vowels  are/air/earxx |

87

# CLASSROOM SNAPSHOT

| Teacher: Mr. B | Lesson Focus: |
|---|---|
| Students: Five students above grade-level expectations | Long *a* |
| Eight students below grade-level expectations | |
| Twelve students meeting grade-level expectations | |
| Four students who are multilingual learners | |

Mr. B has explicitly introduced long *a* spelled *ai* and *ay*. The students have practiced articulating the sound and just finished writing each spelling (*ai* and *ay*) multiple times as they said the sound (/ā/). Now Mr. B is displaying the blending lines on the board. Each student has his or her own copy.

**New Skill: Long *a* spelled *ai*, *ay***

| 1 ran | rain | plan | plain | sad | say |
| 2 may | pay | play | say | stay | stray |
| 3 pail | sail | tail | trail | train | brain |
| 4 chain | tray | faint | nail | paint | raise |

**Review**

| 5 go | she | hope | cute | ride | same |
| 6 bring | ranch | chop | sink | pitch | when |

**Challenge**

| 5 rain | rainbow | day | birthday |

**In Context**

6 "Rain, rain, go away," yelled Gail.

7 I had to wait all day for the train to come.

*Watch and listen as I drag my pointer under each spelling in the first word in Line I as I blend the sounds:* **|rrrraaann|**, **|rraann|**. *The word is* **ran**. *Now your turn.* Mr. B uses his pointer again as students blend the sounds in the word *ran*. *Look at the next word. Watch and listen as I blend it:* **|rrrāāānnn|**, **|rrāānn|**. *The word is* *rain*. *Now your turn.* Mr. B uses his pointer again as students blend the sounds in the word *rain*.

*What do you hear that is different in* **ran** *and* **rain**? *Tell your partner.* Mr. B listens as students discuss the different medial vowel sounds. He observes that some students are struggling, so he grabs a small whiteboard with sound boxes on it. *Help me stretch the sounds in* **ran**. *I will mark one box for each sound we say. Ready? Stretch:* **|rrraaannn|**. As the students stretch the sounds, Mr. B marks three boxes. *What is the middle sound in ran? If you aren't sure watch as I stretch the sounds. What sound do I say when I tap on the middle box?* Mr. B stretches the sounds as he taps the boxes, then pauses for students to answer. *That's right, it's the |a| sound. That's the short **a** sound. Now help me stretch the sounds in* **rain**. *Ready? Stretch:* **|rrrrāāānnn|**." Mr. B repeats the process, guiding students to isolate the medial /ā/ sound in *rain*. *So, the middle sound in* **ran** *is |a|. Say |a|. That's the short **a** sound. The middle sound in rain is |ā|. Say |ā|. That's the long a sound.*

*What do you see that's different in* **ran** *and* **rain**? *Tell your partner.* Mr. B listens as students discuss the short *a* spelling *a* in *ran* and the long *a* spelling *ai* in *rain*. *Remember, that we use the **ai** spelling for long **a** in the middle of a word. We use the **ay** spelling at the end.*

Mr. B then continues with the rest of the words in Lines 1–4. *I will tap on each word and run my pointer under it. I want you to whisper-read it. Then I will tap on the word again and say,* **All together**. *I want you to all read it nice and loud. Ready?* Mr. B taps and says, *Whisper-read.* And then he taps again and says, *All together.* The students do well until they get to the word *trail*. Mr. B stops, reviews the sounds for *tr*, and then asks the students to sound out the word again. When Lines 1–4 are completed, Mr. B points to the words *stay, train,* and *paint* in random order and asks the students to chorally read them. These are words in the upcoming story that students will read after the blending lines.

Mr. B continues with Lines 5–6. *Now, let's review some words with spellings we have been working on for a while. Ready?* Mr. B taps and says, *Whisper-read.* Then he taps again and says, *All together.* He notices that a few students struggled reading *ranch*, so he makes a mental note to provide additional words ending in *-nch* in the week's work.

*Are you ready for a challenge? Let's read some big words with long* **a**. *What's the first word?* Mr. B pauses as students say *rain*. *Look at the next word? Do you see* **rain** *in this word? Tell your partner.* Mr. B then asks for a volunteer to underline the word *rain* in the compound word *rainbow*. *So, the first part of this word is* **rain**. *What is the second part? Tell your partner.* Mr. B pauses. *Let's put these two word parts together:* **rain-bow**. *What's the word?* **Rainbow. Rainbow** *is a word made up of two smaller words. We call these words compound words. Everyone say*

*(Continued)*

(Continued)

*"compound words."* Mr. B repeats the process for *day* and *birthday*. He will work with compound words during small-group time with his above-level students.

*Now, let's read our sentences. I will tap on each word as you read it together.* After students read the sentence on Line 6, he pauses and points out the quotation marks. He explains that they show the words a person says. He then asks the students to read that part to their partners in the way the person speaking might have said these words (e.g., exasperated, not happy). He then has the students reread the sentence chorally in that way. For the sentence in Line 8—a very long sentence—Mr. B chunks it into meaningful parts: *I had to wait / all day / for the train to come.* He reads one part at a time, then has students echo. He highlights how each part adds meaning. ***I had to wait.*** *Your turn.* Mr. B pauses. *When did I have to wait?* ***All day.*** *Read the first two parts of the sentence after me."* Mr. B reads, then pauses for students to echo. *Why did I have to wait? That's right:* ***for the train to come.*** *Now read the whole sentence after me.* Mr. B reads, then pauses for students to echo. *Notice how each part of a sentence answers a question like Who? Did or Do What? When? Why? Where? and How? We will practice writing longer sentences today about our story by answering these questions. But first, we need to read our story. Please open your book,* **The Train Ride.**

**NOTE:** Students will practice reading these words during whole-group time as a daily warm-up and then interact with them during independent work time by completing various activities.

# FIVE KEY TAKE-AWAYS

1. Devote five to ten minutes each day to teaching small groups of students who need to catch up on alphabet and letter-sound mastery.

2. In addition to articulation support while sounding out the words in the blending lines, many multilingual students will need vocabulary support.

3. Daily partner work and independent practice at school and at home are essential in getting students to the goal of automatic, fluent reading.

4. Check students' mastery of blending words containing taught phonics skills each week using a cumulative fluency check and a reading observation checklist.

5. Use the weekly data to adjust whole-group work, form skills-based small groups for the upcoming week, and when conferencing with students.

# CHAPTER SIX

# High-Frequency Words Routine

## And How to Differentiate

## WHAT IS IT?

High-frequency words are the words we see most often in printed English, such as *and, can, for, it, of, that, the*. They often become sight words, but they aren't the same thing as sight words. Sight words are *any* words we have stored in our long-term memory and automatically recognize while reading.

## RESEARCH HIGHLIGHTS

- In the active view of reading model (Duke & Cartwright, 2021), developing learner's sight word vocabulary and command of high-frequency words fall under the "word recognition" component. The goal of reading instruction is to teach students to recognize a lot of words automatically—both high-frequency words and many others. This automaticity leads to and, in a sense, overlaps with reading fluency.

- The best instructional practices related to high-frequency words are those that accelerate learning and focus on mastery. Research shows that readers store "irregular" words in their memory in the same way they store "regular" words (Gough & Walsh, 1991; Lovett, 1987; Treiman & Baron, 1981). That is, readers pay attention to each letter and the pattern of letters in a word and associate these with the sounds that they represent (Ehri, 1992).

- The process by which we store words into memory is called "orthographic mapping," a term coined by Linnea Ehri to describe the three ways the brain commits a new word to memory. A reader uses the oral language processing part of the brain to map (connect) the sounds of words they already know (the phonemes) to the letters in a word (the spellings). They then permanently store the connected sounds and letters of words (along with their meanings), as instantly recognizable words (Sedita, 2022). Brain research has shown that because a person must attend to the sounds, the spelling, and meaning of a new word—whether it's phonetically regular (e.g., *cat*) or not (e.g., *they*) instruction that focuses on high-frequency words as a whole or their shape is generally inadvisable. These teaching routines make it difficult for students to map words orthographically into memory and easily distinguish them from other similar words.

- According to brain research, three distinct regions of the brain must be activated for us to learn and automatically retrieve a word. These parts include where the sounds are stored, where the word's meaning is stored, and where the word's spelling (individual letters) is stored.

- Only 13 words account for more than 25 percent of the words in print (Johns, 1980). These words include *a, and, for, he, is, in, it, of, that, the, to, was,* and *you*. And 100 words account for approximately 50 percent of the words in print (Adams, 1990; Carroll et al., 1971; Fry et al., 1993). About 20 percent of the 250 words most frequently used by students in their writing (70–75 percent of the words they use) are function words such as *a, the,* and *and* (Rinsland, 1945).

Figure 6-1 • How the Brain Stores a Word Through Orthographic Mapping: Sounds, Meaning, and Letters

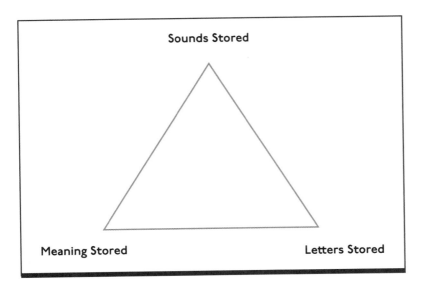

## IMPLICATIONS FOR YOUR INSTRUCTION

- We must teach high-frequency words in a way that activates all three parts of the brain necessary to learn a word.

- It is important to decide which words to teach and when. Several word frequency lists exist, such as the Dolch Basic Sight Vocabulary (Dolch 220), the Fry 100 (and more), and the *American Heritage Word Frequency Book* top 150 words. All serve as great starting points for instructional decisions.

- Teach those words that students will most likely encounter in early reading texts and use in their writing. These are high-impact words in terms of students' reading and writing growth. For example, the word *the* is the most common word in English. Students benefit from learning this word very early in their reading instruction. The word *of* is also one of the most frequent words. However, its use creates more complex sentences than those typical in early kindergarten (e.g., *I see a lot of cats.*). So we might delay its introduction until a bit later in the scope and sequence. As a result, I do not recommend following these high-frequency lists in a sequential lock-step manner.

- Some high-frequency words are "regular," meaning students will learn the phonics skills to sound them out fully, such as *us, see*, and *like*. Others are "irregular," meaning they do not follow the typical sound-spelling we teach in the primary grades or have less-common spellings, such as *they* and *said*.

- High-frequency word instruction should focus on both regular and irregular words. I prefer teaching the irregular words (e.g., *they*) or words that are needed in stories before they become fully decodable based on the scope and sequence that I am using (e.g., *see*). These words are the focus of my direct instruction.

- Then I check my high-frequency word lists for all those words that become decodable at that point in the scope and sequence. For example, if I am teaching short *i*, there might be several high-frequency words that now become fully decodable (e.g., *in, is, it, sit, six, big*). I include those words in my daily activities, such as blending work, dictation, and decodable texts so that students have multiple opportunities to sound them out and use them in writing.

- We know which words are most problematic and require greater review and practice. These include the following: (1) Reversals: *was* and *saw, on* and *no*; (2) Visually similar words without concrete meanings: *of, for, from*; (3) Words with *th* and *wh: there, then, them, that, this, their* and *where, when, what, with, were, why*; (4) Words that vary greatly in their pronunciations but look similar: *one, once*. These words need more intentionality. That is, they need to be addressed multiple times throughout the school year to increase teaching and application to get to mastery. These words should also appear on high-frequency assessments for multiple grades as a lack of automaticity can negatively affect reading fluency.

- Create assessments that mirror the words you teach in kindergarten and Grade 1. You can separate the irregular and decodable high-frequency words on the assessment to assist in analyzing the results. For Grades 2 and up, use one of the high-frequency word lists that follow, such as the "75 High-Frequency Word Hurdles" list. Assess students at the beginning of the year and focus on those words during whole-class lessons for which most students need additional instruction. Form skills-based small groups for students with additional high-frequency word needs.

- In addition, keep a list of the year's high-frequency words in students' writer's notebooks. Periodically (e.g., one a month), review students' recent writings for evidence of consistent and accurate spellings of these words. Circle or put a check mark beside words mastered. Provide additional instruction and practice for words not mastered.

## HELPFUL HIGH-FREQUENCY WORD LISTS

I use multiple high-frequency word lists when planning my instruction, based on my instructional needs. Several of these lists follow. Notice that I've included usage ideas in parentheses to help you access them, but I encourage you to use them flexibly. Your instructional decision-making and assessments often bubble up from what you are seeing in students week to week. In addition, when you choose to select particular words, they should be reflected in the books, poems, and songs you read and write together.

### Top 248 High-Frequency Words in English

**(It often takes students two or more years to learn all these words.)**

Figure 6.2 provides a list of the top 248 words used in English. These words are collected from the three most frequently used word lists in the United States (Fry Words: The First Hundred, Dolch Basic Sight Vocabulary 220, and the "Top 150" in the *American Heritage Word Frequency Book*). The words that are irregular are highlighted. It might take children two or more years to learn all these words.

## A Writer's Notebook

A writer's notebook is usually a simple composition book given to each student at the beginning of the school year. These notebooks can be used by students to

- write when they arrive at school while waiting for the bell—often a prompt is provided by the teacher

- write responses to texts read

- gather notes for larger pieces of writing

- engage in revision assignments connected to target grammar, punctuation, and writing skills

- keep lists of words, such as words with a specific spelling pattern

- write sentences for their new high-frequency words

- engage in self-directed writing for fun or creative expression

- show writing progress to their teacher during conferencing sessions

## Figure 6-2 • Top 248 High-Frequency Words in English

| | | | | |
|---|---|---|---|---|
| a | don't | is | pick | those |
| about | done | it | place | three |
| after | down | its | play | through |
| again | draw | jump | please | time |
| all | drink | just | pretty | to |
| also | each | keep | pull | today |
| always | eat | kind | put | together |
| am | eight | know | ran | too |
| an | even | laugh | read | try |
| and | every | let | red | two |
| another | fall | light | ride | under |
| any | far | like | right | up |
| are | fast | little | round | upon |
| around | find | live | run | us |
| as | first | long | said | use |
| ask | five | look | same | used |
| at | fly | made | saw | very |
| ate | for | make | say | walk |
| away | found | man | see | want |
| back | four | many | seven | warm |
| be | from | may | shall | was |
| because | full | me | she | wash |
| been | funny | more | show | water |
| before | gave | most | sing | way |
| best | get | much | sit | we |
| better | give | must | six | well |
| big | go | my | sleep | went |
| black | goes | myself | small | were |
| blue | going | never | so | what |
| both | good | new | some | when |
| bring | got | no | soon | where |
| brown | green | not | start | which |
| but | grow | now | stop | white |
| buy | had | number | such | who |
| by | has | of | take | why |
| call | have | off | tell | will |
| called | he | old | ten | wish |
| came | help | on | than | with |
| can | her | once | thank | word |
| carry | here | one | that | words |
| clean | him | only | the | work |
| cold | his | open | their | would |
| come | hold | or | them | write |
| could | hot | other | then | years |
| cut | how | our | there | yellow |
| day | hurt | out | these | yes |
| did | I | over | they | you |
| different | if | own | things | your |
| do | in | par | think | |
| does | into | people | this | |

# Irregular High-Frequency Words Mini-List

**(Every learner needs to master these words by the end of Grade 1.)**

It is essential that students master the most common irregular high-frequency words by the end of Grade 1. Figure 6.3 shows 58 "irregular" high-frequency words and is based on the list in Figure 6.2. The words *a* and *I* are relatively easy since they are also letters of the alphabet, but the remaining words include the most common word in English (*the*), question words (*what, where, who*), pronouns (*they, you*), and other high-impact words for reading and writing. These words require special attention, repetition throughout the grade, frequent assessment, and additional practice reading in context.

Figure 6-3 ◆ Irregular High-Frequency Words

| A–E | F–J | K–O | P–T | U–Z |
|---|---|---|---|---|
| a | four | laugh | people | very |
| again | from | live | pretty | want |
| are | give | many | put | warm |
| been | have | most | said | was |
| both | I | of | shall | wash |
| buy | | once | some | water |
| carry | | one | the | were |
| come | | other | their | what |
| could | | | there | where |
| do | | | they | who |
| does | | | through | word |
| don't | | | to | words |
| done | | | today | work |
| eight | | | together | would |
| | | | two | you |
| | | | | your |

Since some decodable texts contain fewer repetitions of these words than is ideal, other texts might be needed for students who require extra support. These words are some of the most common words students will encounter in texts outside the decodable reading done during phonics lessons; the words also regularly appear on assessments, including high-stakes assessments.

## The 75 High-Frequency Word Hurdles

**(Use this list to teach and to create assessments in Grades 1–3.)**

These 75 words in Figure 6.4 contain irregular spellings (e.g., *said*), are confusing reversals (e.g., *was/saw, on/no*), are visually

Figure 6-4 • The 75 High-Frequency Word Hurdles

| | | |
|---|---|---|
| again | laugh | they |
| also | live | they're |
| any | most | today |
| are | no | together |
| because | of | two |
| been | on | very |
| both | once | want |
| buy | one | warm |
| carry | other | was |
| come | people | wash |
| could | pretty | water |
| different | put | were |
| do | said | what |
| does | saw | when |
| don't | should | where |
| done | some | who |
| eight | that | why |
| every | the | with |
| for | their | won't |
| four | them | word |
| from | then | work |
| give | there | would |
| have | this | you |
| know | through | your |
| many | to | you're |

similar (e.g., *of/for/from*), or are too far removed from their sounds (e.g., *one/once*). This list is an expansion of the one presented in Figure 6.3 and contains a few decodable words that fit into at least one of the hurdle categories (e.g., reversals: *on/no*). I use this list to create assessments for Grade 1 through 3. These are the words for which I most frequently need to extend student instruction, practice, and application.

## Decodable High-Frequency Words

**(Use the words for blending lines, dictation, word sorts, decodable texts, and so on.)**

The chart in Figure 6.5 shows possible decodable words for each key phonics skill covered in kindergarten and Grade 1 in most instructional programs. The chart is divided into columns of complexity—simple VC and CVC words (good for kindergarten and early Grade 1), more complex one-syllable words (good for Grades 1–2), and multisyllabic words (good for Grades 2 and up). I use this chart to fold in decodable high-frequency words in my blending lines, dictation, word sorts, decodable texts, and so on. This list is drawn from ONLY the one presented in Figure 6.2—the top 248 most frequently used words in English. Add to this list other high-frequency words beyond that list.

## Irregular High-Frequency Words by Related Concepts

**(Accelerate reading and spelling by grouping spelling patterns and generalizations.)**

Although some high-frequency words are categorized as "irregular," many of those share common spelling patterns with other words (e.g., *could/would/should, do/who/to, some/come, give/live*). The chart in Figure 6.6 helps me group related "irregular" words so that I can take advantage of these spelling patterns and generalizations, teach them to students, and help accelerate their reading and spelling of these words. It also details the instructional conversations I have when teaching each cluster of words to aid in student learning.

Figure 6-5 ♦ Decodable High-Frequency Words

| PHONICS SKILL | SIMPLE WORDS K-1: vowel spelling and single consonants | COMPLEX WORDS Grade 1-2: vowel spelling and blends and digraphs | MULTISYLLABIC WORDS Grade 2-3: multisyllabic words |
|---|---|---|---|
| short a | am an as at can had has man ran | and ask back black fast than that | after |
| short e | get let red ten yes | best help tell them then well went when | better even every myself never open seven yellow |
| short i | big did him his if in is it sit six | bring drink its pick things think this which will wish with | different into little |
| short o | got hot not on | long off stop | upon |

| PHONICS SKILL | SIMPLE WORDS<br>*K–1: vowel spelling and single consonants* | COMPLEX WORDS<br>*Grade 1–2: vowel spelling and blends and digraphs* | MULTISYLLABIC WORDS<br>*Grade 2–3: multisyllabic words* |
|---|---|---|---|
| short *u* | but<br>cut<br>run<br>up<br>us | jump<br>just<br>much<br>must<br>such | funny<br>number<br>under<br>upon |
| *s*-blends | | best<br>fast<br>first<br>must<br>stop | |
| *r*-blends | | bring<br>brown<br>green<br>grow | |
| *l*-blends | | black<br>blue<br>clean<br>place<br>please<br>sleep | |
| *sh* | | she<br>wish | |
| *ch, tch* | | each<br>much<br>such<br>which | |
| *wh* | | when<br>which<br>white<br>why | |

*(Continued)*

(Continued)

| PHONICS SKILL | SIMPLE WORDS<br>*K–1: vowel spelling and single consonants* | COMPLEX WORDS<br>*Grade 1–2: vowel spelling and blends and digraphs* | MULTISYLLABIC WORDS<br>*Grade 2–3: multisyllabic words* |
|---|---|---|---|
| *th* | | than | |
| | | thank | |
| | | them | |
| | | then | |
| | | these | |
| | | things | |
| | | think | |
| | | this | |
| | | those | |
| | | three | |
| | | with | |
| *ng, nk* | long | bring | |
| | sing | drink | |
| | | thank | |
| | | that | |
| | | things | |
| | | think | |
| three-letter blends | | three | |
| soft *c* | | place | |
| soft *g* | | | |
| final e | ate | place | |
| | came | these | |
| | five | those | |
| | gave | used | |
| | like | white | |
| | made | write | |
| | make | | |
| | ride | | |
| | same | | |
| | take | | |
| | time | | |
| | use | | |

| PHONICS SKILL | SIMPLE WORDS<br>*K–1: vowel spelling and single consonants* | COMPLEX WORDS<br>*Grade 1–2: vowel spelling and blends and digraphs* | MULTISYLLABIC WORDS<br>*Grade 2–3: multisyllabic words* |
|---|---|---|---|
| long *a* | day<br>may<br>say<br>way | play | always<br>away |
| long *e* | be<br>eat<br>he<br>keep<br>me<br>read<br>see<br>we | clean<br>each<br>green<br>here*<br>please<br>she<br>sleep<br>three<br>years* | any<br>because<br>before<br>even<br>every<br>funny<br>only |
| long *i* | by<br>light<br>my<br>right | find<br>fly<br>kind<br>try<br>why | myself |
| long *o* | go<br>no<br>own<br>so | cold<br>goes<br>grow<br>hold<br>know<br>old<br>show | also<br>going<br>only<br>open<br>over<br>yellow |
| long *u* | | | |
| *r*-controlled vowel: *ar* | far<br>part | start | |
| *r*-controlled vowel: *or* | for<br>more<br>or | | before |

*(Continued)*

(Continued)

| PHONICS SKILL | SIMPLE WORDS K–1: vowel spelling and single consonants | COMPLEX WORDS Grade 1–2: vowel spelling and blends and digraphs | MULTISYLLABIC WORDS Grade 2–3: multisyllabic words |
|---|---|---|---|
| r-controlled vowel: er, ir, ur | her<br>hurt | first | after<br>another<br>better<br>different<br>every<br>never<br>number<br>over<br>under |
| r-controlled vowel: are, ear, ere | | there*<br>where* | |
| long oo | new<br>soon<br>too | blue | into |
| short oo | good<br>look | full<br>pull | |
| diphthong: oi, oy | | | |
| diphthong: ou, ow | down<br>how<br>now<br>our<br>out | brown<br>found<br>round | about<br>around |
| variant vowel: /ô/ | all<br>call<br>fall<br>saw | called<br>draw<br>small<br>walk | also<br>always<br>because |
| silent letters | | know<br>write | |
| plurals | | | |
| contractions | | | |
| schwa | | | about<br>another<br>around<br>away |
| other | | | |

Figure 6-6 ◆ Common Phonics Rules and Generalizations
          Worth Teaching

| RELATED HIGH-FREQUENCY WORDS | INSTRUCTIONAL CONVERSATIONS |
|---|---|
| **1**<br><br>could<br><br>should<br><br>would | Teach *could, should,* and *would* together.<br><br>Emphasize the *-ould* spelling pattern and highlight the silent *l,* which many students leave out of their spellings. |
| **2**<br><br>come<br><br>some<br><br>done<br><br>one<br><br>once | Connect *one* to *done* and *once.*<br><br>Contrast *one* with *won*—discuss meaning and spelling differences.<br><br>Connect *come* and *some* and highlight the *o_e* spelling for the /u/ sound. |
| **3**<br><br>do<br><br>who<br><br>to<br><br>two<br><br>today<br><br>together<br><br>through | Connect *to, do,* and *who.* Discuss confusion with *go, no,* and *so*—words many students learn early on.<br><br>Contrast *to* with *two* and *too.* Discuss the different spellings and meanings. |
| **4**<br><br>of<br><br>from<br><br>for<br><br>four | Contrast *for* and *four.* Discuss the different spellings and meanings.<br><br>Have students create exemplar sentences for *of, for,* and *from* to connect to meaning and usage. |
| **5**<br><br>give<br><br>live<br><br>have | No English words end in the letter *v.* If you hear the /v/ sound at the end, you must add an *e.*<br><br>Connect to other words such as *love, glove, above, gave,* and *save.* |

*(Continued)*

(Continued)

| RELATED HIGH-FREQUENCY WORDS | INSTRUCTIONAL CONVERSATIONS |
|---|---|
| **6**<br><br>you<br>your<br>you're<br>they're<br>their<br>there<br>where | Contrast *your/you're* and *their/there/they're*. Discuss the different spellings and meanings. Point out that the spelling is a clue to the meaning and that's why there are different spellings.<br><br>Connect *there* and *where* and their shared spelling pattern *-ere*. |
| **7**<br><br>the<br>them<br>then<br>when<br>what<br>that<br>this<br>with | Words that begin with *th* and *wh* can cause challenges for readers and spellers, especially when these words vary only slightly (e.g., *then/when* or *that/what*).<br><br>Do lots of word-building activities with these words and have students create high-frequency word phrase cards to practice reading. |
| **8**<br><br>don't<br>won't<br>most<br>both<br>also | Connect *don't* and *won't*. |
| **9**<br><br>saw<br>was<br>on<br>no<br>know | Discuss reversals *was/saw* and *on/no*.<br><br>Highlight *a* for /u/ and *s* for /z/ in *was* and compare to *is* and *has*.<br><br>Contrast *no* and *know*. Discuss the different spellings and meanings. |
| **10**<br><br>word<br>work | Discuss the sounds for *or*, which might cause confusion because they sound the same as the *er*, *ir*, and *ur* spellings. |

| RELATED HIGH-FREQUENCY WORDS | INSTRUCTIONAL CONVERSATIONS |
|---|---|
| **11**<br><br>said<br><br>they<br><br>been<br><br>again<br><br>put<br><br>buy<br><br>why | Highlight specific sound-spellings that are frequently misspelled, such as *ai* for /e/ in *said* and *again* and *ey* for /ā/ in *they*.<br><br>Highlight the initial schwa sound for *a* in *again*.<br><br>Contrast *buy* with *by* and *bye*. Discuss the different spellings and meanings. |
| **12**<br><br>any<br><br>many<br><br>carry<br><br>very<br><br>every<br><br>pretty | Connect *any* and *many*.<br><br>Highlight the /ē/ sound spelled *y* at the ends of these words.<br><br>Point out the *e* in the middle of *every*, which most people do not pronounce (/evrē/) and is likely to be missing from students' spellings. |
| **13**<br><br>people<br><br>because<br><br>different<br><br>other<br><br>eight<br><br>laugh | This is an especially difficult group of words for students to master in spelling.<br><br>Highlight specific sound-spellings that are frequently misspelled, such as the *e* in the middle of *different*, which most people do not pronounce (/difrunt/) and is likely to be missing from students' spellings. |
| **14**<br><br>wash<br><br>water<br><br>want | Focus on words that begin with *wa-* and how to pronounce the vowel sound. |
| **15**<br><br>are<br><br>were<br><br>warm<br><br>does | This is another difficult group of words for students to master in spelling.<br><br>Highlight specific sound-spellings that are frequently misspelled, such as the *oe* spelling for /u/ in *does*. Contrast with *goes*. |

In addition, there are only a handful of spelling generalizations that are truly useful to teach students to help them spell words, but many are related to these high-frequency words. Below is a list of the most common rules or generalizations that are worthwhile to teach formally.

## ROUTINE 2: HIGH-FREQUENCY WORDS (READ, SPELL, WRITE, EXTEND)

Here is my preferred instructional routine for high-frequency words because it examines the word at the sound, spelling, and meaning level—necessary to accelerate orthographic mapping.

# Common Phonics Rules and Generalizations Worth Teaching

1. English words don't end in the letter *v*. You must add an *e* to any word ending in the /v/ sound (e.g., *have, give, gave, love*).

2. English words don't end in the letter *j*. You must use *ge* or *dge* (e.g., *large, fudge*).

3. The position of spellings in words matters (e.g., long *a* spelled *ai* never appears at the end of *a* word but *ay* does).

4. The FLSZ or Floss Rule (these letters are doubled after a short vowel, e.g., *stiff, well, kiss, jazz*).

5. Letters *c* and *g* before *e, i,* or *y* (e.g., *city, germ;* exception: *girl*)

6. The letter *q* is followed by *u* (e.g., *quick*).

7. The *y* at the beginning is a consonant (e.g., *yes*); at end, the *y* is a vowel (e.g., *fly, happy*).

8. The *ck* and *tch* are used after a short vowel (e.g., *sick, catch*); otherwise use *k* and *ch* (e.g., *park, lunch*). For a word that begins with the /k/ sound, we use the letter *c* if the next letter is *a* (*cat*), *o* (*cot*), or *u* (*cut*). We use the letter *k* if the next letter is *e* (*key, Ken*) or *i* (*kit*).

| ROUTINE STEPS | SAMPLE TEACHER TALK |
|---|---|
| **Read:** Write the word in a context sentence and underline the word. Read aloud the sentence; then point to the target underlined word and read *it* aloud. Have students chorally say the word. Then, guide students to say or tap the sounds they hear in the word. | Write and read the sentence.<br><br>*"I see a cat,"* **said** *Pam.*<br><br>Point to the word said. *This is the word* **said**. *What is the word?*<br><br>*What sounds do you hear in the word* **said**? *Let's say them together: /s/ /e/ /d/.* |
| **Spell:** Spell the word aloud and have students repeat. If students are just learning their letters, do an echo spell.<br><br>Briefly point out any known spellings and then highlight the irregular or unknown spellings that need to be remembered "by heart." Underline, write in a different color, or draw a heart above these letters. | *The word* **said** *is spelled* **s–a–i–d**. *Spell it with me:* **s–a–i–d**. *What is the first sound in the word* **said**? *What letter do we write for the /s/ sound? What is the last sound in the word* **said**? *What letter do we write for the /d/ sound? Notice that the middle /e/ sound in* **said** *is spelled* **ai**. *That's not how we usually spell the /e/ sound; we usually spell it with the letter* **e**. *So that's the part of the word we will need to remember. I'm going to draw a heart above these letters to help you remember them by heart.* |
| **Write:** Ask students to write the word multiple times as they spell it aloud. This can be done on dry erase boards or on paper. It is best to have students physically write the word with a pencil or marker rather than write the word in the air. | *Watch as I write the word. I will say each letter as I write it.* Model this.<br><br>*Now it's your turn. Write the word two or three times. Say each letter as you write it.* |
| **Extend:** Connect the word to other words students have learned. For example, if you have a high-frequency word chart organized by spelling patterns (e.g., *could/should/ would, come/some*), work with students to place the word in the correct spot on the chart. Then ask students to generate oral sentences using the word. Have students work with a partner, and provide sentence frames as support, if needed. Then have students write their oral sentence. Build on these sentences as appropriate. These extension activities can be done on the days following the initial instruction when you have additional time to extend in this way. | *Turn to a partner and finish this sentence:* **I said** _____. Provide time for partners to share. *Now, write on your paper the sentence you just said.* Wait for students to finish. |

**NOTE:** High-frequency words that become decodable at each point in the phonics scope and sequence should be added to blending lines, dictation activities, word building, word sorts, decodable texts, and other places in the lessons to ensure coverage of these words as well. Since these words are decodable, the **Read, Spell, Write, Extend routine** won't be necessary. Rather, model for students how to sound out these words.

## ROUTINE 2: HIGH-FREQUENCY WORDS—TEACHER ALERTS AND PRINCIPAL/COACH LOOK-FORS

| TEACHER ALERTS<br>Things to consider | PRINCIPAL/COACH<br>LOOK-FORS |
|---|---|
| [ ] Go beyond introductions with only context sentences.<br><br>[ ] Reteach and review those words that are more challenging. Many require repetition at intervals throughout the year. One week is NOT enough.<br><br>[ ] Teach "irregular" words as word families, where possible. | [ ] Are teachers using a research-based routine like Read, Spell, Write, Extend to accelerate mastery?<br><br>[ ] Are more challenging words cycled through the year and assessed more frequently? |

# DIFFERENTIATE IT!

| WHO? | HOW? |
|---|---|
| **Students Above Grade-Level Expectations** | While many of these students will read the targeted high-frequency words with ease, some will struggle when spelling words that are "irregular." These students benefit from whole-group instruction. When they write sentences for each word in their writer's notebook, have them also write sentences for any high-frequency words addressed during small-group instruction using their advanced decodables. |
| **Students Below Grade-Level Expectations** | These students benefit from the Read, Spell, Write routine but might need sentence stems and frames when writing sentences using the words. Provide these on the board. Also, review the words during small-group instruction. When you get to the "Write" portion of the Read, Spell, Write routine, guide students to create flashcards for independent practice. Give students index cards. On one side have them write the word. On the other side, co-construct a simple sentence with them using the word. Students then practice reading the words in isolation and in context during independent and partner work. These flashcards are ideal for sending home for additional support. |
| **Multilingual Learners** | These students benefit from the Read, Spell, Write routine but might need sentence stems and frames when writing sentences using the words. Provide these on the board. Also, review the words during small-group instruction. When you get to the "Write" portion of the Read, Spell, Write routine, guide students to create flashcards for independent practice. Give students index cards. On one side have them write the word. On the other side, co-construct a simple sentence with them using the word. Have them create a simple illustration to accompany the sentence to further connect the target word to meaning. Students then practice reading the words in isolation and in context during independent and partner work. These flashcards are ideal for sending home for additional support. They can also help students understand how words function in English, such as distinguishing *of* and *from*. |

# JOYFUL LEARNING VARIATIONS

While instructional routines are important for the efficiency of our teaching and for aiding in student learning, sometimes I like to mix it up and do an alternate activity with the same instructional focus and goal. Here are some possibilities for teaching high-frequency words.

## Read It, Build It, Write It

This popular Orton-Gillingham technique asks students to read a word shown, build it with letter cards or tiles, and then write the word.

## Mix It, Fix It

Build a word with letter cards. Ask students to close their eyes as you scramble the letters. Then have students fix the word so it is spelled correctly. This requires students to quickly recall the word's spelling pattern, which is necessary for reading and writing these high-frequency words efficiently—especially the irregular ones.

## What's Missing?

Build a word with letter cards. Ask students to close their eyes as you remove one or more of the letters, such as **a** from **was** or **ai** from **said**. Then students must replace the missing letter or letters to spell the word correctly. If you remove irregular spellings in those irregular high-frequency words, students will need to give their attention to the part of the word that is more challenging—the part they need to remember.

## Writer's Notebook Sentences

Write the week's target high-frequency words on the board at the beginning of the week. Ask students to write one sentence for each word in the back of their writer's notebook. It is best to reserve a section in the back for this purpose. Then, later in the week, ask students to find a partner during independent work time and read all their high-frequency words from the beginning of the year. This increases the number of repetitions students get reading the words in context—important for building fluency. Periodically, check students' sentences. As they progress throughout the school year, their attention to spelling, grammar, and punctuation will develop. Notice how students begin to self-correct sentences written earlier in the year as their reading and writing skills grow. Praise them for these efforts.

## Say It, Tap It, Write It

Say a high-frequency word and have students repeat. Then have them tap the sounds and mark them using counters on sound boxes (Elkonin boxes). Then have students replace the counters with the spellings for each sound.

## Reader's Theater

Find short reader's theater plays that focus on sentences with the target high-frequency words or create your own. They can be as simple as a few comic strip panels for two readers. Have students practice reading their parts; then provide time for them to share their readings. Celebrate their progress.

## CLASSROOM SNAPSHOT

| | |
|---|---|
| **Teacher:** Mr. B | **Lesson Focus:** The words *some, come, said,* and *again* |
| **Students:** Five students above grade-level expectations | |
| Eight students below grade-level expectations | |
| Twelve students meeting grade-level expectations | |
| Four students who are multilingual learners | |

*(Continued)*

(Continued)

Mr. B is introducing four new high-frequency words for the week. On the whiteboard, he displays each word in a simple sentence. He tries to repeat words across the sentences to make them easier for his multilingual and below grade-level students to read and/or remember.

*I have **some** books.*

*I will **come** and pick a book.*

*"I like that book!" **said** Sam.*

*Can I read that book **again**?*

Mr. B introduces each word using the Read, Spell, Write, Extend routine, which all students can benefit from. For example, for the word **some**, he follows this routine:

**Read:** *I have **some** books.* Mr. B points to the word *some. This is the word **some**. What is the word?* He pauses for the class to chorally respond. *What sounds do you hear in the word **some**? If you need to use your sound boxes and mark the sounds as you stretch them, please do.* Mr. B pauses while each student segments the word individually, and he suggests using manipulatives for students needing that level of support. Students already have these at their tables. *Now let's say the sounds together: /s/ /u/ /m/.* Mr. B holds up one finger for each sound as it is stated. *That's right. The word **some** has three sounds. Let's say them again: /s/ /u/ /m/.* Mr. B wiggles one finger at a time as the class chorally says the sounds. He does NOT join in, so he can hear if students make errors.

**Spell:** *The word **some** is spelled **s–o–m–e**.* Mr. B spells it first as he points to each letter because there are some students who are still learning letter names, so an echo spell supports their needs better than a choral spell. *Now spell it with me: **s–o–m–e**.* Mr. B points to each letter as the students chorally spell it. He does NOT join in on this spelling so he can clearly hear if students make errors. It also gives him a chance to see who is participating and who is not.

*What is the middle sound in **some**? Tell your partner.* Mr. B pauses for students to respond with a partner. He notices that a few students are struggling to answer correctly. *If you aren't sure, watch and listen as I mark (tap) the sounds: /s/ /u/ /m/. What was the middle sound I said?* Mr. B pauses for students to chorally respond. *That's right, the middle sound in **some** is /u/. How do we usually spell the /u/ sound? Tell your partner.* Mr. B pauses for students to share their answers with partners. *That's right, we usually spell the /u/ sound with the letter **u**, but not in this word. In the word **some**, the letters **o** and **e** work together as a team to stand for the /u/ sound. So, that's the part of the word we will need to remember. I'm going to draw a heart above these letters to help you remember them by heart.* Mr. B draws a heart above the letters o and e in *some.* He makes a mental note to compare *some* and *come* when he introduces the second word later in the lesson. *What's this word again?* Students chorally say *some*.

**Write:** *Watch as I write the word **some**. I will say each letter as I write it.* Mr. B models writing the word. He reiterates the handwriting chant as he writes the letter e because some students have been struggling forming this letter. *Now it's your turn. Write the word **some** two times. Say each letter name as you write it.* Mr. B circulates and listens in. He targets students who are struggling with letter names and offers them additional feedback. He states the letter names and has them repeat these as they write each letter. He points to the alphabet chart for any student who needs to refer to the directional arrows when writing one or more of the letters.

Mr. B continues with the words *come*, *said*, and *again*. Mr. B is short on time, so he cannot do the "Extend" activity on this day. He jots a note to remind himself to complete the activity on the next day when he reviews the words. While students are reading the decodable text—which contains these words—he offers spelling-focused feedback if students struggle identifying the words. For example, one student got to the word *some* and mispronounced the vowel sound. Mr. B says this: *Remember, in this word the **o** and **e** work together to stand for the /u/ sound. Now sound out the word again.*

**Extend:** *Turn to a partner and finish this sentence: **I have some** _____.* Mr. B provides time for partners to share their sentences. He circulates and listens in. He calls on two or three students to share their sentences quickly. *Now, write on your paper or dry-erase board the sentence you just said. If you need some help, look on the board. I have written the beginning of the sentence for you.* Mr. B writes the sentence starter *I have some* _____ on the board for his multilingual and below-level students and waits for students to finish writing their sentences. *Read your sentence to your partner.* Mr. B pauses as students share their sentences. *I heard some of you say you have some books; others said you have some other things. I want to know more about what you have. Tell your partner about these things. What do they look like?* Mr. B pauses for students to share. *During our writing lessons, we have been working on writing more detailed and descriptive sentences. So now, underneath your first sentence, I want you to write what you said—that more detailed and descriptive sentence. If you need some help, look at the sentence frames on the board.* Mr. B knows that some of his multilingual learners and students below grade-level expectations benefit from some additional writing support. So he writes two frames on the board and reviews them: *I have some* _____. *I have some* _____ *that are* _____. He provides time for students to write their extended sentences. He circulates and encourages his above-level students to use some of the new words they have been learning during small-group time. *Remember to add details like this to your sentences when we write about our story today. Adding details makes your writing more precise, or specific, and more interesting.*

# FIVE KEY TAKE-AWAYS

1. Teaching words effectively is about layering instruction with previously taught and new words—and giving students loads of practice with the new words. The lessons are just the starting points for where real learning happens.

2. More challenging words will need teaching and assessing more frequently throughout the year.

3. Increase multisensory teaching and learning. Use tactile tools like flash cards and sentence frames; write out words and sentences for all students to see; and display the growing list of words your class is learning. Read, spell, write, clap, and sing the high-frequency words in meaningful contexts. Remember, our brains store words in long-term memory when we activate sound, spelling, and meaning.

4. Think of students' writer's notebooks as one of many differentiation tools. This is where students above grade-level expectations can tackle the more complex activities you give them and where students below grade-level expectations can practice during and after small-group instruction targeting their needs.

5. Use reader's theater as one of a handful of favorite activities for teaching phonics, reading, and writing. Students love it; it builds classroom community along with literacy skills.

# CHAPTER SEVEN

# Reading Decodable Text Routine

## And How to Differentiate

## WHAT IS IT?

Decodable texts are critical practice tools used during phonics lessons to accelerate students' mastery of reading words with taught skills. These texts contain a large percentage of words that can be fully sounded out based on previously taught phonics skills. Often these texts focus on a new target skill and enable a significant amount of practice reading words using that skill.

## RESEARCH HIGHLIGHTS

- Not all decodable texts are created equal. Here are some common errors in decodable texts:
  1. Using low-utility words to try to squeeze in more words containing the target skill (e.g., I can lug the cat with the rug.)
  2. Using nonstandard English sentence structures (e.g., The pup did run at Kit.)
  3. Using nonsensical sentences or tongue twisters (e.g., Slim Stan did spin, splat, stop.)

4. Using too many referents or pronouns instead of concrete words, making the meaning difficult to figure out (e.g., She did not see it but she did kick it.)

5. Using language that is too simple to explain scientific concepts accurately, due to phonics constraints (e.g., The sun will make plants rise.)

6. Using odd names to get more decodable words in the story (e.g., Ben had Mem. Zam had the pup.)

7. Avoiding using the word "the"—the most common word in English—to meet state decodability minimum counts

Texts with these issues need to be avoided (Blevins, 2020a).

- State reading adoption requirements (e.g., in California and Texas) have established that 75–80 percent of the words in a text must be decodable (i.e., words students can fully sound out). The other 20–25 percent of the words can be irregular high-frequency words and story words that make a text more interesting, although words in this last category may be used only occasionally.

- There is no research that says a decodable text must be 100 percent comprised of words that can be fully sounded out (Blevins, 2020a). In fact, this text often lacks the necessary connector words to sound like common English sentence patterns. Early reading texts should match oral language speech patterns. Of the top 250 words in English, about 60 of them are characterized as "irregular." These must be taught and learned efficiently early on, as they affect students' reading fluency and are needed in writing.

- Technically, decoding involves accessing the words on the page. It can include fully sounding out the words but also recalling those irregular high-frequency words that have been orthographically mapped into memory. Some researchers are starting to provide decodable text counts that include both types of words. For my work, I use **decodability** to refer to the percentage of words that can be fully sounded out based on the phonics skills previously taught and **accountability** to describe the percentage of words that can be fully sounded out PLUS those irregular high-frequency words that have been formally taught. This helps me determine how challenging a text might be for students and which words will most likely need support, such as story words (Blevins, 2020a).

- While there is surprisingly little research on decodable texts, what *has* been done highlights its impact on phonics learning. The research also points to areas in need of further exploration. The chart below provides a summary of some of the key research studies on decodable texts. For additional background information on decodable text, see *A Fresh Look at Phonics* and *Choosing and Using Decodable Texts* by Wiley Blevins.

| STUDY | BIG TAKE-AWAY |
|---|---|
| **Juel and Roper-Schneider** (1985)<br><br>*Reading Research Quarterly* | The texts we use in phonics lessons have a powerful effect on how students attack words while reading. In essence, the words determine how students must access them and affect the habits students develop in reading new words. Using decodable texts encourages the sounding out of words, which is a more reliable strategy than using picture or context clues and guessing. |
| **Blevins** (2000)<br><br>*A Research Study on the Effects of Using Decodable Texts With Systematic Phonics Instruction* | Decodable texts have a positive effect on students' ability to read and spell words using the grade-level phonics skills already taught, as well as on their motivation to read. For details about this study, see *Phonics from A to Z*, 4th edition, by Wiley Blevins. |
| **Mesmer** (2005)<br><br>*Reading & Writing Quarterly* | Decodable texts increase students' phonics-application opportunities, which can lead to greater decoding accuracy. |
| **Jenkins, Peyton, Sanders, and Vadasy** (2004)<br><br>*Scientific Studies of Reading* | This intervention study (*not* whole-class Tier I instruction) found benefits for reading both highly decodable and less decodable texts for students receiving extra phonics support, with more positive—but not statistically significant—outcomes using decodable texts. The study raises questions about the quality of texts read and the need for intervention students to read texts with both decodable and irregular high-frequency words to fully meet their reading needs. |
| **Cheatham and Allor** (2012)<br><br>*Reading and Writing* | Decodable texts increase students' decoding practice because so many words can be sounded out. However, early reading texts should *not* be completely (100 percent) decodable as that is not the only criteria for making a strong early reading text. |

*(Continued)*

(Continued)

| STUDY | BIG TAKE-AWAY |
|---|---|
| **Chu and Chen** (2014)<br><br>*Psychological Reports* | This study examined the positive effects of adding decodable texts to phonics lessons for students learning English as a second or additional language. |
| **Frey** (2012)<br><br>PhD dissertation (*Rethinking the Role of Decodable Texts in Early Literacy Instruction*) | This study supported the benefits of decodable readers for on-level students. However, it noted the difficulties below-level students had with these texts because (1) these students hadn't mastered previous phonics skills but were expected to keep up with the grade-level pace and (2) the texts were of poor quality, e.g., repeatedly including low-frequency words and lacking in repetition across texts. The study also noted the "nonlinear" increase in difficulty in these texts in the second half of Grade 1, when multiple spellings were introduced for one sound at a rapid pace, which was challenging for the struggling (below-level) readers. This study highlights the importance of differentiating phonics instruction, including by using decodable texts, and the need to scaffold the reading of these texts for struggling readers. |
| **Pugh, Kearns, and Hiebert** (2023)<br><br>*Reading Research Quarterly* | In an intervention meta-analysis, benefits were found for reading a variety of texts—"decodable" texts limited to only words with taught phonics skills and "nondecodable" texts not limited solely by taught phonics skills. As in the Jenkins et al. study, it is hypothesized that both types of texts provide practice with the types of words these students need support with—decodable words and irregular high-frequency words. The analysis suggests more studies need to be conducted on the texts used for teaching students during intervention. |
| **Leitch** (2023)<br><br>Thesis (*Decodable Readers Versus Leveled Texts*) | In a study to increase the reading fluency of developing readers still struggling to read at grade level, the use of decodable texts allowed for a quicker and more substantial increase in words per minute for students. |

The 1985 criteria came with the following warning: The important point is that a high proportion of the words in the earliest selections children read should conform to the phonics they have already been taught. Otherwise, they will not have enough opportunities to practice, extend, and refine their knowledge of letter-sound relationships. However, a rigid criterion is a poor idea. Requiring that, say, 90 percent of the words used in a primer must conform would destroy the flexibility needed to write interesting, meaningful stories.

- In 1985, the government document *Becoming a Nation of Readers* (Anderson et al., 1985) provided a set of criteria for creating controlled, decodable text. This type of text should include the following three criteria:

  **comprehensible** (vocabulary is understandable, and stories make sense and follow the natural-sounding patterns of spoken and written English), **instructive** (a majority of the words are decodable based on the sound-spellings previously taught), and **engaging** (stories are interesting and worth reading and rereading for building fluency, talking about, and writing about). Figure 7.1 shows an example from the Dynamite Decodables series, which I wrote for Benchmark Education.

Figure 7-1 • Sample Spread From *Zoom Room Adventure*

Illustrations courtesy of Benchmark Education Company LLC

## IMPLICATIONS FOR YOUR INSTRUCTION

- I refer to decodable texts, or phonics readers, as *accountable texts*. Why? There is a strong connection between what you teach and what you have students read, so you can reasonably hold them *accountable* for successfully reading these texts. These daily, successful reading experiences help to build early confidence in students—an "I Can Do It" attitude that is critical to early reading success and aids in motivation. In addition, if students struggle with these texts, they hold the teacher accountable as they alert him or her to areas in which students need more support.

- How decodable a text is is context specific—that is, it's based solely on what skills have been previously taught. Therefore, a decodability account requires the use of a phonics scope and sequence.

- Once students learn a large set of phonics skills (often around mid–Grade 1 when they have learned short and long vowel spellings, consonant digraphs, and a few more complex vowel spellings such as those for *r*-controlled vowels), it is important to introduce **bridging texts** along with the decodable texts. While the decodable texts provide that valuable and intentional practice mastering the new phonics skills, the bridging texts are slightly less controlled and transition students into traditional trade books.

## Enhanced Decodable Text Lessons (to Meet Wider Student Needs)

In this chapter and the next, I offer ideas for an enhanced approach to using decodable texts in the classroom, an approach that spans reading and writing and folds in all phonics work as well. Figure 7.2 illustrates this vision.

Figure 7-2 ◆ Enhanced Decodable Text Lessons (to Meet Wider Student Needs)

Phonics Application

Building Fluency

Decodable Text

Vocabulary/ Oral Language

Syntax and Text Cohesion

Comprehension and Early Reading Behaviors

Writing and Spelling

"Decodables must be used for more than just phonics practice!"

—Wiley Blevins

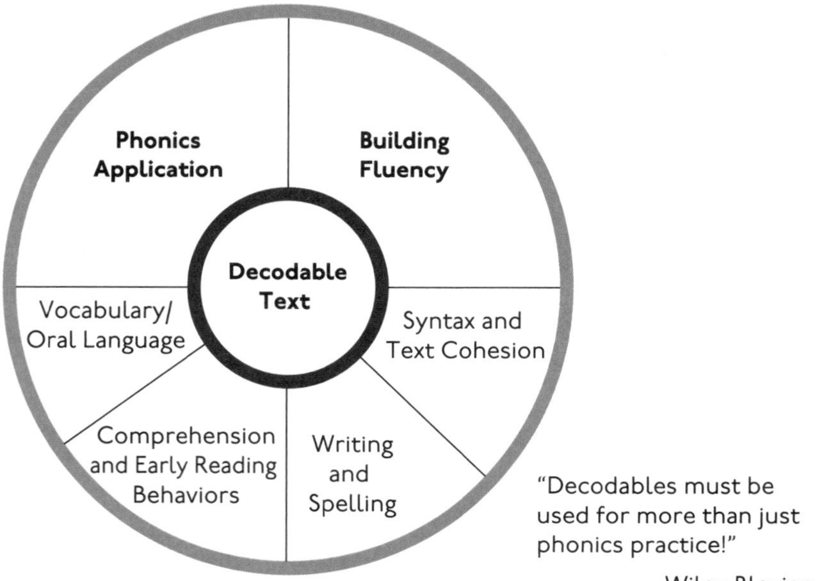

## Reading Throughout the Week

Decodable texts should be read multiple times throughout the week to build fluency. (See also the next chapter, on applying decodable texts to writing.) In addition, students need to read previously read decodable texts during independent and partner work to extend their practice time and build fluency. I recommend creating a rereading fluency routine for these books. For example, after a decodable text is read, you can place a copy of the book in students' decodable reader folders or type the story on a sheet or paper, number it, and place it in the students' folders. Each day of the week, assign stories for students to read with partners during independent work time. For example, on Monday have them reread the story or stories from the previous week. On Tuesday, have them read the story or stories from two weeks ago, and so on until the stories have been cycled through for multiple weeks. Learning phonics requires intentionality to attain fluency.

| MONDAY | TUESDAY | WEDNESDAY | THURSDAY | FRIDAY |
|---|---|---|---|---|
| **Whole Group** | **Whole Group** | **Whole Group** | **Whole Group** | **Whole Group** |
| Read Text I<br><br>Connect text to writing, e.g., through retelling | Reread Text I<br><br>Deepen comprehension and develop syntax | Read Text 2<br><br>Connect text to writing, e.g., through retelling | Reread Text 2<br><br>Deepen comprehension and develop syntax | Reread Texts I and 2 (or a new text or set of decodable sentences) while teacher listens to students read and completes a student observation form |
| **Independent Work Time** | **Independent Work Time** | **Independent Work Time** | **Independent Work Time** | **Independent Work Time** |
| Read texts from one week ago | Read texts from two weeks ago | Read texts from three weeks ago | Read texts from four weeks ago | Read texts from five weeks ago |

## More Tips for Success

- Often programs do *not* have enough decodable texts for reading practice and each program uses a different and unique scope and sequence. So while it is essential to have students practice frequently with the texts that *are* available, reading and rereading them for different purposes (e.g., read with a partner one day, read and find words with a spelling pattern another day, read and complete a writing prompt an additional day), new additional texts are beneficial. Find other decodables with a similar scope and sequence (it won't be an exact match) or create cumulative decodable sentences for reading practice. For example, write five sentences on chart paper or the board for students to practice reading. Each sentence contains at least one word using the new target phonics skill and other words containing previously taught phonics skills, as well as irregular high-frequency words already taught.

- Decodable texts have become a primary practice tool in kindergarten and Grade 1 and a tool during small-group instruction in Grade 2 and up for students needing that level of differentiated support. We need to make these decodable texts more impactful on many components of literacy learning. While the focus of reading decodable text is the application of phonics skills in connected text and developing fluency in using these skills while reading, there are other skills and early reading behaviors that can and should be developed using these instructional tools. These include an increased emphasis on writing, comprehension, vocabulary, and syntax. The following pages include examples of what to do before, during, and after reading a decodable text to expand its impact. The sample lesson template at the end of the book (see page 222) incorporates these aspects of early reading to enhance your decodable text lessons.

> [The] selection of text used very early in first grade may, at least in part, determine the strategies and cues children learn to use, and persist in using, in subsequent word identification. . . . In particular, emphasis on a phonics method seems to make little sense if children are given initial texts to read where the words do not follow regular letter-sound correspondence generalizations. . . . [T]he types of words which appear in beginning reading texts may well exert a more powerful influence in shaping children's word identification strategies than the method of reading instruction.
>
> —Juel and Roper-Schneider (1985, 150–51)

- A variety of texts is needed in early reading instruction, each with a specific purpose. One type of text cannot meet all the reading demands of our early readers. Decodable texts are essential for phonics practice. Complex trade book read-alouds, organized around topics or concepts, are essential for systematically building knowledge while students decoding skills are developing.

- I'm often asked about strong decodables for classroom use. While there are many problematic and poorly created decodables on the market, publishers are beginning to create stronger decodable readers. I have used and like strong decodables from Sadlier, Benchmark Education, and

Scholastic. Teachers I work with also like GEODES and Flyleaf decodables. My absolute favorites are a new set of decodables called Dynamite Decodables from Benchmark Education. These trade-book quality books cover engaging topics in fun formats—innovative nonfiction, comic strips with recurring characters, riddles, poems, mazes, and so on. They are the kind of decodables students will race to read. Use these during instruction, or add them to your classroom library for fun independent reads. See https://www.benchmarkeducation. com/all-series/dynamite-decodables.html for more details.

- As students learn more phonics skills, they will begin to learn spellings that can stand for multiple sounds, such as *ea* for long *e* and short *e*, or *ow* for /ou/ and /ō/. Therefore, students might use the incorrect sound for a spelling on their first attempt reading a word with one of these spellings. Provide mispronunciation correction, known as "Set for Variability." For example, if students read the word *b-r-e-a-k-f-a-s-t* using the long *e* sound for the *ea* spelling (a statistically more prevalent sound for that spelling), point to the *ea* spelling and ask, *What other sound can this spelling stand for? Try that sound.* This modeling increases students' flexibility in using taught sound-spellings while reading.

*Photo Source:* Rick Harrington, Rick Harrington Photography

# ROUTINE 3: READING DECODABLE TEXT

| BEFORE READING | |
|---|---|
| **Introduce the New Phonics Skills** | Provide an explicit introduction of the target sound-letter or sound-spelling that is the focus of the decodable text. |
| **Model Blending** | Provide practice reading words containing the target phonics skills via blending lines. These word sets contain minimal contrast word chains as well as review words to extend previous learning. |
| **Introduce the New High-Frequency Words** | Introduce the new high-frequency words using the Read, Spell, Write, Extend routine that focuses on the meaning, sounds, and individual spellings of the word, highlighting the irregular or untaught spellings that students need to remember. |
| **Preteach Academic Vocabulary** | Select and preteach one Tier 2 academic word that is *not* in the decodable text but can be used to discuss the text. Use the Define, Example, Ask routine developed by Isabel Beck. This will elevate the conversation and further build oral language during the reading of these simple texts. |

| DURING READING | |
|---|---|
| **Read the Book**<br><br>Read the title. Have students repeat. Describe the cover illustration using key words to frontload vocabulary. Ask students to tell what they think the story will be about and why (noting details in the art and title). | Have students whisper-read the text as you circulate and listen in. Have students point to each word as they whisper-read it. It is essential that students hear themselves as they work through the sounding out of words. This helps to orthographically map the words into memory.<br><br>Circulate, listen in, and provide corrective feedback. If students have difficulty with any word, stop and model how to sound it out. Then have students reread the sentence with the corrected word.<br><br>You might wish to stop periodically and check general understanding as students read. For example, have them whisper-read one or two pages at a time, stop, and ask a general question. Include questions using the Tier 2 academic vocabulary word that you pretaught.<br><br>Follow this up with a choral read or an echo read. Echo reads are ideal if many students struggled with the first reading or if there are aspects of fluency you want to model (e.g., reading sentences with different end punctuation). |
| **Provide Corrective Feedback** | Target your feedback on reinforcing any missed sound-spellings in the word. State the missed sound-spelling, have students repeat, then guide students to use the correction to reblend the word. The student then rereads the sentences with the word correction before moving on. |
| **Text Cohesion** | Often students struggle carrying ideas across sentences when they are focusing so intensely on decoding. When a concrete noun is replaced by a pronoun in a subsequent sentence, model for students how to connect the two. Here is an example.<br><br>Sentences: *Pam ran to the dog. She pet it.*<br><br>Ask: *Who is she?*<br><br>If necessary, draw an arrow from *she* to *Pam* to connect the two. Then reread the second sentence, replacing *she* with *Pam* to confirm the connection. |

| AFTER READING | |
|---|---|
| **Revisit to Check Comprehension** | Revisit the text by asking questions that require students to reread the text and support their answers with text evidence. Below are sample questions I asked students after reading a decodable text about a girl visiting Spain (phonics focus: long *a*). After I asked each question, I allowed time for students to discuss their answers with partners before asking volunteers to share their answers. This ensures all students are rereading, processing their understanding, and using language. |

| | |
|---|---|
| 1. *Where did the girl go? Point to the country's name in the story.*<br><br>**Phonics Focus** | This question focuses children's attention on a word containing the new phonics skill. |
| 2. *What did the girl do in Spain? Find the sentences that tell you this.*<br><br>**Detail With Text Evidence** | This question directs children's attention to details in the text and requires them to provide text evidence to support their answers—an important early literacy behavior necessary for both reading and writing. |
| 3. *What problems did the girl have? Circle them. Why were they problems?*<br><br>**Higher-Order Thinking** | This is a higher-order thinking question requiring children to pull together various pieces of information and directing them to find the details that will help them. |
| 4. *Where might the girl go next? Why do you think this?*<br><br>**Inference** | This is a more complex question that requires students to make an inference based on text evidence and their personal knowledge. Model for students how to make an inference as needed. The questions offer opportunities to check comprehension AND model comprehension strategies. |
| 5. *Where might you like to go on a big trip? What would you like to* **explore** *there? Tell your partner why.*<br><br>**Connect to Students' Lives, Reinforce Academic Vocabulary** | This question connects the story to children's lives. It also includes the pretaught Tier 2 academic word (*explore*) to extend students' opportunities to use the more complex language. |

| | |
|---|---|
| **Write to Deepen Understanding**<br><br>Have students retell the story to a partner in their own words. They can use the illustrations as clues to their retellings. Then have students write about the story. They can write their retelling, a story extension, a new story with the same characters, or what they learned from the book (if nonfiction). For extra support, use sentence starters or summary/retelling frames and allow drawings.<br><br>Writing about a decodable text requires students to use words they've decoded with the target phonics skill and deepens comprehension. It is a highly scaffolded activity because students have the book as a support when writing, further helping them | *See the next chapter for more details.* |

*(Continued)*

(Continued)

| | |
|---|---|
| transition the newly acquired phonics skill from reading to writing. It is unnecessary to do dictation on the days in which students are writing about the decodable texts, as this writing is an authentic application of their growing phonics and spelling skills and offers ample opportunities to model how to segment and spell new words, as well as to reinforce developing writing skills (e.g., capitalization, punctuation, using vivid verbs). | |
| **Reread to Build Fluency** | Have students reread the book to a partner. Circulate, listen in, and provide corrective feedback.<br><br>Reread this book on subsequent days to develop fluency. You might have partners reread it on one day as you circulate and listen in, and then have students reread the text independently on a later day and do an activity, such as create a list of words with a target spelling pattern (e.g., words with -*ain* and -*ay*).<br><br>These repeated readings of a text are a key part of developing fluency reading words in context, words that reinforce the new phonics skill. This rereading routine occurs during whole-group time for the new decodable text and during independent time for previously read decodable texts. |
| **Engage in Encoding Activities** | Engage students in follow-up activities, such as dictation and word building, that focus on spelling words containing the new phonics skill. Start with words from the text and build from there. |

## ROUTINE 3: READING DECODABLE TEXT—TEACHER ALERTS AND PRINCIPAL/COACH LOOK-FORS

| TEACHER ALERTS<br>Things to consider | PRINCIPAL/COACH<br>LOOK-FORS |
|---|---|
| [ ] Make sure accountable text is a part of the daily phonics instruction and independent or partner follow-up work. | [ ] Are decodable/accountable texts a daily part of the phonics lessons? |
| [ ] Make sure you are using strong, accountable texts, i.e., comprehensive, engaging, and filled with enough words students can decode based on the phonics skills they have been taught.<br><br>[ ] Strengthen connections between phonics lesson reading and small-group lesson reading, especially if using leveled texts (which may contain few or no words containing the target phonics skill).<br><br>[ ] Build comprehension (through rich questioning) AND vocabulary (through preteaching words in the selection to use in discussions).<br><br>[ ] Use decodable texts as springboards for writing. | [ ] Does the reading of these texts focus on decoding strategies, checking comprehension, and building vocabulary? |

# DIFFERENTIATE IT!

| WHO? | HOW? |
|------|------|
| **Students Above Grade-Level Expectations** | Listen to students read the decodable text on the first day to confirm fluency. On subsequent days, have students reread the more advanced decodable text from the small-group lessons (or a book the student chooses) while the other students reread the week's decodable text. |
| **Students Below Grade-Level Expectations** | Use the Preview routine shown below. On subsequent days when students are rereading the text to partners, have these students reread only a portion of the text (e.g., a page or spread) to minimize frustration. Students will be able to complete this task in the time provided, and it won't be as overwhelming as reading the entire story during that time. Continue to have them listen to an audio recording and follow along, reading with the narrator as possible. |
| **Multilingual Learners** | Use the following **Preview routine** for any decodable books or passages in your reading program or set of materials. <br><br> **Introduction:** Introduce the story by reading aloud the title and explaining that students will be reading this story to (1) practice their skill in sounding out words and (2) check their understanding of what they read. Remind them that we also read stories for fun and to learn new things. Praise students for their efforts, and remind them that you are there to help with any challenges. <br><br> **First Read:** Have students listen to the audio recording (e-book version, if available) and follow along during independent work time prior to the whole-class reading. <br><br> **Second Read:** Guide students through an echo reading during small-group time before the whole-group lesson. Focus on vocabulary and general understanding. <br><br> **Third Read:** Have students read the book during the whole-group lesson with their peers. This careful scaffolding should enable them to have a more successful whole-group reading experience. |

## JOYFUL LEARNING VARIATIONS

While instructional routines are important for the efficiency of our teaching and for aiding in student learning, sometimes I like to mix it up and do an alternate activity with the same instructional focus and goal. Here are some possibilities for decodable texts.

### Decodable Reader's Theater

Create reader's theater experiences using the decodables (especially those with dialogue), or use published decodable reader's theater plays. Assign students parts to practice during independent or partner work, and set aside time at the end of the week for students to share their group readings. Reader's theater can also be conducted using simple phonics poems, rhymes, and songs.

### Our Audio Library

Have students record themselves reading decodables and create a digital collection that students can listen to for pleasure.

## CLASSROOM SNAPSHOT

| **Teacher:** Mr. B | **Lesson Focus:** *The Big Trip* |
|---|---|
| **Students:** Five students above grade-level expectations | |
| Eight students below grade-level expectations | |
| Twelve students meeting grade-level expectations | |
| Four students who are multilingual learners | |

*(Continued)*

(Continued)

Mr. B has introduced the new phonics skill (long *a*) and the high-frequency words (*away, one, doesn't*, and *something*) using the Read, Spell, Write, Extend routine. He is now distributing the decodable text for today: *The Big Trip*.

**The Big Trip**

*Page 1: Last May, I went to Spain. It was a fun trip. What did I do there? Take a look!*

*Page 2: One day, I rode a train. I paid a lot for the ride. I went to see a museum. I had to wait in a long line to get inside.*

*Page 3: The next day, it rained. I went to see a castle. A castle is a big home for a king and queen. But the King of Spain doesn't live in this one.*

*Page 4: Spain is a fun place to visit. When I go away next spring, maybe I will go back. But I hope it doesn't rain again!*

Mr. B asks student to put their fingers on the title, as he leads them in a choral reading of *The Big Trip*.

*Today we are going to read a story about a girl going on a trip to a faraway country and learn about the many things she will explore there. Everyone say,* **explore***.* Mr. B pauses for students to state the new Tier 2 vocabulary word that will be the focus during the discussion of this decodable text and corrects pronunciation as needed. He then introduces the word using the Define, Example, Ask routine. When he asks the question in the "Ask" portion of the routine, he reinforces the definition of *explore* to make sure all students understand the question.

**Define:** *Explore means "to find out more about something."*

**Example:** *We will explore the pond near our school during science class.*

**Ask:** *What would you like to explore, or find out more about, at a pond? Tell your partner.*

Since this is the first long vowel decodable book students have read and there are two spellings for long *a* included in the book (*ai* and *ay*), Mr. B decides to begin with an echo read. He reads one sentence at a time as students point to each word, and he then asks students to read the sentence to him as they point to each word. When he finishes each page, he asks the students to whisper-read the page on their own before asking general comprehension questions or engaging them in a conversation about the story.

To make sure students are connecting ideas across sentences (text cohesion), Mr. B stops after page 1 for a check. *Look at this sentence:* **What did I do there?** *What place does the word* **there** *connect to? Point to the name of the place and show your partner.* Mr. B pauses as partners answer the question. He then draws an arrow to connect *there* with **Spain**. *The place the girl is going is the country of Spain. Listen as I replace* **there** *with in* **Spain: What did I do in Spain?** *Does that make sense? Yes! Spain is a country far away in Europe. Look at our world map. This is where Spain is located, or found.* Mr. B traces a path with his finger from the state in which his students live to the country of Spain.

Mr. B continues echo reading page 2 with students and then asks the students to whisper-read. He stops for questions after page 2. *What is the girl exploring on this page? Tell your partner. Discuss what she might find out more about in this place. Use the word* **explore** *in your conversation.*

Mr. B continues echo reading page 3 with students and then asks the students to whisper-read. He stops and asks this. *What is the girl exploring on this page? Tell your partner.* He listens in on the conversation and then calls on a volunteer to share her answer. He continues discussing this page by using different forms of the word **explore**. *A castle is a great place for an exploration. I would love exploring a castle. What would you like to explore in a castle? Tell your partner. Use the word* **explore** *in your conversation. If you need help, begin your sentence with* **In a castle, I would explore** _____. Mr. B is slowly trying to introduce more complex sentence structures into students' oral language.

Mr. B concludes by echo reading page 4 with students, then asking the students to whisper-read. He stops for questions. *How do you think the girl feels about her big trip to Spain? Why do you think this? Tell your partner. Use information from the text, the illustration on this page, and what you know about visiting places.* Mr. B circulates and listens in on the conversation. He sees that he is short on time, so he ends the lesson there.

*Tomorrow, we will revisit the story and dig in a little deeper. We will also write about what we read. Please close your books and place them in the bin on your tables. You will reread the story with a partner during independent work time.*

**Note:** On the next day, Mr. B will guide students in a series of questions about the story that requires them to reread portions of the text to build fluency and develops some important early reading behaviors. The questions he will ask are below. This engaging conversation includes a lot of reading, thinking, and talking—the kind of work with these texts Mr. B knows his students need.

1. Phonics focus: *Where did the girl go? Find the country's name in the story.*

2. Detail with text evidence: *What did the girl do in Spain? Find the sentences that tell you this.*

3. Higher-level thinking question: *What problems did the girl have? Circle them.*

4. Higher-level thinking question (inference): *Where might the girl go next? Why do you think this?*

5. Connect to children's lives: *Where would you like to go on a big trip? What would you like to explore there?*

Mr. B will also prompt the students to write about the story. The story prompt is below. See the next chapter for details on this part of the lesson.

*What did the girl do in Spain?*

FIVE KEY TAKE-AWAYS

1. Most programs do not provide enough decodable texts, and most schools are still building their collections of them. Augment what you have with high-quality texts from publishers like Benchmark, Scholastic, and Sadlier.

2. Use decodable texts before, during, and after reading to deepen their impact on students' decoding, comprehension, vocabulary development, writing, and spelling.

3. In whole-group instruction, have students whisper-read the full text at some point in the lesson to accelerate orthographic mapping of fully decodable words. Model blending and aspects of fluency.

4. Use small-group instruction to build fluency with skills—either previously taught skills not yet mastered or newly introduced skills.

5. Decodable texts are effective for a relatively brief window of time. Often by midyear in Grade I, students are ready for instruction with bridging texts. While the decodable texts continue to provide that valuable and intentional practice in mastering the new phonics skills for the entire year of kindergarten and Grade I, the bridging texts are slightly less controlled, transition students into traditional trade books, and can be slowly added to the decodable text readings.

# CHAPTER EIGHT

# Writing About Decodable Text Routine

## And How to Differentiate

## WHAT IS IT?

Writing about a decodable text offers a unique opportunity to combine comprehension and encoding practice for students. As students write, they show their developing understanding of the story while engaging in a structured exercise that requires them to use decodable words with the new target phonics skill. Learners are encouraged to reread the text as they write, which benefits both their reading and their spelling. The words and sentences in the decodable text give students a "running start" on their writing, making the task of composing ideas less daunting for them.

## RESEARCH HIGHLIGHTS

- Writing development lags behind reading development (Moats, 1995). Students need more opportunities to use their growing phonics skills in writing to develop their spelling abilities. Activities such as writing about decodable texts, dictation, and word building with letter cards can be used throughout the instructional cycle to achieve this goal.

- *The Writing Rope*, by Sedita (2022), provides a framework that identifies the major components of skilled writing: critical thinking (generating ideas and gathering information, writing process), syntax (grammar, sentence elaboration, punctuation), text structure (narrative, informational, opinion; paragraph structure; organizational patterns such as cause/effect or sequence; linking and transition words), writing craft (word choice; awareness of task, audience, and purpose; literary devices), and transcription (spelling, handwriting, keyboarding). Work with many of these components can be a focus of the writing work done as a follow-up to the reading of decodable texts.

## IMPLICATIONS FOR YOUR INSTRUCTION

- Have students write about every decodable text they read.

- Don't approach these writings as one-off assignments. Revisit the writings on subsequent days, and have students revise them based on aspects of writing you are teaching in your writing lessons at other times during your literacy block, such as correcting punctuation or capitalization errors, combining sentences, or adding more vivid verbs.

- Include structured work with syntax to get students proficient in understanding how different parts of sentences add meaning, as well as to increase students' ability to create more complex sentences. This work also increases students' sentence-level comprehension and sets them up for unpacking more complex sentences and paragraphs in later grades. Sentences increase in complexity based on their length, number of clauses, distance between the subject and verb, advanced connectives (e.g., *however*, *although*), pronoun references, less common verb tenses, and use of the passive or active voice. Some of these syntactic enhancements can be addressed as early as kindergarten.

- When reading, guide students to **deconstruct** complex sentences. For example, take a complex sentence in the text and chunk it into meaningful parts by drawing lines to divide the parts: *Pam had to wait / in a long line / to get inside the museum.* Read the first part of the sentence (the "who" and "did what" portions), and have students echo. Then ask, *Where did Pam wait?* Point to the second part of the sentence and guide students to read it. Then read the first two parts and ask, *Why did Pam wait?* Point to the third part of the sentence and guide students to read it. Then read all the parts together.

- After reading, **construct** sentences with students using content from the story. For example, if you read a story about a brother running in a race, you might guide students to complete the following sentence frames orally and in writing as you go from simple to more complex sentences. Repeat usage of this activity enables students to more easily construct longer more complex sentences with ease.

  My brother ran.

  My brother ran _____ (when).

  My brother ran _____ (where).

  My brother ran _____ (when) (where).

  My brother ran _____ (when) (where) (how).

  My brother and _____ ran.

  My brother and _____ (who) ran _____ (when) (where).

You can also guide students to change sentences by changing punctuation (e.g., changing a statement into a question, which requires them to move around parts of the sentence and add a word or two—for example, *My brother ran to the park becomes Did my brother run to the park?*). You can also guide students to move around parts of sentences to go from sentences that resemble spoken language (e.g., *My brother ran to the park*) to sentences that resemble book language, which is more challenging for students (e.g., *To the park, my brother ran*).

# DIFFERENTIATE IT!

| WHO? | HOW? |
|---|---|
| **Students Above Grade-Level Expectations** | Add the pretaught Tier 2 academic word to a word bank, and encourage students to include the word in their writing. |
| **Students Below Grade-Level Expectations** | Provide sentence frames and sentence starters for students needing that level of support. Encourage students to go beyond the frames and starters. Also, add words to a word bank and prompt students to include them in their writing. For example, select two key decodable words containing the new phonics skill and one of the new high-frequency words.

Some students will need paragraph retelling frames for extra support, especially those who feel frustrated by the amount of writing required to write an adequate retelling. These frames can include simple connector words:

First, _____.

Then, _____.

Next, _____.

At last, _____.

Include more details as needed by students. Then have them practice rereading their retellings based on these frames. These extended frames can also be used as guides for oral retellings. |
| **Multilingual Learners** | Provide sentence frames and sentences starters at different levels of language acquisition for students needing that level of support. Encourage students to go beyond the frames and starters. Also, add words to a word bank and prompt students to include them in their writing. For example, select two key decodable words containing the new phonics skill and one of the new high-frequency words. Allow time for students to discuss their writing in their primary language first—especially if you or a student speaks that language. |

# JOYFUL LEARNING VARIATIONS

While instructional routines are important for the efficiency of our teaching and for aiding in student learning, sometimes I like to mix it up and do an alternate activity with the same instructional focus and goal. Here are some possibilities for writing complex sentences.

## Word Card Sentence Build

Write nouns (who), verbs (do/did what), and phrases that tell where, when, or how on separate index cards. Place each type of sentence part in a column in a pocket chart (e.g., all the "who" parts in the same column). Guide students to build sentences using parts from each column. Read the completed sentences. Move around the parts in a completed sentence to see if you can create variations of the same sentence. Keep blank index cards handy in case you need to add words. Make sure you have punctuation index cards visible as well.

## Trio Sentence Building Train

Whiteboards are ideal for this activity. Create a sentence building train with three students, one for each "car" of the train. The first student (car) writes the "who" and the "do/did what" portion of the sentence. The next person writes the "where" portion. The last person writes the "why" or "how" portion. Have the trios read and share their completed sentences. Repeat having students switch roles in the sentence build.

# CLASSROOM SNAPSHOT

| | | **Lesson Focus:** |
|---|---|---|
| **Teacher:** Mr. B | | *The Big Trip* |
| **Students:** | Five students above grade-level expectations | (continued) |
| | Eight students below grade-level expectations | |
| | Twelve students meeting grade-level expectations | |
| | Four students who are multilingual learners | |

*(Continued)*

(Continued)

Mr. B read the decodable text, *The Big Trip*, with students on the previous day and had students read the story with partners during independent work time. Today, he has already guided students through a revisit of the text to deepen comprehension using the questions below.

Comprehension Questions

1.  Phonics focus: *Where did the girl go? Find the country's name in the story.*

2.  Detail with text evidence: *What did the girl do in Spain? Find the sentences that tell you this.*

3.  Higher-level thinking question: *What problems did the girl have? Circle them.*

4.  Higher-level thinking question (inference): *Where might the girl go next? Why do you think this?*

5.  Connect to children's lives: *Where would you like to go on a big trip? What would you like to **explore** there?*

The students are now ready to write about the text. Mr. B knows that this will give them an opportunity to use words containing the new target skill (long *a* spelled *ai* and *ay*) in writing—a valuable encoding activity. Since students are just learning how to use these two spellings for the long *a* sound in writing, the text offers a built-in scaffold. Students can revisit the text to help them spell words like *Spain* and *train*, or to confirm their spellings.

*Now I want you to write about the story. I want you to write about what the girl did in Spain. Before you write, I want you to turn to your partner and tell them what you remember from the story. Look back at the story if you need help.*
Mr. B circulates as students discuss what the girl did in Spain. He provides enough time for them to have a rich conversation and revisit the text because he knows that talking about what they will write to clarify their ideas will improve the content of their writing.

While students are concluding their conversations, he records a few words in a word bank on the board. These words include *explore* (the Tier 2 academic word), *Spain* and *day* (two decodable words with the new phonics skill) and *one* (a new high-frequency word). He also writes a couple of sentence frames on the board for students who will need that level of support:

*The girl _____ in Spain.*

*The girl _____ and _____ in Spain.*

*In Spain _____, the girl _____.*

*Before you start writing, take a look at today's word bank. The first word is **explore**. Say, **explore**. Let's read the next three words together. Ready? Read.* Mr. B guides students through a reading of *Spain, train,* and *one. Try to include as many of these words as you can in your writing. Also, if you need help as you write, take a look at these sentence frames. You can use these as you need. Listen as I read them.*

As students begin writing, Mr. B circulates. He stops by his above-level students and encourages them to include *explore* in their writing. He makes sure his multilingual learners and below-level students are using the sentence frames if they show a need.

*For those of you who finish early, reread your writing then add a picture with lots of details to show what the girl did in Spain.*

NOTE: On the next day, Mr. B has the students revisit their writings. He asks them to read their writings to their partners. Then he gives them a revision assignment:

*We have been working on using capital letters at the beginnings of sentences, for the word I, and for the first letter in names in our writing lessons. I want you to revisit this writing about* The Big Trip *and make sure you used capital letters correctly.*

Mr. B provides time for students to revise their writings.

He then guides students through a syntax-focused writing activity. He writes the following sentence frames on the board.

The girl saw (what).

The girl saw (what) (where).

The girl saw (what) (when).

The girl saw (what) and (what).

Mr. B reads and asks students to complete the first frame orally with their partners. He then calls on a few volunteers to show the range of responses. He asks the students to write their sentences. Then he asks them to write that sentence again but to leave off the period at the end because he wants to add more information. He asks, *Where did the girl do what you wrote? Share that with your partner.*
Mr. B circulates and listens in as students share; then he calls on volunteers to share. Students then complete their expanded oral sentence in writing (e.g., *The girl saw a little dog at the park*). *Count the number of words in your new sentence.* Mr. B does this in these activities to show students they are capable of writing long, complex sentences by adding parts to their simple sentences that answer questions (e.g., Where? Why? How?). He often asks students to revise their writing to add sentence parts that answer these questions. His students are getting comfortable writing longer sentences than ever before.

Mr. B continues with the sentence frames. To conclude the activity, he models for students how to take their second sentence and start it with the "where" part. *I noticed that some of you wrote* **The girl rode a train in Spain**. *Watch as I write this sentence on the board. Which part of this sentence tells "where"? That's right:* **in Spain**. *I am going to rewrite this sentence to begin with the "where" part. Watch as I do this:* **In Spain, the girl rode in a train**. *Let's read these two sentences together. Ready? Read.* **The girl rode a train in Spain. In Spain, the girl rode a train**. *Do these sentences mean the same thing? Yes! When we read books, the sentences don't always sound like how we talk. Sometimes parts of sentences are moved around. We call that book language. We will listen for examples of this when I read our read-aloud today. Please add today's writings to your writing folders.*

# FIVE KEY TAKE-AWAYS

1. Inviting students to write about texts helps them strengthen decoding and encoding skills. Students need to engage in purposeful reading and writing daily.

2. Create a tight knit between the new phonics skill, decodable words you expect students to be able to spell, and the questions you ask them to write about. Doing so makes it easier for students to learn, giving them a greater sense of cohesion.

3. Support all students before, during, and after the lesson with tactile scaffolds such as word banks on the classroom wall, sentence and paragraph frames, and writer's notebooks.

4. While students work collaboratively and independently, continuously watch and provide brief, targeted assistance to students who need it.

5. When students write about decodable texts, each day look for ways to differentiate the experience in terms of sentence structure or syntax tasks, vocabulary work, and composing. Students above grade-level expectations can extend their writing by composing their own versions of the featured story, writing a "new chapter" for it, and so on.

# CHAPTER NINE

# Dictation Routine

## And How to Differentiate

## WHAT IS IT?

Dictation is guided spelling practice. It is your way of modeling and providing supported practice for a student in how to transfer phonics skills from reading into writing. The great benefit of dictation is that it can accelerate students' use of taught phonics skills in their spelling.

## RESEARCH HIGHLIGHTS

- In the primary grades, students' spelling ability generally lags behind their reading ability (Moats, 1995). That is, students can read words by applying specific phonics skills before they can consistently write words accessing those same skills. This is beneficial for us to know. For example, if we see students correctly and consistently using consonant digraphs like *ch* or *sh* in their writing, then we know they can read words with these same sound-spellings.

- Most state standards connect phonics reading skills to spelling skills in the early grades. However, in most phonics programs, there is an imbalance between decoding (reading) activities and encoding (spelling) activities. Generally, there are far more decoding activities in each lesson. We need to correct the imbalance so students efficiently master phonics skills in both reading and writing. Too often, students continue to struggle to apply a taught phonics skill to spelling words long after that skill has been introduced. This is why intentional review, repetition, and application of the skill for at least four to six weeks after the introduction is important.

- While most states link their phonics and spelling standards, especially at the primary grades, some researchers have chosen to separate their phonics lessons from their spelling lessons using a spelling scope and sequence that is based on a developmental sequence (e.g., Bear et al., 2019; Moats, 2000).

- Research and classroom practice show that students learn letter-sound relationships and spellings as they write. Formal, sequential dictation practice each week provides students with structured opportunities to develop their writing and spelling skills, with your guided support and corrective feedback.

- Dictation relies on students' knowledge of letter-sound and spelling-sound relationships as well as on students' ability to segment words orally—a key phonemic awareness skill. Getting students to attend to words at the phoneme, or sound, level must be a priority in early kindergarten in order for students to begin spelling words. Numerous recent studies, research documents, and academic blog postings have focused on this issue. These include the following and others:

  1. **"Building Phoneme Awareness" by the International Dyslexia Association:** This new fact sheet on phonemic awareness highlights the importance of working with words on the phoneme, or sound, level early on and skipping over those less-impactful phonological sensitivity activities (e.g., rhyme) if students are struggling with them. It also

emphasizes combining this phonemic awareness instruction with letter (grapheme) work and handwriting.

2. **"Phonological Awareness Materials in Utah Kindergartens: A Case Study in the Science of Reading":** This article in the *Reading Research Quarterly* by Brown et al. (2021) found "no empirical support" for oral-only phonemic awareness instruction and warned about overdoing the amount of time spent on phonemic awareness activities when these take "valuable instructional time away from research-tested instruction in phonics and the reading of connected text."

3. **"Current Knowledge About Instruction in Letter Knowledge, Phoneme Awareness, and Handwriting: What to Teach, When to Start, and Why to Integrate":** This academic paper by Brady (2021) emphasizes matching the phonemic awareness tasks to students' reading and writing demands, "the strong benefits of instruction in the first year of school that focuses on awareness of phonemes and links phonemes with letters," and the compelling research that shows phoneme awareness (at the sound level) can be taught to students who lack phonological sensitivity (for example, those who struggle with rhyming activities).

4. **"They Say You Can Do Phonemic Awareness Instruction 'In the Dark,' But Should You? A Critical Evaluation of the Trend Toward Advanced Phonemic Awareness Training":** This article by academics Nathan H. Clemens, Emily Solari, Devin M. Kearns, Hank Fien, Nancy J. Nelson, Melissa Stelega, Matthew Burns, Kimberly St. Martin, and Fumiko Hoeft found that "proficiency on so-called advanced phonemic tasks is not more strongly related to reading or more discriminative of difficulties than other phoneme-level skills.". It also warns against the push to include these activities for all students in Grades 2 and up, as mandated by at least one state, and discusses how "reading outcomes

are stronger when phonemic awareness is taught with print" (Clemens et al., 2021, p. 2).

5. **"RIP to Advanced Phonemic Awareness"**: This blog posting by Dr. Timothy Shanahan (on *Shanahan on Literacy*) was the result of a conversation and debate among Tim Shanahan, David Kilpatrick (a strong advocate of advanced phonemic awareness skills), and Linnea Ehri (who coined the term *orthographic mapping*). They agree that getting students to the point where they can fully segment a word is a reasonable goal in phonemic awareness instruction early on. They also generally agree that these "advanced phonemic awareness" skills (e.g., oral substitution, deletion, addition) would not be needed for all students—only for those who struggle with the orthographical mapping of words into memory so these words can be automatically accessed as "sight words." In addition, they agree that "advanced phonemic awareness mandates" by state departments of education lack current evidence to support them (Shanahan, 2021).

- If students are unable to segment words at the phoneme level orally by the time your curriculum requires them to read and spell simple VC (vowel-consonant) and CVC (consonant-vowel-consonant) words (often a couple of months into a kindergarten curriculum), use the activity below to get these children over that hurdle. In this activity, students are given a word orally (e.g., *sat*), guided to stretch the sounds in the word (e.g., /ssssaaaat/) as they move one counter into each sound box (Elkonin box) to physically mark the sounds. They are then guided to replace each sound (counter) with the corresponding letter/spelling (e.g., What's the first sound in *sat*? [/s/] What letter do we write when we hear the /s/ sound? [s] Write *s* in the first box. What's the middle sound in *sat*? . . .). This teaches students how to break apart and put together words—a critical understanding for phonics instruction to be impactful. Figure 9.1 shows an example.

Figure 9-1 • Sound/Elkonin Boxes

| Model | ◯ | ◯ | ◯ |
|---|---|---|---|
| Connect Sound to Letter | **s** | **a** | **t** |

Use sound boxes to help students segment the sounds in words.

# IMPLICATIONS FOR YOUR INSTRUCTION

- Dictation should be a part of your weekly phonics instruction as it is a systematic way for you to show your students how to use their growing phonics skills in their writing.

- Encoding activities, such as dictation, should be a part of each day's phonics lessons. But given time constraints, you might not be able to do dictation in every lesson. If you don't have time to do dictation daily, there are options. I recommend the schedule below when time is an issue. Also, make sure that at least one encoding activity is done each day, such as dictation, word building with letter cards, word sorts with conversations about spelling patterns, and writing about decodable texts.

    **Day 1:** Whole group/all students (focus on new target skill)

    **Day 2:** Small group/below- and above-level students (do quick five-minute differentiated dictation work)

    **Day 3:** Whole group/all students (focus on new target skill)

    **Day 4:** Small group/below- and above-level students (do quick five-minute differentiated dictation work)

**Day 5:** Whole group (dictate cumulative sentences as part of the weekly spelling assessment) Note: These sentences contain words that have both the target skill and previously taught skills, so you can track progress over time to ensure mastery and/or catch decayed learning and make timely course corrections. This is the ONLY weekly dictation used for assessment—the others are guided spelling exercises in which you support students in transferring their reading skills to writing).

- The more opportunities students have to write and "try out" their developing skills, the better. In the early grades, this "invented spelling" or "phonic spelling" will provide you valuable formative assessment information on each student and assist you as you tailor your instruction—and provide appropriate differentiated support.

- While the whole-group dictation generally consists of individual words and, perhaps, a sentence, make sure you fold in some words that contain previously taught skills as a way to differentiate the learning and practice. I recommend analyzing students' writing at least once a month (e.g., in their writer's notebooks) and noting skills previously taught that you don't see students consistently and accurately applying in their spelling. Add words containing these skills to the whole-group dictation word list. If only a few students are struggling applying a specific skill, use that information to form a targeted, skills-based differentiated small group.

- Dictation is meant to be used both as guided practice in writing words and to check students' understanding of sound–spelling correspondences. Since many of the words in the dictation exercises contain the new, target sound-spelling introduced, students are not expected to have mastered that sound-spelling. It is for this reason that dictation is not to be used as an assessment tool. The only time I use dictation as assessment is when I dictate cumulative sentences at the end of the week (instead of using a spelling list based on only the week's target skill).

- Allow students to use supports such as sound boxes to segment the sounds and an alphabet chart to get reminders on how to form the letters. The chart below provides an example dictation word list for kindergarten, Grade 1, and Grade 2.

# DICTATION WORD LIST FOR KINDERGARTEN, GRADE 1, AND GRADE 2

| Kindergarten | **Target Skill: *t*** <br><br> **Review Skills: *a, s, m*** <br><br> (say sound) <br><br> *s*      *t*      *m* <br><br> (words with new and review skills) <br><br> ***am***      ***at*** <br><br> (simple sentence) <br><br> ***Sam sat.*** | • Dictate sounds and have students write the corresponding letters. <br><br> • As students progress, add a few words to the dictation. <br><br> • When ready, add a simple sentence. |
| --- | --- | --- |
| Grade 1 | **Target Skill: Short *u*** <br><br> **Review Skills: Short *e* and *i*** (students have yet to master) <br><br> (words with new skill) <br><br> ***sun***      ***bug*** <br><br> (words with skills needing additional support) <br><br> ***red***      ***hid*** <br><br> (sentence with high-frequency words added) <br><br> ***They have fun in the mud.*** | • Dictate a couple of words containing the new target phonics skill. <br><br> • Add a couple of words containing previously taught skills that students have yet to master as evidenced by their writings. <br><br> • Add a sentence and include one or more of the new high-frequency words being taught. |
| Grade 2 <br><br> Teacher Note: Students are struggling with many earlier skills from Grade 1. | **Target Skill: Words with prefix *re-*** <br><br> (a LEVEL UP dictation) <br><br> ***rain*** (focus on long *a* spellings by reinforcing *ai* in middle, *ay* at end) <br><br> ***train*** (focus on the initial blend and orally segmenting the sound and distinguishing it from /*ch*/) <br><br> ***training*** (add suffix, reinforcing it is a separate and recognizable syllable) <br><br> ***retraining*** (add prefix to get to grade-level word in a step-by-step attainable manner, reinforce meaning of *re-* [again]) <br><br> **Target Skill: Changing *y* to *i* before adding suffix** <br><br> (a dictation focusing on spelling rules and generalizations) <br><br> *happy*     *happily*     *happiness* <br><br> *funny*     *funnier*     *funniest* | • Dictation can take many forms in Grade 2. <br><br> • Use the LEVEL UP version of dictation to differentiate the support. Dictate a word chain that begins with simpler words and builds toward a grade-level more complex word. Do three to five word chains based on time available. <br><br> • Use dictation to practice spelling challenges, such as spelling changes when adding a suffix (e.g., change the *y* to *i*, drop the *e*, double the final consonant). |

*(Continued)*

(Continued)

| | | |
|---|---|---|
| | **Target Skill: Multisyllabic words with prefix *re-*** <br><br> Teacher asks students to clap each syllable and spell one syllable at a time. <br><br> (Chunk longer words into recognizable and common word parts.) <br><br> *re-read* <br><br> *re-cook-ing* <br><br> *re-main-ing* <br><br> **Target Skill: Related words with confusing spellings** <br><br> (a related words dictation to build morphophonemic awareness) <br><br> *sign    signal    signature* <br><br> *limb    limber* <br><br> *heal    health    healthy* | • Use dictation to chunk longer words and see those chunks as common word parts. <br><br> • Use dictation to increase students' morphophonemic awareness. Dictate a series of related words that illustrate how spellings are maintained across related words. |

- For the end-of-the-week, whole-group dictation of cumulative sentences, circle words misspelled and record skill errors (e.g., long *e* spelled *ea*, diphthongs *ou* and *oi*). Add more of these words to whole-group dictation if lots of students are showing the same types of errors. If not, use the information to form skills-based differentiated small groups for targeted dictation activities. See the sample cumulative sentences in the chart below. Note that skills should be assessed in the cumulative sentence dictation for four to six weeks after they are introduced.

## Examples of Cumulative Sentences for Kindergarten, Grade 1, and Grade 2

| Kindergarten | **Target Skill: Short *o*** <br><br> **Review Skills: *h, d, n, f, c,* short *i*, short *a*** <br><br> 1. *Dan is not hot!* <br> 2. *The hat can fit on me.* |
|---|---|
| Grade 1 | **Target Skill: /ou/ spelled *ou* and *ow*** <br><br> **Review Skills: Long and short *oo*; r-controlled vowel spellings *or/ore*, *er/ir/ur*, *ar*; long *u* spelled *ew/ue*** <br><br> 1. *My house is made of wood.* <br> 2. *The girl ran down the street.* <br> 3. *I found a few more books.* <br> 4. *It is dark outside.* |

| Grade 2 | **Target Skill: Diphthongs /ou/ and /oi/** |
|---------|---------|
| | **Review Skills: Long and short _oo_; _r_-controlled vowel spellings _or/ore_, _er/ir/ur_, _ar_** |
| | 1. _I have a loose tooth in my mouth._ |
| | 2. _The cowboy rode his horse downtown._ |
| | 3. _The mouse chewed a hole in the corner of my shoe._ |
| | 4. _Is it hard to join the school's soccer team?_ |

To differentiate each student's spelling needs effectively, you need activities such as dictation and cumulative sentences to monitor progress over time in a systematic and intentional way. You also need tools to stay on top of what students can and cannot do in their spelling, as compared to grade-level expectations. The simplest tool I use is a spelling checklist that I place in the front of each student's writer's notebook as shown on the following pages.

# Tips for Using a Spelling Checklist

- The spelling checklist contains a list of the phonics skills (therefore, the spelling skills needed to be mastered) for the grade, along with a column to check when movement toward mastery is shown and a column to record sample words correctly used in students' writing.

- When a phonics skill is introduced, the students circle it on their spelling checklist. This is an indicator to them that I will hold them accountable for correctly using that skill in their writing.

- At least once a month, I review students' most recent writings, including those in their writer's notebooks. I look at the circled skills on the spelling checklist to notice words containing those skills.

- If students are consistently and accurately spelling words containing any of the circled skills, I add a check mark in the "Mastery" column to show movement toward proficiency in applying that skill to writing. I then record some of the correctly spelled words demonstrating that skill in the last column. I use this information when conferencing with students to celebrate their successes and to set new, individualized spelling goals.

- The following is an example of a marked-up spelling checklist for one student. Notice that the student is still struggling with applying two previously taught skills, spelling words with short _e_ and short _i_, as well as with applying a recently taught skill, spelling _l_-blends. (Mastery of this last skill is not unexpected since it takes some students many weeks of intentional work on a skill to transfer it efficiently to writing.)

# GRADE 1

## Marked-Up Spelling Checklist

| SKILL | MASTERY | EXAMPLES | SKILL | MASTERY | EXAMPLES |
|---|---|---|---|---|---|
| (Short a) | ✓ | am, man, sad | Long e (ee, ea) | | |
| (Short i) | | | Long o (oa, ow) | | |
| (Short o) | ✓ | on, hop, lot | Long i (y, igh) | | |
| (Short u) | ✓ | run, sun, but | Long u (u, ew, ue) | | |
| (Short e) | | | r-controlled ar | | |
| (l-blends) | | | r-controlled er, ir, ur | | |
| (s-blends) | ✓ | stop, sled, step | r-controlled or, ore, oar | | |
| r-blends | | | Short oo (book), long oo (oo, ou, ew, ue, u_e) (room) | | |
| Digraph sh Digraph th (both sounds) | | | Diphthong /ou/ (ou, ow) | | |
| Digraph ch, tch Digraph wh | | | Diphthong /oi/ (oi, oy) | | |
| Digraph ng (also cover nk) | | | Complex vowel /â/ [au, aw, a(lk), a(lt), a(ll)] | | |
| Final e (a_e, i_e) | | | r-controlled are, air, ear | | |
| Final e (o_e, u_e, e_e) | | | Long i and o [i(ld), i(nd), o(ld)] | | |
| Single letter long vowels e, i, o | | | Long i and o (ie, oe) | | |
| Long a (ai, ay) | | | Long e (y, ey, ie, ei) | | |

The following are sample spelling checklists for kindergarten, Grade 1, Grade 2, and Grade 3. Modify these checklists based on the phonics scope and sequence for your grade. You can download these from the companion website, as well.

The simplest tool I use is a spelling checklist that I place in the front of each student's writer's notebook.

## KINDERGARTEN

## Writer's Notebook Spelling Checklist

| SKILL | MASTERY | EXAMPLES | SKILL | MASTERY | EXAMPLES |
|---|---|---|---|---|---|
| Mm | | | Bb | | |
| Short *a* | | | Ll | | |
| Ss | | | Kk | | |
| Tt | | | Short *e* | | |
| Pp | | | Gg | | |
| Nn | | | Ww | | |
| Short *i* | | | Xx | | |
| Cc | | | Vv | | |
| Ff | | | Short *u* | | |
| Dd | | | Jj | | |
| Hh | | | Qu | | |
| Short *o* | | | Yy | | |
| Rr | | | Zz | | |

## GRADE 1

### Writer's Notebook Spelling Checklist

| SKILL | MASTERY | EXAMPLES | SKILL | MASTERY | EXAMPLES |
|---|---|---|---|---|---|
| Short *a* | | | Long e (*ee, ea*) | | |
| Short *i* | | | Long o (*oa, ow*) | | |
| Short *o* | | | Long i (*y, igh*) | | |
| Short *u* | | | Long u (*u, ew, ue*) | | |
| Short *e* | | | *r*-controlled ar | | |
| *l*-blends | | | *r*-controlled er, ir, ur | | |
| *s*-blends | | | *r*-controlled or, ore, oar | | |
| *r*-blends | | | Short oo (*book*), long oo (*oo, ou, ew, ue, u_e*) (*room*) | | |
| Digraph *sh* Digraph *th* (both sounds) | | | Diphthong /ou/ (*ou, ow*) | | |
| Digraph *ch*, *tch* Digraph *wh* | | | Diphthong /oi/ (*oi, oy*) | | |
| Digraph *ng* (also cover nk) | | | Complex vowel /â/ [*au, aw, a(lk), a(lt), a(ll)*] | | |
| Final *e* (*a_e, i_e*) | | | *r*-controlled are, air, ear | | |
| Final *e* (*o_e, u_e, e_e*) | | | Long *i* and *o* [*i(ld), i(nd), o(ld)*] | | |
| Single letter long vowels e, i, o | | | Long *i* and *o* (*ie, oe*) | | |
| Long a (*ai, ay*) | | | Long e (*y, ey, ie, ei*) | | |

# GRADE 2

## Writer's Notebook Spelling Checklist

| SKILL | MASTERY | EXAMPLES | SKILL | MASTERY | EXAMPLES |
|---|---|---|---|---|---|
| Short vowels | | | *r*-controlled *ar* | | |
| *l*-blend, *r*-blends, *s*-blends | | | *r*-controlled *er, ir, ur* | | |
| Final blends | | | *r*-controlled *or, ore, oar* | | |
| Final *e* (*a_e, i_e, o_e, e_e, u_e*) | | | *r*-controlled *are, air, ear* | | |
| Digraph *sh* | | | Short *oo* (*oo*) and long *oo* (*oo, ou, ew, ue, u_e*) | | |
| Digraph *ch, tch* | | | Diphthong /*ou*/ (*ou, ow*) | | |
| Digraph *th* | | | Diphthong /*oi*/ (*oi, oy*) | | |
| Digraph *wh* | | | Complex vowel /â/ [*au, aw, a(lk), a(lt), a(ll)*] | | |
| Digraph *ph* | | | Multisyllabic words | | |
| Digraph *ng* (also cover *nk*) | | | Open syllables | | |
| Long *a* | | | Closed syllables | | |
| Long *e* | | | Consonant + *le* syllables | | |
| Long *i* | | | Vowel team syllables | | |
| Long *o* | | | *r*-controlled vowel syllables | | |
| Long *u* | | | Final *e* syllables | | |

## GRADE 3

### Writer's Notebook Spelling Checklist

| SKILL | MASTERY | EXAMPLES | SKILL | MASTERY | EXAMPLES |
|---|---|---|---|---|---|
| Short vowels | | | Closed syllable | | |
| Long *a* | | | Open syllables | | |
| Long *o* | | | Final stable syllables | | |
| Long *e* | | | Vowel team syllables | | |
| Long *i* | | | *r*-controlled vowel syllables | | |
| Long *u* | | | Final *e* syllables | | |
| *r*-controlled vowel *ar* | | | Inflectional endings (*-ed, -ing*) with spelling changes | | |
| *r*-controlled vowel *or*, *oar, ore* | | | Irregular plurals | | |
| *r*-controlled vowel *er*, *ir, ur* | | | Prefixes | | |
| Short *oo* and long *oo* | | | Suffixes | | |
| Diphthong /ou/ (*ou, ow*) | | | Homophones and homographs | | |
| Diphthong /oi/ (*oi, oy*) | | | Compound words | | |
| Complex vowel /â/ [*au, aw, a(lk), a(lt), a(ll)*] | | | Contractions | | |

# ROUTINE 4: DICTATION

| ROUTINE STEPS | SAMPLE TEACHER TALK |
|---|---|
| State aloud the first word in the dictation line, and have students repeat it. For those who have difficulty hearing the sounds in the words, you can provide three levels of support.<br><br>• One level involves saying the sounds more slowly while moving your hands from right to left while facing the class to illustrate beginning, middle, and end.<br><br>• A second level of assistance involves modeling the blending for each sound in the word. In effect, students are helped to hear and write one sound at a time.<br><br>• A third level of support is having students segment the word using sound (Elkonin) boxes and counters, then replacing each counter with a letter or spelling.<br><br>Then have students write the word. | *This time, I want you to write a word that can be sounded out. The word is* **sat**. *Say* **sat**. The students chorally say *sat*.<br><br>• *Sound* **sat**. Here you slowly say the sounds in *sat* without any break and again show beginning, middle, and end with right to left hand motions.<br><br>• Then you move your hand back to the beginning position and ask, *What's the beginning sound?* The students should say */sss/. Write the letter for /**sss**/.* Wait for the students to finish. Then ask, *What word are you writing?* Answer: *Sat. The beginning sound was . . . ?* Answer: */sss/. Next sound?* Answer: */aaa/. Write the letter for /**aaa**/.* Wait for students to finish. *What word are you writing?* Answer: *Sat. What do you have so far?* Answer: */sssaaa/. Last sound?* Answer: */t/. Write the letter for /**t**/.*<br><br>• When they finish, ask students to chorally tell you the sounds in *sat* as you write the word on the board.<br><br>• Note: Guide students using sound boxes and counters to replace each counter with a letter or spelling. |
| Walk around the room and give help as necessary.<br><br>• This may include showing students the correct stroke procedure for writing letters or directing them to the correct spelling on the alphabet wall chart or sound-spelling card.<br><br>• In the case of multiple spellings for a single sound (such as *c*, *k*, and *ck*), tell students which spelling is correct and briefly explain why. For example, the *ck* spelling for */k/* appears at the end of a word and is preceded by a short vowel sound (e.g., *sick, back, rock, luck, deck*). These on-the-spot reminders of rules and generalizations in English spelling are important differentiated additions.<br><br>• Continue this procedure for each word in the dictation line. | Offer corrective feedback. |

| ROUTINE STEPS | SAMPLE TEACHER TALK |
|---|---|
| As each word is completed (or at the end of the activity), provide feedback by writing the answer on the board so that students can correct their work. A key component of dictation is self-correction, in which students begin to notice and correct their errors. This can also aid in continuing the conversation about English spellings. | Write answers on the board for self-correction. |
| For the dictation sentence, read the entire sentence aloud and then focus on one word at a time. For multisyllabic words, do one syllable at a time. While students are writing, walk around and monitor their work, paying more attention to those who are likely to experience difficulty.<br><br>**\*NOTE:** This teacher-assisted sound-by-sound process is critical for students who cannot segment sounds. Don't take shortcuts by just giving students the word, waiting for them to finish, and then writing the answer on the board. Some students will wait and copy what is on the board and will not learn to become independent. This is their time to try, to explore, to make their best attempts. | • For the sentence, say, *Now you will write a sentence with* [three] *words. The sentence is* **Sam is sad**. *Repeat it.* [Sam is sad.] *What is the first word?* [Sam.] *How do we start a sentence?* [With a capital letter.] *Is* **Sam** *a word we can sound out or a word on our high-frequency word chart? Sound* **Sam**. *Use hand motions as before. First sound?* Students say the first sound. *Write it. What word are you writing? What do you have so far? Next sound?* The students respond. *Write it.* Continue in a similar manner until the word is done. *What sentence are you writing?* [Sam is sad.] *What have you written so far?* [Sam.] *What is the next word?* [Is.] *If you know how to spell it, go ahead and write it. If you are not sure, check the high-frequency word chart.*<br><br>• Repeat the above procedure with *sad*, treating it as a word that can be sounded out. |

# ROUTINE 4: DICTATION—TEACHER ALERTS AND PRINCIPAL/COACH LOOK-FORS

| TEACHER ALERTS<br>Things to consider | PRINCIPAL/COACH LOOK-FORS |
|---|---|
| [ ] Model by thinking aloud each week how you write words using the new phonics skill.<br><br>[ ] Make sure spelling is linked to phonics and students' needs based on analysis of their writing.<br><br>[ ] Provide increased opportunities for students to write words containing the new phonics skills (e.g., writing follow-up to decodable text readings).<br><br>[ ] Don't start dictation too late—start at the beginning of K.<br><br>[ ] Spelling words and sentences should be cumulative. Fold in review skills over an extended period of time. Monitor students' writing for information on which skills need the most work. | [ ] Does dictation begin in kindergarten?<br><br>[ ] Does the teacher extend Elkonin box (sound box) activities by having students replace counters with letters?<br><br>[ ] Does the teacher analyze student writing for evidence of use of taught phonics skills and adjust dictation exercises as needed? |

# DIFFERENTIATE IT!

| WHO? | HOW? |
|---|---|
| **Students Above Grade-Level Expectations** | Meet with these students at least one or two times per week during small-group time to conduct dictation activities on more complex skills. During whole-group dictation, dictate a couple of challenge words for students to spell while the other students are checking their work (the answers you wrote on the board). You might also dictate a challenge word for all students to attempt. |
| **Students Below Grade-Level Expectations** | Build in review words in the weekly dictation. Focus on the previously taught skills that many students have yet to master. This intentional, extended process of modeling and practicing guided spelling is the ideal way to embed differentiation into the DNA of your curriculum. Make sure you have sound (Elkonin) boxes and counters available for students needing these hands-on resources. Clap the syllables in longer words and guide students to spell one syllable at a time. Offer other supports as needed. |
| **Multilingual Learners** | Provide articulation support during dictation. Have students clearly repeat the word they are spelling. Discuss how more challenging sounds are formed by pointing out the position of the mouth (lips, teeth, tongue) and whether the sound is voiced (you feel a throat vibration) or unvoiced (you don't feel a vibration). Include supports (e.g., articulation) not only for students whose first or primary language is other than English but also for students speaking different dialects and English variations. |

The chart below shows common sound-spelling variations to address during phonics and spelling activities for students speaking different dialects or variations of English.

## AFRICAN AMERICAN ENGLISH (AAE) PHONICS DIFFERENCES

| ENGLISH/LANGUAGE ARTS SKILL | LINGUISTIC DIFFERENCES AND INSTRUCTIONAL MODIFICATIONS |
|---|---|
| Digraph *th* as in *bathroom* | For many speakers of African American English, the initial /th/ sound in function words, such as *this* and *then*, is often produced as a /d/ sound. In some words, such as *thing* and *through*, the /th/ sound is produced as a /t/ sound. At the ends of words and syllables, such as *bathroom*, *teeth*, *mouth*, and *death*, the /th/ sound is replaced by the /f/ sound. In the word *south*, it is replaced by the /t/ sound (*sout'*). This will affect children's spelling and speaking. Children will need articulation support prior to spelling these words. |
| Final consonant *r* | Many speakers of African American English drop the /r/ sound in words. For example, these children will say *sto'* for *store* or *do'* for *door*. They might also replace it with the *uh* sound, as in *sista* for *sister*. Clearly pronounce these words, emphasizing the /r/ sound. Have children repeat these words several times, exaggerating the /r/ sound, before spelling them. |
| *r*-blends | Many speakers of African American English drop the /r/ sound in words with *r*-blends. For example, these children will say *th'ow* for *throw*. Clearly pronounce these words in the lesson, emphasizing the sounds of the *r*-blend. Have children repeat words several times, exaggerating the /r/ sound. |
| Final consonant *l* and final *l*-blends | Many speakers of African American English drop the /l/ sound in words, particularly in words with *-ool* and *-oal* spelling patterns, such as *cool* and *coal*, and when the letter *l* precedes the consonants *p*, *t*, or *k*, as in *help*, *belt*, and *milk*. The /l/ sound might also be dropped when it precedes /w/, /j/, /r/ (*a'ready*/ *already*); /u/, /o/, /aw/ (*poo*/*pool*), or in contractions with *will* (*he'*/*he'll*). These children will drop the *l* when spelling these words, as well. Provide additional articulation support prior to reading and spelling these words. |
| Final consonant blends (when both are voiced as in *ld* or voiceless as in *sk*) | Many speakers of African American English drop the final letter in a consonant blend (e.g., *mp*, *nd*, *nt*, *nk*, *kt*, *pt*, *ld*, *lt*, *lk*, *sk*, *st*, *sp*) or consonant blend sounds formed when adding *-ed* (e.g., /st/ as in *missed* or /pt/ as in *stopped*). For example, they will say *des'* for *desk*. Clearly pronounce the final sounds in these words and have children repeat these words several times, exaggerating the sound. |

*(Continued)*

(Continued)

| ENGLISH/LANGUAGE ARTS SKILL | LINGUISTIC DIFFERENCES AND INSTRUCTIONAL MODIFICATIONS |
|---|---|
| **Other final consonants** | Many speakers of African American English drop the final consonant in a word when the consonant blend precedes a consonant, as in *bes'kind* for *best kind*. They also drop the final consonant sound in words ending in *-ed*, as in *rub* for *rubbed*. Provide additional articulation support prior to reading and spelling these words. |
| **Plurals** | When the letter *s* is added to a word ending in a consonant blend, such as *test (tests)*, many speakers of African American English will drop the final sound. This is due to the phonological (pronunciation) rules of AAE that restricts final consonant blends. Therefore, they will say *tes'* or *tesses*. These children will need additional articulation support. |
| **Contractions** | Many speakers of African American English drop the /t/ sound when pronouncing the common words *it's*, *that's*, and *what's*. These words will sound more like *i's*, *tha's*, and *wha's*. These children will need additional articulation support in order to pronounce and spell these words. |
| **Short vowels *i* and *e*** | When the /i/ and /e/ sounds appear before the consonants *m* or *n* in words such as *pen/pin* and *him/hem*, many speakers of African American English won't pronounce or hear the difference. Focus on articulation, such as mouth position for each vowel sound, during lessons. |
| **Inflectional ending *-ing*** | Many speakers of African American English will pronounce words with *-ing* as /ang/. For example, they will say *thang* for *thing*. Emphasize the /i/ sound in these words to help children correctly spell and pronounce them. |
| **Stress patterns** | Many speakers of African American English place the stress on the first syllable in two-syllable words instead of on the second syllable (more common in Mainstream English). For example, they will say **po**'lice instead of po**lice**. These children will need additional articulation support in order to pronounce these words. |
| **Homophones** | Due to the phonological rules of AAE, many words that are not homophones in Mainstream English become homophones in African American English. This will affect children's spelling and understanding of these words. Some examples include *find/fine*, *run/rung*, *mask/mass*, *pin/pen*, *coal/cold*, *mold/mole*. Focus on articulation, such as mouth position, and differences in meaning for each word pair during lessons. |

# CHICANO/A (CE) PHONICS DIFFERENCES

| ENGLISH/ LANGUAGE ARTS SKILL | LINGUISTIC DIFFERENCES AND INSTRUCTIONAL MODIFICATIONS |
|---|---|
| **Final consonants** | Many speakers of Chicano English will drop sounds in words or syllables that end with multiple final consonants, thereby reducing the consonant cluster sound to one consonant sound. For example, they will say *mine* instead of *mind* or *harware* for *hardware*. This occurs when consonant clusters are voiced and unvoiced, as in *prized/price*, *worst/worse*, and *strict/ strick*. Other consonant clusters that are problematic include *ft, sk, sp*, and *pt*. This tendency will affect children's spelling and speaking. Children will need articulation support prior to spelling these words. Clearly pronounce these words. Have children repeat them several times, exaggerating the final consonant sounds before spelling these words. |
| **Digraphs /ch/ and /sh/** | Many speakers of Chicano English will switch (or merge) the /ch/ and /sh/ sounds. This is more common in Tejanos (Chicanos from Texas) than Californianos. Some examples include *teacher/teasher, watch/wash, chop/shop, chair/share, shake/ chake, shy/chy, shame/chame, shop/chop, share/chair*. Provide articulation support. Exaggerate the sound and have children repeat words. |
| **Consonants /z/ and /v/** | Many speakers of Chicano English will replace the /z/ sound with /s/ and the /v/ sound with /f/. Examples include *prized/price, fuzz/fuss*, and *raise/race*, as in *When I don't race my hand the teasher makes a fuzz*, or *lives/lifes* and *save/safe*, as in *The hero safe many lifes*. Articulation support connected to word meanings will be beneficial. |
| **Homophones** | Because of the unique phonological rules of Chicano English, many words that are not homophones in Mainstream English will sound like homophones. For example, *fine* will be used for both *fine* and *find*, *tin* will be used for both *tin* and *ten*, and *pen* will be used for both *pen* and *pin*. Clearly pronounce these words and focus on mouth position during articulation. Have children repeat these words several times, exaggerating the sound, before spelling them. |
| **Stress patterns** | In Chicano English, stress is placed on one-syllable prefixes as well as roots. The stress is also often elongated. For example, speakers of Chicano English will say **too**day for *today*, **dee**cide for *decide*, and **ree**peat for *repeat*. Articulation work will be needed. |
| **Intonation** | Many speakers of Chicano English will exhibit a pattern of intonation that is different from Mainstream English. This pattern, derived from the Náhuatl language, involves a rise and sustain (or rise and fall) at the end of a phrase or sentence. For example, these speakers will say, "Doont be baaad." Provide articulation support. Recast children's sentences to emphasize intonation when working with children one on one. |
| **Consonant /w/** | Many speakers of Chicano English will pronounce the /w/ sound with an added breath so that it sounds more like /wh/. As a result, words like *with* sound like *whith* and *will* like *whill*. This might also affect children's spelling. Contrast words beginning with *w* and *wh* and have children keep lists in their writer's notebooks. |
| **Pronouncing *the*** | The word *the* is pronounced in Mainstream English with a schwa sound *(thuh)* before a word beginning with a consonant, and a long-e sound *(thee)* before a word beginning with a vowel. Many speakers of Chicano English will use the schwa pronunciation for all words. Point out the distinction and usage of each pronunciation. |

# Regional/Dialect Phonics Differences

| ENGLISH/ LANGUAGE ARTS SKILL | LINGUISTIC DIFFERENCES AND INSTRUCTIONAL MODIFICATIONS |
|---|---|
| **Short *a*** | When the short *a* sound /a/ is followed by /m/ or /n/ (nasal sounds) or /g/ it can affect the pronunciation of /a/ and make it more challenging to distinguish the sound. Some English speakers will also need extra support distinguishing /a/ and /e/ because they are formed in similar ways and are beside each other on the Vowel Valley Sound Wall chart. |
| **Short *i*** | Some students might confuse or have difficulty distinguishing the /i/ and /e/ sounds because of regional dialects. When the /i/ and /e/ sounds appear before the consonants *m* or *n* in words such as *pen*/ *pin* and *him*/*hem,* many speakers of African American English won't pronounce or hear the difference. Model each sound and focus on the articulation of confusing word pairs. Say: *The /i/ sound makes you grin, while the /e/ sound makes you drop your chin.* |
| **Short *o*** | In some English dialects, when the letter *o* is followed by the letter *g*, as in *dog* and *log*, the sound for the letter *o* is pronounced more like /ô/ than /o/. |
| **Short *e*** | In some regions of the United States, English speakers may pronounce short *e* as long *a*. For example, *egg* might be pronounced as *aeg*. These speakers might write long *a* with an *e* and will need extra support. |
| **Long *u* vs.** **Long *oo*** | The *u_e* spelling can stand for the long *u* sound in words like *use* and *cute* but also the long *oo* sound as in words like *tube* and *rule*. Point this out to children as they encounter these spellings in their readings. Teach mispronunciation correction (set for variability). Say: *What other sound could this spelling stand for? What else could you try?* |
| **Long *i*** | The long *i* sound acts like a diphthong—when making the sound there is movement in the mouth, unlike other long vowel sounds such as long *a* and long *e* where the mouth maintains a consistent position. This might cause children to use more letters to spell the sound or struggle spelling this sound. Point this out when modeling articulation. |
| **Diphthongs /ou/ and /oi/** | Diphthongs are sounds that glide, or move, in the mouth. Some students might struggle attaching discrete spellings to these sounds. Model articulation and point out the movement in the mouth when making the /ou/ and /oi/ sounds. |
| **Variant vowel /ô/** | In some English dialects, the /ô/ sound has been replaced with the short *o* sound /o/ in words like *bought* and *caught*. In other dialects, the short *o* sound /o/ has been replaced with the /ô/ sound, as in words like *cot* and *dog*. This is known as the "*cot-caught*" merger. |

# JOYFUL LEARNING VARIATIONS

While instructional routines are important for the efficiency of our teaching and for aiding in student learning, sometimes I like to mix it up and do an alternate activity with the same instructional focus and goal. Here are some possibilities for dictation.

## Scrambled Words

Provide a word bank on the board. Then give students a set of scrambled words to unscramble. This requires them to attend to each letter/spelling in a word and notice spelling patterns. Some students find scramble words challenging, so offer the first letter (or first and last) as support.

## Missing Letters

Write a series of words on the board but leave out the target spelling pattern (e.g., *oa* or *ow* for long *o* words or the last syllable in consonant + *le* syllable). Then give a meaning (vocabulary) clue for each word. Students must determine the word and fill in the missing letters or spelling pattern. For example:

I am a yummy red fruit: ap __ __ __ (apple)
I am white and fall in the winter: sn __ __ (snow)

## Crosswords

Crosswords make good spelling practice because they require students to attend to each letter in a word and also have an added benefit—vocabulary work.

## Word Searches

Word searches also make good spelling practice because they require students to attend to each letter or spelling pattern in a word. Students repeat this pattern over and over in their minds as they look for the word in the word search. (e.g., *b-o-a-t, b-o-a-t, b-o-a-t, b-o-a-t* . . . Ahhh! There it is: *boat*).

## Sound/Elkonin Boxes

Students stretch the sounds in a word and drag one counter onto each box as they physically mark the sound. They then replace each counter with the corresponding letter or spelling.

## Chopping Words

Students hold their hands together and make a chopping motion as they move both hands from side to side and "chop" (segment) the sounds in a word. They then swoop quickly to say the word. This helps them focus on each sound as they write the letter/spelling for that sound.

Example: *sat*, /s/ (chop), /a/ (chop), /t/ (chop), *sat* (swoop).

# CLASSROOM SNAPSHOT

Mr. B introduced short *u* spelled *u* and is modeling for his students how to transfer this skill from reading into writing. He has about five minutes for dictation today, so he has selected two words with short *u*: *sun* and *bug*. He has also observed after a look at recent writings in the writer's notebooks that quite a few students are still not consistently writing words with short *e* and short *i*—two previously taught skills. So, Mr. B has added two words to the dictation activity to review these skills: *red* and *hid*. He has also included a simple sentence: *They have fun in the mud*. This sentence includes the irregular high-frequency words *they* and *have*. Mr. B knows that for his above-level students this dictation will be fairly easy, except perhaps the spelling of *they*. So he has added a challenge word: *funny*. He is working with students who are above grade-level expectations during small-group time on words with *-y* and *-ly* endings.

**Target Skill: Short *u***

**Review Skills: Short *e* and *i*** (students have yet to master)

Words for new skill: ***sun bug***

Words for review skills: ***red hid***

Challenge word: ***funny***

Sentence with high-frequency words added: ***They have fun in the mud.***

Mr. B starts the lesson by asking students to number their papers from one to six (1–6). He says: *For number one, I want you to write the word* **sun**. *Everyone say,* **sun**. He pauses for the students to repeat the word. *Let's stretch the sounds in* **sun** *as we move our hands from side to side, chopping on each sound. If you want to use your sound boxes and counters to mark the sounds, please do so.* The students have a stack of sound box templates and counters at their tables.

*Now let's write the letter or spelling for each sound. What's the first sound you hear in* **sun**? Mr. B pauses. *If you aren't sure, watch again as I stretch and chop the sounds. What sound do I say on my first chop?* Mr. B repeats stretching and chopping the sounds, emphasizing the first sound /s/. *That's right; it's /**s**/. What letter do we write when we hear the /**s**/ sound?* Mr. B pauses for a choral response. *That's right; it's the letter* **s**. *If you need help writing the letter* **s**, *take a look at our alphabet chart.*

Mr. B continues modeling the rest of the sounds and corresponding letters for the word *sun*.

*Now it's your turn to try it by yourself. I want you to write the word* **bug**. *Everyone say,* **bug**. Mr. B pauses for a choral response. *Make sure you write the letter for each sound you hear. I will circulate and help as needed.*

Mr. B circulates and offers feedback for a few students. He focuses on students who might need the extra modeling. He knows he can't get to every student, but at the end—when students are self-correcting their work—he will attend to more of them.

*Now let's write some words with phonics skills we have been working on.*

Mr. B repeats the above procedure for the words *red* and *big*. He knows some students have been struggling distinguishing the /e/ and /i/ sounds, so he reminds them of a memory device he used during articulation work a couple of weeks ago. He says, *Remember, when you say /**e**/ you drop your chin, but /**i**/ makes you grin. Try it. Say /**e**/. Do you feel your chin drop? We write the letter* **e** *for /**e**/. Now say /**i**/. Do you feel the grin? We write the letter* **i** *for /**i**/.*

Mr. B then dictates the challenge word: *funny.*

*Okay, who is ready for a funny challenge? The challenge word I want you to write today is* **funny**. *Let's clap the syllables together:* **fun-ny**. *Now write the letters for the sounds you hear in each syllable. Give it your best try!*

Finally, Mr. B dictates the sentence.

*Today we are going to write a long sentence. It has not three, not four, not five, but six words! Listen to the sentence and repeat it after me:* **They have fun in the mud**. Mr. B pauses for students to repeat the sentence. *We will write one word at a time. Let's begin. The first word in the sentence is* **They**. *This is one of our new high-frequency words. Look at our high-frequency word chart if you need help. Which part of* **they** *has a heart above it? Why? Tell your partner.*

Mr. B pauses as students find the word *they* on the chart and note that the letters *ey* have a heart above them because they stand for the /ā/ sound, which doesn't "follow the rules"—that's the part they have to remember by heart.

*(Continued)*

(Continued)

Mr. B continues with the next word: *have*. This word is also a high-frequency word. He reminds them of the rule they learned about English words that end in the /v/ sound. *Let's say the sounds in **have** together: /h/ /a/ /v/. What is the last sound? That's right, it's /**v**/. Tell your partner what we need to do when a word ends in the /**v**/ sound. What letter do we need to add?* Mr. B pauses as students discuss the rule that no English words end in the letter *v*, so if a word ends in the /v/ sound, you must add the letter *e* to the end. He prompts students to share with their partners other words they know that follow this rule, such as *give* and *love*.

Mr. B continues with the rest of the words in the sentence. For the words *fun*, *in*, and *mud* he reminds them that they know all the letter-sounds to write this word.

While they are finishing writing the last word in the sentence, he reminds students to check that they began the sentence with a capital letter and ended it with an end mark as he displays the answers to the dictation activity on the board.

*Now it's time to check your work. Mark any corrections you need to make. I will circulate and help as needed. If you finish early, read your words and sentence to a partner.*

Mr. B has time to check in on a few additional students and offer feedback. He concludes the lesson by praising students for their hard work and reminding them that when they write throughout the day, they should think about the sounds in each word and attach a letter or spelling to each one.

# FIVE KEY TAKE-AWAYS

1. Formal, sequential dictation practice each week provides students with structured opportunities to develop their writing and spelling skills, with your guided support and corrective feedback. Students generally need at least four to six weeks of practice after any new skill is introduced.

2. You can offer a lot of differentiation, even in a relatively brief five-minute lesson. As you plan a lesson, check to see that you have built in "I Do, We Do, You Do" moments, so that learners see and hear explicit teacher modeling (I do); are invited to participate, e.g., by choral spelling together (we do); and try it independently (you do). This model allows you to circulate and provide one-on-one support. Also remind students of previous teaching points and point to helpful charts.

3. Review students' writer's notebooks to discover previously taught sound-spellings that students still struggle with; select words for dictation that give students additional practice.

4. Daily dictation practice is ideal, but if you are crunched for time, as long as you do some other encoding work each day, that's okay.

5. Accelerate children's learning by providing fun practice for school and home. Crossword puzzles, word searches, scrambled words, and missing letters are just a few of many classic activities that shore up spelling.

# CHAPTER TEN

# Word-Building Routine

## And How to Differentiate

## WHAT IS IT?

Word building is a routine in which students build a series of words using letter cards. Each word in the series, or word chain, varies slightly. It is an ideal activity for increasing students' word awareness and consolidating their learning of taught sound-spellings.

## RESEARCH HIGHLIGHTS

- Word building is a high-impact routine because it combines three aspects of learning how words work. First it practices high-level phonemic awareness (manipulation skills such as substitution, addition, or deletion) when students must determine the sound or sounds that are different in each word and decide which sound has been substituted, added, or deleted. It then uses students' encoding (spelling skills) as they write the word using letter cards. Finally, it uses students' decoding (reading) skills as they must read the spelled word to confirm it is correct (Blevins, 2017, 2020b).

- Beck and Beck (2013) is one of the originators of word building sequences and popularized their use in phonics instruction. Their focus was on a student's flexible use of the taught sound-spellings when writing words.

- Research shows that connecting phonemic awareness work with letters is far more impactful than oral-only exercises (Brady, 2021; Brown et al., 2021; Clemens et al., 2021; International Dyslexia Association, 2022). Word building and dictation—during which students orally say, segment, and manipulate the sounds in words and then show their thinking using letters—are two primary applications of this research.

- While the initial introduction of phonics skills is best using an explicit approach, that does not mean there shouldn't be a time during the instructional cycle in which students play with and explore letter-sounds. I think this exploration is *critical* for students to consolidate and solidify their learning of how words work. Yes, the initial explicit introduction begins this learning efficiently, but it takes time and loads of experiences reading and writing words for that knowledge to be mastered. These types of "exploratory" activities (e.g., word building) provide essential "thinking" time for students as they incorporate new learning into already established learning. When phonics instruction fails, it often does so because it is rote, unthinking, and not applied to real reading and writing experiences.

## IMPLICATIONS FOR YOUR INSTRUCTION

- In word building, students are given a set of letter cards and asked to create a series of words in a specified sequence. This can occur during both whole- and small-group lessons. Generally, each new word varies by only one sound-spelling from the previous word (there can be more variance as students progress in skills). For example, students might be asked to build, or make with letter cards, these words in sequence: *sat, mat, map, mop.* Notice how each word varies from the preceding word by only one sound-spelling.

- There are two types of word building, each with a clearly defined instructional purpose.

## Type 1. Blending

In this type of word building, students are asked to make a word, such as *sat.* They are then told to change the letter *s* to the letter *m* and read the new word formed. Thus, the primary goal is for them to blend, or sound out, the new word formed. This is the type of blending you might want to start out with at the beginning of an instructional cycle. It allows students time to use the new target phonics skills to spell and decode many words, while also reviewing previously taught skills.

## Type 2. Word Awareness

In this type of word building, students are asked to make a word, such as *sat.* They are then told to change *sat* to *mat.* This is cognitively more demanding than the blending-focused word building. Students have to consider how the words *sat* and *mat* vary (i.e., which sound is different), which letter must be removed from *sat,* which letter must be added to form *mat,* and in which position in the word that letter must be added. That's a lot of thinking about how words work!

- By repeating the word-building sequences, or chains, multiple times throughout the week with different instructional focuses (and slowing the activity down during small-group time with a subset of the words for students who need extra support), you need to create only one set of words and one set of letter cards—saving you valuable planning time.

- Have students build words with partners during independent work or center time. Create a list of possible words for students to self-check. Use the word-building sequences (chains) and add to them other possible words with the letter set.

- In kindergarten, start word building by replacing the initial sound only, then progress to replacing the initial and final sounds. Finally, guide students to replace the initial, medial, and final sounds. **Examples:** (initial only) *sad, mad, bad, had*; (initial and final) *sad, sat, hat, had, mad, mat*; (initial, medial, and final) *sad, sat, sit, hit, hat, hot, hop, top, tip, tap, map, mat*

- In Grades 1 and 2, you can generally substitute, add, and delete sound-spellings in any position of the word.

- You can increase the word-building complexity in Grades 3 and up by building words with syllables. I recommend using the top 322 syllables in English and other syllables taught or needed to make an effective word chain. The 322 most common syllables can be found in the 5,000 most frequent words in English. Research has shown that 92 percent of the top 322 syllables found in primary grade readers have no more than two pronunciations; 66 percent have only one pronunciation (Sakiey & Martin, 1980). This makes them highly reliable to teach. For a list of these syllables, see *Phonics from A to Z*, 4th edition, by Wiley Blevins.

> Research has shown that 92 percent of the top 322 syllables found in primary grade readers have no more than two pronunciations; 66 percent have only one pronunciation. This makes them highly reliable to teach.

- Managing word-building materials can be a challenge, as most classrooms have students store their letter cards in small plastic baggies, leaving the responsibility of gathering these resources to the teacher. And that takes a lot of time! But there is great news. Publishers are starting to create magnetic word-building boards, so all the students have to do is open the board and get started. If you don't have access to magnetic word-building boards yet, slowly turn over the responsibility of gathering each week's letter cards to the students. Even kindergarteners can handle this task by midyear. Write the word-building letter set on the board on Monday. Have students collect the letter cards and place them in their plastic bags as part of their "get ready for school" routine. You can also do this at the end of the week to prepare for the upcoming week as students ready the classroom before going home.

- The chart below shows a suggested schedule to begin folding in word building to your weekly instructional time.

## DIFFERENTIATED WORD-BUILDING SCHEDULE

| DAY 1 | DAY 2 | DAY 3 | DAY 4 | DAY 5 |
|---|---|---|---|---|
| *Repeat the previous week's word building* during small-group time for students needing more support.<br><br>*Limit the activity to five minutes. | *Blending focus* as part of the whole-group phonics lesson. | *Repeat Day 2 word building* during small-group time for students needing more support;<br>Include a challenge word for students ready for more complex skills. | *Word awareness focus* as part of the whole-group phonics lesson. | *Repeat Day 4 word building* during small-group time for students needing more support;<br>Include a challenge word for students ready for more complex skills. |

- The charts below show differentiated word-building samples.

## DIFFERENTIATED SAMPLES

| TARGET SKILL | WORD CHAIN FOR TARGET SKILL ONLY | WORD CHAIN FOR TARGET SKILL AND REVIEW SKILLS | WORD CHAIN FOR TARGET SKILL, REVIEW SKILLS, AND CHALLENGE WORDS |
|---|---|---|---|
| Short *a* | sad, mad, map, tap, tan, man | sad, mad, map, mop, top, tap, tan, man | sad, mad, map, mop, top, tap, tan, man, pan, plan, plant |
| Long *a* | rain, train, brain, rain, pain, paint, saint, stain, stay, say, ray, gray | ran, rain, train, brain, rain, pain, paint, pant, pan, pay, say, stay | ran, rain, train, brain, rain, pain, paint, pant, pan, pay, say, stay, staying, saying, paying, repaying, repaid, unpaid |

## GRADES 3 AND UP SAMPLE

Instead of letter cards, use syllables cards to build words. This reinforces those larger high-utility chunks common to many words.

| TARGET SKILL | SYLLABLE CARDS | WORD CHAIN | EXTENSION |
|---|---|---|---|
| Final stable syllables (e.g., -tion, -tive) | pre, scrip, tive, tion, ven, in, con | prescriptive, prescription, prevention, convention, invention, inventive | You can add in conversations about morphology, such as *scrip* meaning *to write* and *ven* meaning *to come*. |

# ROUTINE 5A: WORD BUILDING—BLENDING FOCUS

| ROUTINE STEPS | SAMPLE TEACHER TALK |
|---|---|
| **Introduce:** Name the task and explain its purpose to students. | *Today we will be building, or making, words using the letters and spellings we have learned.* |
| **Model:** Place letter cards in a pocket chart (or use letter cards on a whiteboard) to form the first word you are building. This can also be done using a digital whiteboard resource. Model sounding out the word. Remember to (a) build words using the new, target sound-spelling; (b) add words to review sound-spellings as appropriate to extend the practice and application of these skills to achieve mastery; and (c) use minimal contrasts to require students to analyze words fully and notice their unique differences (e.g., *sat* and *mat*, *pan* and *pen*, *rip* and *trip*, *hat* and *hate*, *cot* and *coat*). | *Look at the word I've made. It is spelled* **s–a–t**. *Let's blend the sounds together to read the word:* **/sssaaat/**, **sat**. *The word is* **sat**. <br><br>**NOTE:** The series of words used in a word-building activity is also referred to as a **word chain**. |
| **Guided Practice/Practice:** Continue by having students change one (or more) letters in the word (blending focus). Have students chorally blend the new word formed. Do a set of eight to ten words as time permits. | *Using your letter cards, change the letter* **s** *in* **sat** *to* **m**. *What is the new word?* <br><br>Or, if students are more advanced in their understanding, say, *Change the first sound in* **sat** *to* /m/. |
| **NOTE:** A blending focus is best at the beginning of the week when students have just been introduced to the new phonics skill. Then, progress to a word awareness focus, which provides guided opportunities for students to use both the new phonics skill and previously taught skills flexibly. | |

# ROUTINE 5B: WORD BUILDING— WORD AWARENESS FOCUS

| ROUTINE STEPS | SAMPLE TEACHER TALK |
|---|---|
| **Introduce:** Name the task and explain its purpose to students. | *Today we will be building, or making, words using the letters and spellings we have learned.* |
| **Model:** Place letter cards in a pocket chart (or use letter cards on a whiteboard) to form the first word you are building. This can also be done using a digital whiteboard resource. Model sounding out the word. Remember to (a) build words using the new, target sound spelling; (b) add words to review sound-spellings as appropriate to extend the practice and application of these skills to achieve mastery; and (c) use minimal contrasts to require students to analyze words fully and notice their unique differences (e.g., *sat* and *mat*, *pan* and *pen*, *rip* and *trip*, *hat* and *hate*, *cot* and *coat*). | *Look at the word I've made. It is spelled* **s–a–t**. *Let's blend the sounds together to read the word:* **/sssaaat/**, **sat**. *The word is* **sat**.<br><br>**NOTE:** The series of words used in a word building activity is also referred to as a **word chain**. |
| **Guided Practice/Practice:** Continue by stating the next word in the word chain and having students decide what letter or letters must be changed. Have students chorally blend the new word formed. Do a set of eight to ten words as time permits. | *Using your letter cards, change the word* **sat** *to* **mat**. *What is the new word?*<br><br>When the focus on word building is word awareness, tell students what the next word in the sequence is and give them time to form the new word. Circulate and provide assistance and corrective feedback (e.g., modeling your thinking process, modeling how to segment or blend the word). Then build the new word in the pocket chart (or on the whiteboard), modeling aloud your thinking. |
| **NOTE:** When time is tight or the students are in the front of the room on the carpet (instead of at their desks), I will conduct word building using whiteboards. Students erase the part of the word that needs to be changed, then insert the new "missing" letter or spelling. When I conduct a word-building lesson this way, I record the words we build on chart paper as we build them for students to self-correct. We then read the entire list of words we built at the end from the chart paper to conclude the lesson. | |

# ROUTINE 5: WORD BUILDING— TEACHER ALERTS AND PRINCIPAL/COACH LOOK-FORS

| TEACHER ALERTS<br>Things to consider | PRINCIPAL/COACH<br>LOOK-FORS |
|---|---|
| [ ] Use high-utility words in the word-building activities (those words students are most likely to need when reading and writing) to increase student capacity. | [ ] Is word building done every week during whole-group time? |
| | [ ] Is word building used in small groups for students needing more support? |
| [ ] Create review transition activities when distributing and collecting materials for word building. For example, sing the "ABC Song," do an oral phonemic awareness activity, or state a decodable or high-frequency word for students to spell orally. | [ ] Are the word-building word chains cumulative (i.e., is there evidence of previously taught skills in some of the words to extend the guided practice)? |
| [ ] Remember, word building combines phonemic awareness (sound substitution, addition, deletion), decoding, and encoding. You don't need to do additional phonemic awareness or dictation work during a lesson containing word building. This can be a real timesaver. | |

# DIFFERENTIATE IT!

| WHO? | HOW? |
|---|---|
| **Students Above Grade-Level Expectations** | Write or display the completed word chain list used in word building. Have on- and below-level student pairs read and/or sort the words by common spelling patterns while you continue building more complex words with above-level students.<br><br>As an alternative, you can provide a couple of challenge words at the end of the word chain that will be a stretch for on-level students but better meet the needs of your above-level students.<br><br>Quick (e.g., five-minute) small-group word-building sessions can be conducted once or twice throughout the week for above-level students to do additional word chains that contain skills with which they still need support. |
| **Students Below Grade-Level Expectations** | Start with a few easier words in your word chain; then progress to the first few on-level words. Allow below-level students to stop the activity at that point and Read, Build, Write a list of words you have put on the board. These words require students to practice skills you are working on with them during small-group time.<br><br>An alternative is to list spelling patterns for the week on the board during this time and have students work with partners to add letters to create words (e.g., ___ ain, ___ ain, ___ ay, ___ ay). This is less demanding yet still requires them to practice the on-level target skill to read and write some words.<br><br>Quick (e.g., five-minute) small-group word-building sessions can be conducted once or twice throughout the week for below-level students to do additional word chains that contain skills with which they need support. |
| **Multilingual Learners** | Provide articulation and vocabulary support throughout the word-building chain. For example, here is my process when a student writes *n* instead of *m*:<br><br>I will pronounce the /m/ sound and ask the student, *Are my lips together or apart? They are together.* Then I pronounce the /n/ sound and ask the student, *Are my lips together or apart? They are apart.* I continue: *When my lips are together, I write* **m**.<br><br>In addition, quickly define words in the word chain. Here is an example:<br><br>*Say* **sway**. Pause for students to repeat. *The word* **sway** *means to move back and forth. Watch as I* **sway**. Act it out. *What have you seen* **sway** *in the wind? Tell your partner.* |

# JOYFUL LEARNING VARIATIONS

While instructional routines are important for the efficiency of our teaching and for aiding in student learning, sometimes I like to mix it up and do an alternate activity with the same instructional focus and goal. Here are some possibilities for word building.

## Read It, Build It, Write It

This popular Orton-Gillingham technique asks students to read a word shown, build it with letter cards or tiles, and then write the word.

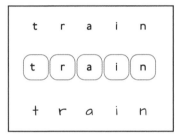

## Word Ladders

Word ladders, created by Dr. Tim Rasinski, are a variation of word building that combines spelling words with vocabulary. A meaning clue is given for the next word to spell, along with a hint about how many letters are added, deleted, or substituted to form the new word. For students in kindergarten and Grade 1, I typically have them replace a letter, add a letter, or delete a letter. For students in Grades 2 and up, I have them change larger word chunks (e.g., spelling patterns, prefixes and suffixes, syllables). Below is an example word ladder. Students love these! I usually save them for the end of the week when students have had multiple exposures to the words and I have done some vocabulary building for my multilingual learners. However, sometimes I introduce a few new vocabulary words in the ladders as well.

Dr. Rasinski has a great website (https://www.timrasinski .com/resources.html) with more examples and, if you follow him on X, the social network formerly known as Twitter (@TimRasinski1), he offers a free word ladder each week. They are also fun to create at grade-level meetings!

Figure 10-1 • Word Ladder

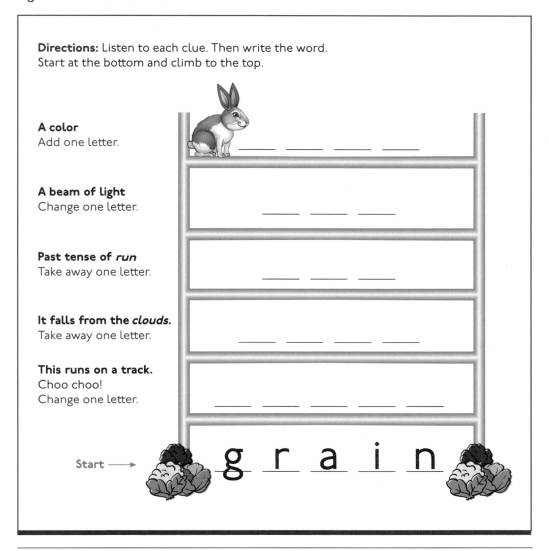

**Directions:** Listen to each clue. Then write the word.
Start at the bottom and climb to the top.

**A color**
Add one letter.

**A beam of light**
Change one letter.

**Past tense of** *run*
Take away one letter.

**It falls from the** *clouds.*
Take away one letter.

**This runs on a track.**
Choo choo!
Change one letter.

Start ⟶

g r a i n

SOURCE: Adapted from timrasinksi.com

## Cubes/Letter Dice and Spelling Patterns

Create simple paper cubes/dice or use the widely available whiteboard cubes (that let you write spellings on each side of the cube but erase them for later use). Use consonants, consonant blends, and consonant digraphs that your students are learning. Then write on the board spelling patterns containing your target skill (e.g., *-ear, -air, -are*). Have students work with partners or in small teams to roll the cubes/dice, and then see how many words they can build using the letters shown and the spelling patterns.

Figure 10-2 • Cubes

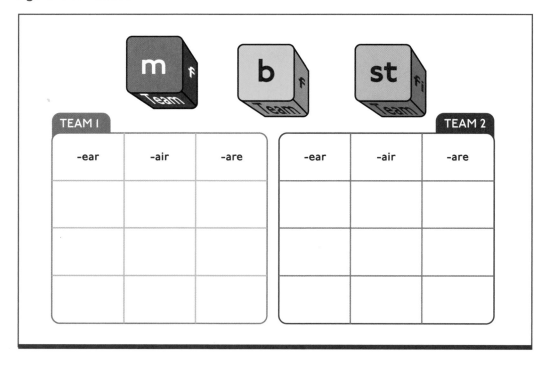

## Living Words

This is my favorite word-building variation. All the students have their letter cards at their desks. I then call a few students to the front of the room. Each child gets to hold a large letter card. I start by saying a word I want to build. The students build it at their seats as the few students at the front of the room also form the word. I ask the students at their seats to be our judges. "Thumbs up if we spelled it right!" I then run my hand above the students' heads as we blend the sounds together to confirm.

Next, I tell students I want to change the word we made (e.g., *sat*) to a new word (e.g., *mat*). I ask them, "What do I need to change and why?" Based on student responses, we then have a conversation about how the (beginning/medial/ending) sound is different in the two words and what letter or spelling we need to replace and with what. This conversation about how words work makes our thinking public, allows me to share needed information about words with students, and solidifies their use of taught sound-spellings. Plus, it's loads of fun!

*Photo Source:* Rick Harrington, Rick Harrington Photography

# CLASSROOM SNAPSHOT

| | |
|---|---|
| **Teacher:** Mr. B<br><br>**Students:** Five students above grade-level expectations<br><br>Eight students below grade-level expectations<br><br>Twelve students meeting grade-level expectations<br><br>Four students who are multilingual learners | **Lesson Focus:**<br>Long *a* |

Mr. B has created a word chain using only seven letters and the suffix *-ing*, which is the suffix he is working on with his above-level students during small-group time. He wants to contrast the short and long sounds of "vowel *a*" to continue working on the language of instruction his students will need as they discuss multisyllabic words (e.g., a closed syllable ends in a consonant and has a "short vowel" sound; an open syllable ends in a vowel and has a "long vowel" sound). Making this contrast is important because he wants to set students up for success in future lessons, and some struggle with the terms used in these lessons. He also wants to reinforce that the *ai* spelling for long *a* only appears in the middle of a word (or syllable) and the *ay* spelling only appears at the end of a word (or syllable).

Letters and Suffix: a, i, r, n, p, t, m, ing

ran

rain

pain

*(Continued)*

(Continued)

paint

pant

pan

man

main

rain

ray

rain

train

tray

train

training

raining

Mr. B introduces the activity and makes sure students have their letter cards at their seats.

*Today we will be building, or making, words using the letters and spellings we have learned. Take the letter cards out of your baggie and place them on your desk. Make sure you have all the letters I have listed on the board.* Once students have their letter cards ready, Mr. B quickly points to the letters on the board and asks students to say the sound for each one.

He then builds the word *ran* using his letter cards. *Look at the word I've made. It is spelled* **r–a–n**. *Let's blend the sounds together to read the word: /***rrraaannn***/,* **ran**. *The word is* **ran**. *Using your letter cards, make the word* **ran**. Mr. B pauses briefly for students to build the word.

*Now, change the word* **ran** *to* **rain**. *Everyone say,* **rain**. Students chorally say the word. *Think about what sound is different—***ran**, **rain**. *What spelling will you use for this new sound?* Mr. B circulates and observes. He notices that some students need help stretching the sounds in *rain*, so he does it with them.

*Look as I change* **ran** *to* **rain**. Mr. B adds the letter *i* after the letter *a*. *Why did I use the* **ai** *spelling for the long* **a** */ā/ sound and not the ay spelling?* The students begin to mumble answers. *Turn to your partner and tell them why.* Mr. B listens in to see which students remember the spelling generalization for these two long *a* spellings. *Who would like to share with the class what you discussed?* Mr. B calls on a volunteer who correctly states that the *ai* spelling appears in the middle of words and the *ay* spelling appears at the end. He then points at students in rapid fire succession and says, *Do you agree? Thumbs up.*

Mr. B continues with the remaining words and the pace quickens. He only stops when he needs to highlight a common confusion. For example, when he gets to the word *pant* he models how a dog pants when it is thirsty and contrasts *pant* with *pants*—something you wear. He also focuses on the meaning of the word *main*. During the vocabulary conversation he noticed a couple of students having a side chat. Mr. B pauses and says, *Macaroni and cheese.* All the students face him and chant, "That means everyone freeze." He then gives the students a sentence starter using the word *main* to complete orally with their partners to refocus their attention.

At the end of the word-building activity, Mr. B displays the word-chain list. *Let's read these words together. Ready? Read!* This takes about 10 seconds. *I will leave this word list on the board. During independent work time I want you to record these words in your writer's notebooks in three columns: words with short **a**, words with long **a** spelled **ai**, and words with long **a** spelled **ay**. Now you can put away your letter cards. Pat yourselves on the back for a great job.*

# FIVE KEY TAKE-AWAYS

1. Word building combines phonemic awareness (sound substitution, addition, deletion), decoding, and encoding. You don't need to do additional phonemic awareness or dictation work during a lesson containing word building.

2. A blending focus is best at the beginning of the week when students have just been introduced to the new phonics skill. Then, progress to a word awareness focus, which provides guided opportunities for students to use the new phonics skill and previously taught skills flexibly.

3. Students consolidate their learning when they are given time to play with and explore letter sounds by building words. Each student should have a baggie of letter cards at the ready and have daily opportunities to make words in whole-group, small-group, partner, and independent settings.

4. Keep your word chains to a maximum of eight to ten words. In the course of the week, have students work with word chains that help students practice the target skill only; the target skill and review skills; and the target skill, review skills, and challenge words.

5. Guide students to write word chains in their writer's notebook. In addition, routinely ask them to use these words in the writing they do in class or on their own. Integrate target sounds and spellings and words into class poetry, nonfiction, fiction—and all genres of writing.

# CHAPTER ELEVEN

# Word Sort Routine

## And How to Differentiate

## WHAT IS IT?

Word sorts involve students arranging a set of words, often on individual word cards, into piles or groupings based on common features (e.g., all contain the same vowel sound but with different spellings, as in *ai* and *ay* words for long *a*; all contain a common prefix or suffix; all are nouns or verbs).

## RESEARCH HIGHLIGHTS

- Word sorts allow students time to think about how words work by drawing their attention to important and common spelling patterns or morphological units (e.g., prefixes and suffixes) (Bear et al., 2019). They offer the teacher an opportunity to share and/or reinforce generalizations about how English words work, details that can aid in spelling (e.g., the *ai* spelling for long *a* appears in the middle of a word and never at the end, whereas the *ay* spelling appears at the end).

- Word sorts can be used during Ehri's (1996) phases of word reading development to help move students from

189

# Ehri's Phases of Word Reading Development

**Phase 1 (Pre-alphabetic):** Beginning readers remember words by their visual attributes and pronunciations or meanings, such as the golden arches for McDonalds or the red STOP sign. They do not use letter-sounds.

**Phase 2 (Partial Alphabetic):** Children begin to use some letter-sound relationships to remember words, such as the first and/or last letters.

**Phase 3 (Full Alphabetic):** Children connect each letter or spelling in a word to its sound and blend the sounds together to read the word. This is typical in kindergarten and Grade I when students are learning the most common sound-spelling relationships.

**Phase 4 (Consolidated Alphabetic):** Children begin to notice and use common chunks in words to read new words. This reduces the cognitive (memory) load needed to read words. For example, in order to read the word *replaying*, instead of sounding out the word letter by letter (e.g., /r/ /ē/ /p/ /l/ /ā/ /i/ /ng/) children would notice larger chunks—*re, play, ing*—and use those pieces to access the word. This is a much easier and efficient task.

fully sounding out words (the full alphabetic phase where students sort by common letters and spellings, such as *ai* and *ay* for long *a*) to beginning to notice larger chunks (the consolidated alphabetic phase where students sort by larger spelling patterns or syllables such as *-ain, ail, -ate* for long *a*), which is essential when reading longer, multisyllabic words more efficiently (i.e., noticing larger chunks of the word and putting those pieces together to sound out the word rather than relying on letter-by-letter sounding out).

## Reading Big Words Strategy

In light of what we know of word reading development, I conceived of a practice called the **Reading Big Words Strategy** to help students attack multisyllabic words by

(1)  looking for known word parts at the beginning of the word (prefixes),

(2)  looking for known word parts at the end of the word (suffixes),

(3)  using knowledge of basic phonics and syllabication strategies to chunk or read the base word,

(4)  putting the parts together to get an approximation, and then

(5)  reading the word parts fast and adjusting pronunciation to match a word in one's speaking and/or listening vocabularies (if it is there).

- Bear et al. (2019) have created word sorts for students at all levels of spelling ability through their *Words Their Way* resources.

Figure II-I • Reading Big Words Strategy

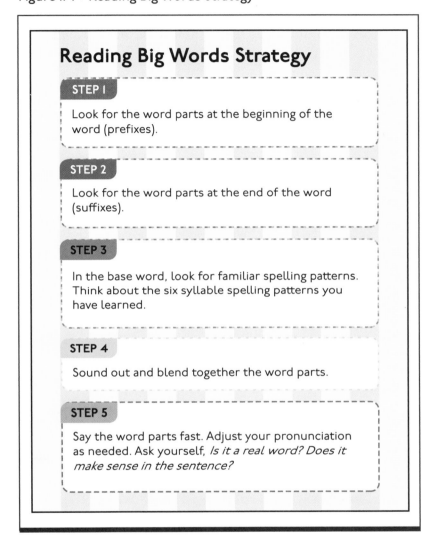

# Reading Big Words Strategy

**STEP 1**

Look for the word parts at the beginning of the word (prefixes).

**STEP 2**

Look for the word parts at the end of the word (suffixes).

**STEP 3**

In the base word, look for familiar spelling patterns. Think about the six syllable spelling patterns you have learned.

**STEP 4**

Sound out and blend together the word parts.

**STEP 5**

Say the word parts fast. Adjust your pronunciation as needed. Ask yourself, *Is it a real word? Does it make sense in the sentence?*

## IMPLICATIONS FOR YOUR INSTRUCTION

- Words sorts can be done using word cards, or you can write the words on the board for students to sort in their writer's notebooks or on dry-erase boards.

- Distribute copies of word card sheets during independent work time and assign students to cut the word cards and place them in their storage bags instead of you having to do this every week. This can be an end-of-week activity to prepare for the upcoming week.

- There are many types of word sorts, each with a distinct instructional purpose. Below are some of the most common types that you can incorporate into your instruction.

## COMMON TYPES OF WORD SORTS TO TRY

Buddy sorts are one of many partner activities that can help students who need extra support get it from a more proficient peer.

*Photo Source:* iStock.com/FG Trade Latin

1. **Open sorts:** In these sorts, students are *not* told how to sort the words. They are allowed to sort them in any way they want. This tells you a lot about how students are thinking about words and what aspects of words they notice.

2. **Closed sorts:** In these sorts, students are told how to sort the words. These are fairly simple and direct sorts since students are visually scanning each word for a specified spelling pattern. The value in this type of sort is the conversation you have with students *following* the sort. For example, you should ask students

questions like these: "What do you notice about these words?" "What do you notice about these spellings for _____ (a skill)?" "Do you know other words with these spellings?"

3. **Timed sorts:** In these sorts, students are told how to sort a set of words but are given a limited amount of time to do so. This is an ideal type of sort to do with a set of words students have been working with all week (having already completed a closed sort). Adding the element of time creates a game-like feel to the task that students enjoy. However, even more, it provides an added and important benefit. Getting students to readily notice larger word chunks in words, such as these common spelling patterns, is essential to reading longer, multisyllabic words.

4. **Sound sorts:** In these sorts, students sort picture cards into piles based on common sounds, such as "words that begin with /m/" in one pile and "words that begin with /s/" in another pile.

5. **Meaning sorts:** In these sorts, students focus on the meanings of words instead of their spelling patterns. These sorts can focus on categories (e.g., words related to plants versus words related to animals) or parts of speech (nouns versus verbs). They help students deepen their understanding of word meanings and usages. They can be done with words in reading lessons as well as in science, social studies, and math lessons to review concepts.

6. **Buddy sorts:** In these sorts, students work with partners as they read and discuss each word. This is an ideal sort for students who need extra support from a more proficient partner.

7. **Blind sorts:** In these sorts, the teacher reads the words to sort, and the students write each one into the correct category. Students do not see the words but must think about and write the spellings as they sort words. This is a variation of dictation (guided spelling)—a powerful encoding activity.

# ROUTINE 6: WORD SORTS

| ROUTINE STEPS | SAMPLE TEACHER TALK |
|---|---|
| **Introduce:** Name the task and explain its purpose. Distribute the word cards and read each with students to make sure they know all the words. If you are doing a closed sort, introduce the categories in which students will be sorting the words.<br><br>**Alternative:** List the words on the board for students to record in categories in their writer's notebooks. | *Now we are going to sort words into two piles. One pile will contain all the long **a** words spelled **ai**; the other pile will have all the long **a** words spelled **ay**.* |
| **Sort:** Have students sort the words. If you are doing a closed sort, model sorting one or two of the words. Then have students sort the remaining words. Circulate and ask students questions about why they are putting specific words into each category. | *Watch as I sort the first word: **gray**. Read the word with me: **gray**. In this word, the long **a** sound is spelled **ay**, so I will put this in the "**ay**" pile.* |
| **Check and Discuss:** Review the words in each sort category. Ask students what they learned about these words from doing the sort. Guide students to the word awareness aspect of each sort that will assist them in reading and writing. Have students store the word cards for future sorts (e.g., a timed sort using these words). | *What do you notice about these long **a** spellings? Look at where each spelling appears in the words.* Provide time for students to discuss. *The long **a** spelling **ai** never appears at the end of a word, but the **ay** spelling does. That is good to remember because it can help us spell new words with long **a**.*<br><br>*For example, I want to spell the word **pray**. Where do you hear the long **a** sound—in the middle or at the end? That's right; it's at the end. So will I spell the long **a** sound in **pray** with the letters **ai**? No. Why? Because that spelling doesn't appear at the end of a word. Which spelling should I use? That's right—**ay**. This spelling does appear at the end of words like **say**, **may**, **gray**, and **play**.* |
| **Notes About Generalizations:** Rather than teaching unreliable or complicated rules, word sorts offer an opportunity to highlight generalizations about how English words work that can greatly benefit students as they spell.<br><br>But always present generalizations as "usually" applying and highlight key exceptions to avoid confusion. | **Common Generalizations to Point Out During Sorts**<br><br>• The position of spellings in words (e.g., *ai* in middle, *ay* at end of long *a* words; *oi* in middle, *oy* at end of diphthong / *oi*/ words; *oa* in middle, *ow* at end or followed by *l, n, er* in long *o* words)<br><br>• The *-igh* spelling is usually followed by the letter *t*<br><br>• The *-er* spelling for /*ûr*/ is common at the end of multisyllabic words (e.g., *never, farmer*) |

| ROUTINE STEPS | SAMPLE TEACHER TALK |
|---|---|
| **Notes About Generalizations** *(continued)* | • FLSZ rule (double consonants at end of short vowel words, such as *sniff, tell, miss, buzz*) |
| | • The *ck* at the end of one-syllable words after short vowels, e.g., *sick*; *k* otherwise, e.g., after consonant in *sink* or vowel team in *keep* or at beginning of some /k/ sound words as in *ki* (*kick*) and *ke* (*kept*)—note that *c* for /k/ is often in words that begin with *ca* (*cat*), *co* (*cot*), and *cu* (*cut*) |
| | • No English words end in the letter *j* or the letter *v*. If a word ends in the /v/ sound you must add an *e* (e.g., *have, live*); *-dge* at the end of a one-syllable word after a single short vowel (e.g., *fudge*) |
| | • The *-tch* at the end after a short vowel as in *patch*; otherwise, it's *-ch* as in *bench* and *beach* |
| | • The *y* as the consonant sound /y/ at the beginning of a word like *yes* but as a vowel sound at the end of words (e.g., long *i* sound as in *my, why, try*—one-syllable words; long *e* sound as in *happy, funny, tricky*—two-syllable words) |
| | • Soft *c* and *g* (usually /s/ or /j/ after *e, i,* or *y* but there are notable exceptions such as *girl*—focus on the spelling patterns *ce, ci, cy, ge, gi, gy*) |
| | • The /ûr/ sounds are often spelled *-or* after the letter *w* as in *word* and *work* |
| | • Related words can help students understand how spellings in base words are maintained across words such as *sign/signal/signature* (why silent letter *g* is used), *limb/limber* (why silent letter *b* is used), and *different/difference, excellent/excellence, fragrant/fragrance* (*ent/ence* versus *ant/ance*) |

# ROUTINE 6: WORD SORTS—TEACHER ALERTS AND PRINCIPAL/COACH LOOK-FORS

| TEACHER ALERTS<br>Things to consider | PRINCIPAL/COACH<br>LOOK-FORS |
|---|---|
| [ ] Remember that word sorts are far more than moving cards into piles—it's all about the talk about how words work.<br><br>[ ] Use high-utility words in the sorts to increase student capacity when reading and writing.<br><br>[ ] Create review transition activities when distributing and collecting materials for word sorts. | [ ] Do the word sorts include follow-up discussions about what students learned about how words work (not an independent activity)? |

# DIFFERENTIATE IT!

| WHO? | HOW? |
|---|---|
| **Students Above Grade-Level Expectations** | Replace half of the grade-level words with more complex words, such as multisyllabic words. For example, for long *a* use *rain, train, paint, play, stay*, and ADD *unpaid, unafraid, remain, repay*, and *subway*. |
| **Students Below Grade-Level Expectations** | Use half of the grade-level words—the most common ones that students will likely encounter in readings or use in writings—then replace the others with short *a* words to contrast with an earlier skill. For example, for long *a* use *rain, train, paint, play*, and *stay*, and ADD *ran, plan, trap, pan*, and *stack*. |
| **Multilingual Learners** | Preview the words for the sort during small-group time and focus on meaning. For example, use illustrations for *rain, train, paint*, and *play*. Guide students to complete sentence starters or frames using each word: *The paint is* _____ (color word), *I like to play* _____, or *I* _____ *when it rains*. Connect the same words to students' primary language using a translation app. |

# SAMPLE DIFFERENTIATED WORD LISTS

| Long *A* | **Above Grade Level:** |
|---|---|
| | rain, train, paint, play, stay, |
| | unpaid, unafraid, remain, repay, subway |
| | **On Grade Level:** |
| | rain, train, paint, play, stay, |
| | brain, nail, pail, gray, way |
| | **Below Grade Level:** |
| | rain, train, paint, play, stay, |
| | ran, plan, trap, pan, stack |
| **Long *O*** | **Above Grade Level:** |
| | boat, coat, goat, row, grow, |
| | raincoat, rowboat, railroad, rainbow, below |
| | **On Grade Level:** |
| | boat, coat, goat, row, grow, |
| | toast, coast, show, slow, snow |
| | **Below Grade Level:** |
| | boat, coat, goat, row, grow, |
| | box, top, mop, got, hot |

*(Continued)*

(Continued)

| Long *E* | **Above Grade Level:**<br>read, team, keep, week, seed,<br>unreal, unclear, sixteen, oversleep, agreed<br>**On Grade Level:**<br>read, team, keep, week, seed,<br>beach, clean, dream, three, sleep<br>**Below Grade Level:**<br>read, team, keep, week, seed,<br>red, bed, let, met, ten |
|---|---|
| Long *I* | **Above Grade Level:**<br>light, night, high, my, try,<br>midnight, sunlight, butterfly, July, reply<br>**On Grade Level:**<br>light, night, high, my, try,<br>bright, flight, sky, shy, why<br>**Below Grade Level:**<br>light, night, high, my, try,<br>six, big, fit, zip, will |
| Long *U* | **Above Grade Level:**<br>cute, use, huge, few, menu,<br>rescue, argue, continue, usual, museum<br>**On Grade Level:**<br>cute, use, huge, few, menu,<br>cube, mule, unit, human, music<br>**Below Grade Level:**<br>cute, use, huge, few, menu,<br>cut, us, hug, but, bug |

# JOYFUL LEARNING VARIATIONS

While instructional routines are important for the efficiency of our teaching and for aiding in student learning, sometimes I like to mix it up and do an alternate activity with the same instructional focus and goal. Here are some possibilities for word sorts.

## Find Your Family

Give each student a word card. Tell students they need to "find their family." That is, they need to find other students whose words on their cards have the same spelling pattern. Guide students to read their word and the words of classmates as they slowly form small groups of students with words containing the same spelling pattern. When the task is completed, have students in each group read their words and identify the common spelling pattern.

## Meaning Sort

It is important that students view words through multiple lenses—pronunciation and meaning. This will help students as they begin to read multisyllabic words when they will use word parts, such as affixes, for both reading/pronouncing the words and determining their meaning. Find categories to sort the words based on meaning, such as sorting all the nouns (naming words) versus the verbs (action words) or sorting words that tell about animals versus words that tell about people.

## Part of Speech Sort

This is ideal for older students. Have students sort words into parts of speech: noun, verb, adjective, adverb. Discuss how certain word parts, such as suffixes, form specific kinds of words. For example, words that end in *-tion, -ment,* and *-ness* form nouns. For a challenge, have students write related words in other sorting columns. For example, if students sort the word *happiness* into the noun column, ask them to write a version of the word in the columns for adjectives (*happy*), adverbs (*happily*), and verbs (none). Not all columns will have a related word.

## Timed Sorts

Following a closed sort, repeat the sort on a later date and make it game-like. Give students a specific time to sort the words (e.g., one minute), and see if they can "beat the clock." This type of sort helps students visually notice larger spelling patterns (e.g., phonograms, prefixes, suffixes) faster and is ideal for the second half of Grade 1 and beyond when you want students to start noticing these larger word chunks and move into the consolidated alphabetic phase of word reading development.

# CLASSROOM SNAPSHOT

| **Teacher:** Mr. B | **Lesson Focus:** Long *a* spelled *ai* and *ay* |
| --- | --- |
| **Students:** Five students above grade-level expectations | |
| Eight students below grade-level expectations | |
| Twelve students meeting grade-level expectations | |
| Four students who are multilingual learners | |

Mr. B is conducting a closed sort for long *a* words spelled *ai* and *ay*. He writes the words for the sort on the board in three columns

**TRIANGLE GROUP** (above level): ***rain***, ***train***, ***paint***, ***play***, ***stay***, *unpaid*, *unafraid*, *remain*, *repay*, *subway*

**SQUARE GROUP** (below level) : ***rain***, ***train***, ***paint***, ***play***, ***stay***, *ran*, *plan*, *trap*, *pan*, *stack*

**CIRCLE GROUP** (on level): ***rain***, ***train***, ***paint***, ***play***, ***stay***, *brain*, *nail*, *pail*, *gray*, *way*

**NOTE:** Multilingual learners are placed in the appropriate group based on their reading needs.

Why is Mr. B not using word cards for this activity today? Recently, his district reading supervisor criticized him for giving more work to above-level students and not just more challenging work. In a previous sort, he had these students sort the ten on-level words, and then he added five more complex words. The district reading supervisor also didn't like him circulating and removing five cards from the below-level students because she felt it drew too much attention to them.

To accommodate the supervisor's feedback, Mr. B now gives ten words to all student groups. He writes them on the board. Five words are shared by all groups (e.g., *rain, train, paint, play, stay*). The above-level students get five additional words that are more challenging and reflective of skills further in the scope and sequence (e.g., multisyllabic words). The on-level students get five additional words that are grade-level appropriate. The below-level students get five simpler words that contrast the new skill with a previously taught skill to extend that practice and review.

Mr. B decided to write these words on the board because creating these separate word cards was too time-consuming for him. Since the words are on the board instead of on word cards, students must write the words in their writer's notebooks and then mark the common spelling patterns. Mr. B likes this. However, it requires more time than sorting cards into piles and having a quick discussion. As a result, he has had to trim time from other parts of his lesson.

Note that Mr. B met with his multilingual learners for a few minutes before the sort that morning. They practiced echo reading the words; then he used pictures and simple actions to address the meaning of several words, such as *rain, train, paint,* and *play*.

**Introduce**

Mr. B tells the students that they will be doing a closed sort of long *a* words—the words they have been reading and writing this week. He draws their attention to the three columns of words on the board and reminds them of their different groups for this week—Triangle, Square, or Circle. Groups are flexible and change weekly based on students' specific needs.

Mr. B reads the first five words in each column with all the students. These are the words that all three groups have in common.

*Let's read the first several words in each column together as I point to them. Okay, Triangle Group, you're up first.* Mr. B points to *rain, train, paint, play,* and *stay* in succession as the students chorally read them. He corrects pronunciation errors as needed. *Now, Square Group it's your turn.* Mr. B repeats the above. *Finally, I want to hear from the Circle Group. Square Group, please join in with them and read the words together.* Mr. B directs the on-level and below-level students to read the words together. This gives the below-level students a second opportunity to practice these words before the sort. *All groups have five additional words. These are for you to read on your own. I will circulate, listen in, and help as needed.*

**Sort**

Before the students begin the sort, Mr. B models how to sort one of the words.

*We are going to sort these long **a** words into two piles. One pile will contain all the long **a** words spelled **ai**; the other pile will have all the long **a** words spelled **ay**.*

*(Continued)*

(Continued)

*Watch as I sort the first word:* **rain**. *Read the word with me:* **rain**. *In this word, the long* **a** *sound is spelled* **ai**, *so I will put this in the "ai" pile. Now it's your turn. Continue with the rest of the words.*

Mr. B circulates and asks questions such as these: *Why did you put this word in this group? What do all these words have in common?*

**Check and Discuss**

Mr. B has some early finishers, so he prompts them to read the words and underline the spellings as they say the sounds.

*If you finish sorting the words, underline the* **ai** *or* **ay** *spelling in each word as you say the /ā/ sound. This will help you connect that spelling to its sound.*

Mr. B then reviews the words in each sort category.

*It looks like everyone is finished sorting. If you haven't finished underlining the common spellings, you can do that during independent work time. For now, though, I want to hear each group read the words in their sort. Let's start with the Circle Group. Read the words you listed in the* **ai** *column.* Mr. B pauses for students to read. He listens in and offers feedback. *Now read the words in the* **ay** *column.* Mr. B repeats the process, being careful to just listen and not join in unless students need corrective feedback. He then calls on the Square and Triangle Groups to read their words.

Mr. B then asks students what they learned about these words from doing the sort. This is the word awareness aspect of the sort that will assist them in spelling long a words because the position of each spelling in a word matters.

*Take a look at the words in each column. What do you notice about these words? What did you learn about these spelling patterns?* Mr. B pauses. One student notices that the letters *ai* are always in the middle of a word and the letters *ay* are always at the end.

*Great observation! That's correct. When we hear the long* **a** *sound /ā/ in a word, if the sound is at the end, then the* **ay** *spelling is a better choice because the* **ai** *spelling and the* **a_e** *spelling, which we learned a few weeks ago, never appear at the end of a word.* Mr. B writes three words on the board to illustrate this: *say, rain, make. Which word ends in the /ā/ sound? How do we spell the /ā/ sound in this word? Yes,* **ay**. *So, remember this when you are writing long* **a** *words.*

*For example, you want to spell the word* **sway**. *Where do you hear the long* **a** *sound—in the middle or at the end?* Mr. B pauses for student response. *That's right, it's at the end. So will I spell the long* **a** *sound in* **sway** *with the letters* **ai**? Mr. B pauses for student response. *No. Why? Because that spelling doesn't appear at the end of a word. Which spelling should I use? Tell your partner.* Mr. B pauses for student response. *That's right—* **ay**. *This spelling does appear at the end of words like* **say**, **day**, **stay**, *and* **play**.

FIVE KEY TAKE-AWAYS

1. There are many types of word sorts, each with a distinct instructional purpose. For example, you could focus on meaning, parts of speech, sounds, and spelling patterns. You could focus on high-utility words for reading, for writing, and so on.

2. The underlying rationale for word sorts is to give students think time with words. And a very big part of this think time occurs *through discussion*. So throughout the modeling and practice, ask questions. *What do you notice about these words? Do you know other words with these spellings? Why did you sort the way you did?* Students need to verbalize their thinking about words. The discussion helps all children learn the important features of the spellings and patterns.

3. Plan on creating word-building sequences (chains) and word-sort lists for each week's target skills, plus review words.

4. You can create word lists for word building by consulting resources such as http://resources.corwin.com/blevinsphonics.

5. Differentiate word sorts by providing all students with one set of words matching grade-level content and another set matching the specific needs of groups of students (e.g., enrichment, additional grade-level practice, review).

# CHAPTER TWELVE

# Phonological and Phonemic Awareness

## And Why They Are Necessary Adjustments to Instruction

Phonemic awareness is one of the two best predictors of early reading success. The other is alphabet recognition. Phonemic awareness activities should be connected to the specific reading and writing goals you set for your students at each point in the instructional year. Too often, phonemic awareness is treated as a separate, or siloed, activity. We achieve the maximum benefit when phonemic awareness and phonics are tightly connected.

Oral blending and oral segmentation are the two "power" phonemic awareness skills critical for early reading and spelling success. If students cannot orally blend together sounds, then they won't be able to decode (sound out) a word in print. Likewise, if students cannot orally segment a word into its individual sounds, they will struggle writing the word because in order to learn a word's spelling we must think about the individual sounds in that word and attach a letter or spelling to each sound.

Often, I enter classrooms where there is no connection between what is happening in phonemic awareness and what is expected in the phonics lesson. For example, during phonemic awareness, students might be engaging in activities that focus on rhyming and clapping syllables, but during the phonics lessons they might be required to read and spell short vowel CVC words. Thus, the phonemic awareness activities aren't addressing the students' immediate needs. Below is a chart showing what is expected in kindergarten and what phonemic awareness skills are necessary for the phonics lessons to have impact. We must get students to attend to words at the phoneme level very early in kindergarten.

| READING/WRITING TASK | NECESSARY PHONEMIC AWARENESS |
|---|---|
| Reading (Blending) CVC Words | Oral Blending at the Phoneme, or Sound, Level |
| Writing (Spelling) CVC Words | Oral Segmentation at the Phoneme, or Sound, Level |

Assess students' phonemic awareness skills at the beginning of the year and provide additional differentiated small-group work for students needing extra support. The activity presented in Chapter 9 (on dictation), which has students use sound boxes and counters and then write the letter for each sound, is a powerful activity to do daily until students understand how words work.

Often, I enter classrooms where there is no connection between what is happening in phonemic awareness and what is expected in the phonics lesson.

During whole-group lessons, target those skills most of your students need. You can, at times, build levels into these activities, such as, in the same activity, blending words by syllable (e.g., *pan-cake*), then using onset-rime (e.g., *s-at*), and then phoneme-by-phoneme (e.g., *s-a-t*). Doing so will help you check which students still struggle working at the phoneme level. Note, for example, that once students can orally blend sounds, it's more impactful to spend their time using that skill to sound out words. Therefore, there isn't the need to do whole-group oral blending. You can reserve that activity for small groups for any students needing that support.

Don't overdo the amount of time spent on phonemic awareness each day. About five minutes a day is plenty. Also, keep in mind that many of the encoding activities have built-in phonemic awareness work, such as dictation (during which students are orally segmenting sounds) and word building (which has students orally substituting, adding, or deleting sounds).

Combine phonemic awareness with work on letters and hand-writing (e.g., say the sound as you write the letter).

The following are routines for each type of phonemic awareness task. These include multimodal and multisensory supports, as well as suggestions for how to include print more appropriately.

> During whole-group lessons, target those skills most of your students need.

## ROUTINE 7: PHONEMIC AWARENESS—RHYME

| ROUTINE STEPS | SAMPLE TEACHER TALK |
|---|---|
| **Step 1: Introduce**<br><br>Tell students the purpose of the activity. | *Today we will listen for words that rhyme. Then we will generate, or make, a list of rhyming words.* |
| **Step 2: Model (I Do)**<br><br>Model why words rhyme. | *Do the words **sat** and **mat** rhyme? Listen: /s/ . . . /at/, **sat**; /m/ . . . /at/, **mat**. Do you hear /at/ at the end of **sat** and **mat**? Yes! **Sat** and **mat** rhyme because they both end in /at/. Rhyming words have the same ending sounds. What other words do you know that end with the /at/ sounds?* |
| **Step 3: Guided Practice (We Do, You Do)**<br><br>State a pair of words such as *man* and *fan*. Ask students if the words rhyme. If yes, point out the rhyming part (/an/). Progress to providing a series of words (e.g., three words like *sit*, *sad*, and *bit*), and ask students to identify the two words that rhyme. Once students are skilled at identifying rhyming words, progress by having them generate words that rhyme with a word or series of words you provide: e.g., *What words rhyme with **big** and **dig**?* | **Corrective Feedback**<br><br>When students make mistakes, break apart the words by onset and rime to highlight the rhyming portion. |
| **Multimodal and Multisensory Supports**<br><br>Use color cards. Break apart a word by onset and rime (e.g., /s/ /at/) and place a color card for each part. Use the same color for the rime (e.g., at) in words that rhyme (e.g., *sat* and *mat*).<br><br>When generating rhyming words, list on the board or chart paper the words students say. Underline the rhyming part, or write it in a different color to reinforce why words rhyme. | |

# ROUTINE 8: PHONEMIC AWARENESS—ORAL BLENDING

| ROUTINE STEPS | SAMPLE TEACHER TALK |
|---|---|
| **Step 1: Introduce**<br><br>Tell students the purpose of the activity. | *We will be blending, or putting together, sounds to make words.* |
| **Step 2: Model (I Do)**<br><br>Say each sound in a word. Model how to blend the sounds to make the whole word. Start with two-letter words (e.g., *am, is*), progress to consonant–vowel–consonant (CVC) words (*sat, man*) starting with continuous sounds that can be stretched (e.g., /f/, /l/, /m/, /n/, /r/, /s/, /v/, /z/), progress to words that begin with stop sounds (e.g., *bad*), and then progress to words beginning with consonant blends (e.g., *slip*). You will progress as students begin showing consistent success with the current level of activity. For some students, this may occur quickly, within a few weeks. For others, it will take much longer. The goal is to stretch students continually and gradually by introducing activities of slightly more complex skill demands. | *I am going to put sounds together to make a word. I'll say each sound in the word. Then I will blend the sounds together to say the word. Listen:* /s/, /a/, **/t/**, /sssaaat/, *sat. The word is* **sat**. |
| **Step 3: Guided Practice (We Do, You Do)**<br><br>Provide a word sound by sound for students to practice putting together (blending the sounds) to form a whole word. | *Listen to the sounds. Blend, or put together, the sounds to say the whole word:* /f/, /i/, /sh/.<br><br>**Corrective Feedback**<br><br>When students make mistakes, stretch together (or sing) the sounds. Move your hands from right to left as you move from sound to sound to emphasize the changing sounds. Repeat the routine using the same word, asking students to respond without you. |
| **Multimodal and Multisensory Supports**<br><br>Move your hands from right to left (which will appear as left to right to students viewing you) as you move from sound to sound to emphasize the changing sounds. You can also move down your arm to model. Do not tap the sounds you are blending as some students struggle holding onto the sounds and will generate a word with the last sound they hear (Gonzalez-Frey & Ehri, 2021). | |

# ROUTINE 9: PHONEMIC AWARENESS—ORAL SEGMENTATION

| ROUTINE STEPS | SAMPLE TEACHER TALK |
|---|---|
| **Step 1: Introduce**<br><br>Tell students the purpose of the activity. | *Today we will be segmenting, or taking apart, a word sound by sound.* |
| **Step 2: Model (I Do)**<br><br>Model how to segment the sounds in a word. Use sound (Elkonin) boxes and counters. Start with two-letter words (e.g., *am*, *is*), progress to CVC words (*sat*, *man*) starting with continuous sounds that can be stretched (e.g., /f/, /l/, /m/, /n/, /r/, /s/, /v/, /z/), progress to words that begin with stop sounds (e.g., *bad*), and then progress to words beginning with consonant blends (e.g., *slip*). | *I am going to say a word, then I will say it sound by sound. As I say each sound, I will place one counter in each box. Listen:* **sat**. *Now I will say* **sat** *sound by sound* [stretch each sound three seconds so students can hear each discrete sound]: /**s**/ [place counter in first box], /**a**/ [place counter in second box], /**t**/ [place counter in third box]. *The word* **sat** *has three sounds:* /**s**/, /**a**/, *and* /**t**/ [point to each box as you say the sound]. |
| **Step 3: Guided Practice (We Do, You Do)**<br><br>State words (at least six to ten) for students to segment phoneme by phoneme, or sound by sound. Do the first word with students. | *Listen to the word. Segment, or break apart, the word sound by sound.* Use sound (Elkonin) boxes as a support early on. You can use sound boxes for CVC words, short-vowel words with consonant blends and digraphs, and even some simple long-vowel words. However, as spellings become more complex, such as words with a final e, the boxes will be less useful, and students should have enough experience segmenting words to not need them for all oral activities. You can continue using them during dictation as needed.<br><br>**Corrective Feedback**<br><br>When students make mistakes, stretch the word using the rubber band technique (pretend you are holding an imaginary rubber band and stretch it as you stretch the sounds). Have students repeat. Then use the sound boxes to model how to place one counter on each box as you stretch the word and move from sound to sound. Repeat the routine using the same word, asking students to respond without you. |

*(Continued)*

(Continued)

| ROUTINE STEPS | SAMPLE TEACHER TALK |
|---|---|
| **Connect to Spelling**<br><br>Use segmentation and the sound boxes to help students transition to spelling words. After students have segmented a word, have them replace each counter with a letter (or letters) to spell the word. This breaking apart and then putting together of words using printed letters will accelerate students' understanding of how words work. | |
| **Multimodal and Multisensory Supports**<br><br>When segmenting by syllables, teach students the "chin drop" technique. Have them place their hands underneath their chins and count the number of chin drops (vowel sounds) as they say the word. Remind students that each syllable has one vowel sound.<br><br>When segmenting by sounds, use tapping, sound boxes, and color cards for students needing additional support. This is an effective modification to a whole-group lesson during small-group time. | |

# ROUTINE 10: PHONEMIC AWARENESS— PHONEME MANIPULATION (SUBSTITUTION)

| ROUTINE STEPS | SAMPLE TEACHER TALK |
|---|---|
| **Step 1: Introduce**<br><br>Tell students the purpose of the activity. | *Today we will be replacing sounds in words. I will say a word. Then I will say a sound. You will replace the first sound in the word with the sound I say.* |
| **Step 2: Model (I Do)**<br><br>Model how to substitute the initial sound in a word. Start with continuous sounds that can be stretched (e.g., /f/, /l/, /m/, /n/, /r/, /s/, /v/, /z/) and then progress to words that begin with stop sounds (e.g., *bad*). | *Listen to this word: **mad**. I will substitute, or replace, the first sound in **mad** with the /s/ sound. What word did I make? That's right. I made the word **sad**. If students struggle, continue the model using letter cards. How did I do it? Say the word **mad** again: **mad**. Watch as I make the word **mad** with letter cards: m-a-d. Show the letter cards. What is the first sound in **mad**. Yes, /**mmm**/. What letter do we write for the /**mmm**/ sound? Yes, **m**. I need to replace this sound, so I will take away the letter **m**, which stands for the /**mmm**/ sound. Remove the m card. What sound do I need to replace /**m**/ with? Yes, /**s**/. What letter do we write for the /**s**/ sound? Yes, **s**. So, I will place the **s** letter card where the **m** card was. Add the **s** card. What is the word I made? Sound it out. Exactly! The word I made is **sad**.* |

| ROUTINE STEPS | SAMPLE TEACHER TALK |
|---|---|
| **Step 3: Guided Practice (We Do, You Do)**<br><br>State a series of words, one at a time. Tell students that you want them to substitute, or replace, the first sound in each word with _____. Do the first word with students.<br><br>You can also substitute medial and final sounds in words as students progress. | *Mat*. *Replace the first sound in **mat** with /**s**/. What is the new word?*<br><br>**Corrective Feedback**<br><br>When students make mistakes, walk through the process of replacing the sound step by step, as shown in the "Model" row (step 2). Provide as many explicit models, especially models with letter cards, as needed. |
| **Multimodal and Multisensory Supports**<br><br>Use letter cards or color cards for students needing additional support. For example, build a word using letter cards, and then replace its letter or letters with those corresponding to the sound substituted. Guide students to blend the new word formed. For words whose spelling differences might confuse students, use colored cards. Say a word and have students place one color card for each sound they hear. It is best to use the same color for all the sounds in the initial words and then use another color for the letters of the substituted sound. Ask students to point to and say the sound where the substitution will occur (e.g., students say the medial sound). Then remove that color card and replace it with the new color card for the sound substituted in. Have students point to the new color card, say the new sound, and then slide their fingers under the color cards as they use the new sound to say the new word formed. | |

# ROUTINE 11: PHONEMIC AWARENESS—
# PHONEME MANIPULATION (ADDITION)

| ROUTINE STEPS | SAMPLE TEACHER TALK |
|---|---|
| **Step 1: Introduce**<br><br>Tell students the purpose of the activity. | *Today we will add sounds to words (or word parts). I will say a word. Then I will say a sound. You will add the sound to the beginning of the word.* |
| **Step 2: Model (I Do)**<br><br>Model how to add an initial sound to a word. Start with continuous sounds that can be stretched (e.g., /f/, /l/, /m/, /n/, /r/, /s/, /v/, /z/); then progress to words that begin with stop sounds (e.g., *bad*). | *Listen to this word:* **at**. *I will add the* **/s/** *sound to the beginning of* **at**: **/s/** *. . .* **at**. *What word did I make? That's right. I made the word* **sat**. *If students struggle, continue the model using letter cards. How did I do it? Say the word* **at** *again:* **at**. *Watch as I make the word* **at** *with letter cards:* **a-t**. *Show the letter cards. Now I want to add the* **/s/** *sound to the beginning. What letter do we write for the* **/s/** *sound? Yes,* **s**. *So I will place the* **s** *letter card at the beginning. Add the s card. What is the word I made? Sound it out. Exactly! The word I made is* **sat**. |
| **Step 3: Guided Practice (We Do, You Do)**<br><br>State a series of words or word parts, one at a time. Tell students that you want them to add the _____ sound to the beginning of the word or word part. Do the first word with students.<br><br>You can also add sounds to the end of a word as students progress. | **End**. *Add the* **/s/** *sound to the beginning. What is the new word?*<br><br>**Corrective Feedback**<br><br>When students make mistakes, walk through the process of adding the sound step by step as shown in the model. Provide as many explicit models, especially models with letter cards, as needed. |
| **Multimodal and Multisensory Supports**<br><br>Use letter cards or color cards for students needing additional support. For example, use letter cards to build the word, and then add the letter or letters for the sound added. Guide students to blend the new word formed. For words whose spelling differences might confuse students, use colored cards. Have one colored card represent the initial word (or sounds). Then choose another color for the sound to be added. Place the card representing the new sound at the beginning (or ending) of the word (in front of or behind the initial color card), and model blending the sounds to form the new word. | |

# ROUTINE 12: PHONEMIC AWARENESS— PHONEME MANIPULATION (DELETION)

| ROUTINE STEPS | SAMPLE TEACHER TALK |
|---|---|
| **Step 1: Introduce**<br><br>Tell students the purpose of the activity. | *Today we will delete, or take away, sounds from words. I will say a word. Then I want you to take away the first sound in the word and tell me what's left.* |
| **Step 2: Model (I Do)**<br><br>Model how to delete the first sound from a word that begins with a single consonant (e.g., *mad, bit*). Then progress to deleting other sounds in words (e.g., an ending sound, the first sound in a word that begins with a consonant blend). | *Listen to this word:* **bend**. *I will delete, or take away, the first sound. What word did I make? That's right. I made the word* **end**. *If students struggle, continue the model using letter cards. How did I do it? Say the word* **bend** *again:* **bend**. *Watch as I make the word* **bend** *with letter cards:* **b-e-n-d**. *Show the letter cards. Now I want to delete the first sound. So I will take away the first letter card* **b** *since it stands for the first sound in* **bend**: */b/. What is left? Sound it out. Exactly! The word that remains is* **end**. |
| **Step 3: Guided Practice  (We Do, You Do)**<br><br>State a series of words or word parts, one at a time. Tell students that you want them to delete the first sound in each word. Tell them that what is left might be a real word or just a word part.<br><br>You can also delete the final sound in a word or the first or last sound in a blend in a word (whether at the beginning or end of the word) as students progress. | **Pitch**. *Delete, or take away, the first sound. What is left? Is it a real word?*<br><br>**Corrective Feedback**<br><br>When students make mistakes, walk through the process of deleting the initial sound step by step as shown in the model. Provide as many explicit models, especially models with letter cards, as needed. In addition, orally segment the word by onset and rime to highlight the initial sound that should be removed. Here's an example. ***Send**: /s/ /end/, **send**.* |
| **Multimodal and Multisensory Supports**<br><br>Use letter cards or color cards for students needing additional support. For example, use letter cards to build the word,  and then remove the letter or letters for the sound to be deleted. Guide students to blend the remaining word or word part. For words whose spelling differences might confuse students, use colored cards. Use one card for each sound. Have students tap on each card as they say the word, moving from sound to sound. Then remove the color card for the sound deleted and have students repeat the new word, tapping on each remaining card as they say and then blend the remaining sounds. | |

# FIVE KEY TAKE-AWAYS

1.  Assess students' phonemic awareness skills at the beginning of the year, and provide additional differentiated small-group work for students needing extra support.

2.  Connect phonemic awareness activities to the reading and writing goals of your students at each point in the instructional year.

3.  Oral blending and oral segmentation are the two "power" phonemic awareness skills critical for early reading and spelling success.

4.  Multimodal and multisensory supports are not nice-to-have instructional components; they are *need*-to-have components.

5.  The "I Do, We Do, You Do" model (Pearson & Gallagher, 1983) is a touchstone for effective teaching of phonemic awareness—and virtually all content. Students need clear demonstrations, ample guided practice, and independent work time *at school*—and at home.

# PART III

# Tools to Use

*Photo Source: iStock.com/SolStock*

# CHAPTER THIRTEEN

# Sample Weekly Lesson Templates

## And How the Routines Flow for Maximum Impact

Use the following sample lessons to plan your differentiated instruction to meet the widest range of student needs during whole-group lessons. These templates follow a suggested lesson sequence while incorporating aspects of the high-impact routines and how to differentiate them. Use as is or modify based on your specific school's time constraints and available resources.

Full-scale, blank versions of the following example templates can be downloaded from the online companion website at resources.corwin.com/differentiatingphonics. online resources

# PART 1: WARM-UP

Choose from one of these activities.

| | |
|---|---|
| **Quick Read**<br><br>Have students do a brief whisper-read of a previously read text. Allow no more than three to four minutes. If the text is long, limit the amount students are expected to read given the time.<br><br>"He Will Go!" | **Below-Level Support**<br><br>Have students read only a small portion of the text or reread a text from small-group time focusing on a previously taught skill.<br><br>Read the first two pages to partners. |
| | **Above-Level Support**<br><br>Have students read the text from small-group time focusing on a more challenging skill further in the scope and sequence.<br><br>Read "On the Farm." |
| | **Multilingual Learner Support**<br><br>If needed, you can use this time to frontload content for the day's lesson, such as by introducing or confirming understanding of a few vocabulary words in the upcoming decodable text.<br><br>Preteach vocabulary: *rain, trip, train, pay, line*. |
| **Cumulative Phonics Fluency**<br><br>Display letter, spelling, or syllable cards for up to 20 previously taught skills. Rapidly flip through the cards as students chorally say the sound or sounds. Note skills students struggle with and fold in more instruction and guided practice. Allow no more than 60 seconds.<br><br>*a_e, i_e, o_e, u_e, e_e, ng, ch, tch, sh, th, wh, br, tr, dr, sl, sp, st, fl, gl, pl* | |
| **Cumulative High-Frequency Fluency**<br><br>Display word cards for up to 20 previously taught words. Rapidly flip through the cards as students chorally say them. Note words students struggle with and fold in more instruction and guided practice. Allow no more than 60 seconds.<br><br>*put, other, said, they, water, of, carry, was, who, there, where, from, many, very, have* | |

## PART 2: PHONEMIC AWARENESS

Choose one or more of these activities based on time and student needs. Connect the phonemic awareness work to the reading and writing demands your students are expected to meet. (If students are spelling CVC words, for example, then they need to be segmenting words at the phoneme, or sound, level.)

| Oral Blending | Multisensory Variation for Extra Support |
|---|---|
| Do this until students can readily blend sounds. No need to continue after that since blending the sounds in printed words accomplishes the same goal and is more impactful. | |
| | **Articulation Point to Address** |
| **Oral Segmentation** | **Multisensory Variation for Extra Support** |
| Do this with each new skill because spelling lags behind reading and this extra attention to the individual sounds and their spellings will accelerate learning. | Use sound boxes and counters. |
| | **Connection to Print** |
| | Spell words in sound boxes. |
| *ray, rain, train, brain, pain, paint* | **Other Differentiators** |
| | Model articulation using sound wall cards and articulation videos; point out mouth position. |
| **Phonemic Substitution** | **Multisensory Variation for Extra Support** |
| **Phonemic Deletion** | |
| **Phonemic Addition** | |
| (Choose one of the above.) | **Connection to Print** |
| Delete initial sound: *ray, rain, train, brain, pain, paint* | Model using letter cards. |
| | **Other Differentiators** |

# PART 3: INTRODUCE SKILL AND BLENDING

Introduce the skill on Day 1. Briefly review it on Day 2. Blending work is done every day.

## Introduce the Skill

Provide an explicit introduction of the sound and its spellings. Point out any generalizations that will help students use this skill to read and write words, such as that the *ai* spelling for long *a* always appears in the middle of a word or syllable and the *ay* spelling always at the end. Connect directly to handwriting. Have students write the spellings as they say the sounds.

Long *a* spelled *ai* (train) and *ay* (play)

## Articulation

Model articulation using sound wall cards and articulation videos; point out mouth position.

## Handwriting

Have students write *ai* and *ay* five times as they say /ā/; reinforce letter formation as needed.

## Multilingual Learners

In Cantonese, Vietnamese, and Hmong, there is only an approximate sound transfer.

## Blending

Make sure the blending practice is cumulative and differentiated. It should include at least eight to twelve words containing the target skill and the review skills, as well as a few challenge words for enrichment.

1. ran rain plan plain sad say
2. may pay play say stay stray
3. pail sail tail trail train brain
4. chain tray faint nail paint raise

**Review**

5. go she hope cute ride same
6. bring ranch chop sink pitch when

**Challenge**

7. rain rainbow day birthday

**In Context**

8. "Rain, rain, go away," yelled Gail.
9. I had to wait all day for the train to come.

## Above Grade-Level Support

Use "Challenge" line: compound words.

## Below Grade-Level Support

Use "Review" lines.

Highlight *ran* (short *a*) versus *rain* (long *a*) in line I.

## Multilingual Learner Support

Preteach vocabulary: *stay, tail, brain, faint, tray, paint, raise.*

## Follow-Up Independent or Partner Assignment

Day I: Read to a partner.

Day 2: Circle and read all the words with ai and underline all the words with ay.

Day 3: Select five words and quiz a partner to spell them.

Day 4: Use three to four words to create a story about a train ride.

Day 5: Take home an exercise for extra practice.

## PART 4: ENCODING

Choose from one of these activities each day.

| | |
|---|---|
| **Dictation With Embedded Phonemic Segmentation**<br><br>First<br><br>*chain, gray, train*; add review words *hope, brave*<br><br>One day, I will ride a *train*.<br><br>Second<br><br>*may, pain, brain*; add review words *cute, slide*<br><br>I like to play in the *rain*. | **Support Tools**<br>Sound boxes and counters |
| | **Articulation Point to Address**<br>Address how wide open the mouth is. |
| | **Spelling Point to Address**<br>*ai* in middle; *ay* at end |
| **Word Building With Embedded Phonemic Manipulation**<br><br>*pay, lay, play, plain, pain, rain, train, strain, stain, stay, say, may, ray, gray* | **Support Tools**<br>Letter cards and/or chart paper |
| | **Above Grade-Level Support**<br>Add *saying, staying, playing, raining, training.* |
| | **Below Grade-Level Support**<br>Read, Build, Write: *ran, man, pan, plan, plant* (*a, n, r, m, p, l, t*) |
| **Word Sort With Follow-Up Discussion on Spelling Patterns**<br><br>*rain, train, paint, play, stay, brain, nail, pail, gray, way* | **Above Grade-Level Support**<br>*rain, train, paint, play, stay, unpaid, unafraid, remain, repay, subway* |
| | **Below Grade-Level Support**<br>*rain, train, paint, play, stay, ran, plan, trap, pan, stack* |
| **Discussion Point**<br><br>*ai* in middle; *ay* at end | **Alternate Sort (e.g., by meaning or function)**<br>nouns (naming words) versus verbs (action words) versus other |

## PART 5: READ DECODABLE TEXT

| | |
|---|---|
| **Phonics Focus**<br><br>**Words Decodable Using Target Skill**<br><br>*rain, day, train, paid, wait, Spain, May, maybe*<br><br>**New High-Frequency Words**<br><br>*away, one, doesn't, something*<br><br>**Story Words (if any)**<br><br>*museum, castle* | |
| **Academic Vocabulary Word to Preteach**<br><br>This vocabulary word is not from the book but is about the book and can be used during the conversations about the book to elevate the oral language.<br><br>*Explore*<br><br>　**Define:** *Explore* means "to find out about something"<br><br>　**Example:** We will *explore* the pond near our school during science class.<br><br>　**Ask:** What would you like to *explore* at a pond? | |
| **During Reading Technique** (circle method to use)<br><br>***Whisper Read*** (accelerates orthographic mapping of decodable words)<br><br>First read<br><br>***Choral Read*** (ideal for rereading to build fluency after an initial read)<br><br>***Echo Read*** (use to provide initial reading support or to model an aspect of fluency)<br><br>Second read, model reading questions versus statements | **Below-Level Supports**<br><br>Have students listen to the audio recording the day before.<br><br>Do an echo read and discussion (including about vocabulary) during a quick small-group lesson prior to whole-group instruction.<br><br>**Multilingual Learner Supports**<br><br>Have students listen to the audio recording the day before.<br><br>Do echo read and discussion (including about vocabulary) during a quick small-group lesson prior to whole-group instruction. |

**Comprehension—Deep Dive Questions**

Be sure to include the academic vocabulary word in one of the questions.

1.  Phonics focus:

    Where did the girl go? Find the country's name in the story.

2.  Detail with text evidence:

    What did the girl do in Spain? Find the sentences that tell you this.

3.  Higher-level thinking question:

    What problems did the girl have? Circle them.

4.  Higher-level thinking question:

    Where might the girl go next? Why do you think this?

5.  Connect to children's lives:

    Where would you like to go on a big trip? What would you like to explore there?

**Text Cohesion Point to Address**

*Pam rode on a train. **She** had a fun ride.*

**Ask:** Who is she?

**Sentence to Deconstruct**

*Pam had to wait / in a long line / to get inside the museum.*

**Ask:** Where? Why?

# PART 6: WRITING, SYNTAX, AND FLUENCY PLAN

| | |
|---|---|
| **Writing Prompt**<br><br>For fiction, have students write a retelling. For nonfiction, have students list facts they learned.<br><br>Write what the girl did in Spain. | **Sentence Frames and Stems (Multilingual Learner Support)**<br><br>In Spain _____.<br><br>The girl _____ in Spain.<br><br>The girl _____ and _____ in Spain. |
| | **Word Bank (Above-Level Support)**<br><br>*explore* |
| | **Word Bank (Below-Level Support)**<br><br>Decodable: *train, day*. High-frequency: *one* |
| **Syntax Focus**<br><br>Construct complex sentences using content from the decodable text.<br><br>(Circle the method to use.)<br><br>***Build Basic Who? Do What? Sentence***<br><br>Add Where?<br><br>Add When?<br><br>Add How?<br><br>***Create Compound Sentence*** (e.g., using *and* to join subjects)<br><br>***Switch Parts of Sentences*** (e.g., start with the "Where" part)<br><br>***Change Sentence Punctuation*** (e.g., change a statement to a question) | **Sentence Stems for Support**<br><br>The girl saw (what).<br><br>The girl saw (what) (where).<br><br>The girl saw (what) (when).<br><br>The girl saw (what) and (what).<br><br><br>Move the parts in the second sentence stem—*The girl saw* (what) (where)—to start with the "where" part. |
| **Fluency Plan**<br><br>(Circle the method to use.)<br><br>***Reread*** with a partner on Day 2<br><br>***Find words*** containing the target skill and list by spelling pattern. List words with *ai* and *ay*<br><br>***Reread decodable texts*** from previous week: #14. | |

# CHAPTER FOURTEEN

# Phonics Primer for Upper-Grade Teachers

## And Why So Many Students in the Intermediate Grades Are Behind

Regardless of where I go in the United States, the number of students in Grades 3 and up who have not mastered the basic phonics skills taught in Grades K–2 has grown. This is due, in part, to the effects of the COVID pandemic. Most students were introduced to the basic phonics skills but did not get the instructional intensity and number of reading and writing opportunities to develop fluency. As a result, they cannot access these skills with the degree of ease necessary when reading and spelling. This has significantly increased the challenges for teachers in the upper elementary grades as they try to assist their students in reading and writing about grade-level, complex texts. So what can you do if you have students with basic foundational skill fluency issues? I recommend following the tips found on the next few pages.

# TIPS FOR ADDRESSING FOUNDATIONAL SKILL FLUENCY ISSUES

1. Establish a protected time each day to work with students on the foundational phonics skills they need. You might have only 10–15 minutes per day, perhaps during a portion of the day when you are conducting small groups and students are working independently (e.g., reading or working on projects in small teams). Or this might be the first 10–15 minutes of the day as the other students are writing in their writer's notebooks or independently reading and annotating a selection you will discuss later in the day.

2. Assess students' individual foundational phonics skill needs using a cumulative phonics and spelling quick survey. (See the provided assessments if you don't have ones in your resources. These are designed to be quick checks to determine skill need categories, such as long vowels, in order to provide a starting point for instruction. They are not designed to provide a detailed assessment of each skill in each category.) This assessment will give you a starting point for individual or small groups of students.

3. Create a weekly instructional schedule. See the schedule provided, or use it as a springboard to create one that works for your students and within your instructional schedule.

4. Provide short, targeted lessons focused on building fluency in the foundational phonics skills, but *also* scaffold to grade-level expectations.

5. Focus on acceleration. That requires both frequent assessment (e.g., quick checks) to determine the impact of your instruction and observations of students reading and analysis of their writing to monitor and adjust the instruction offered as needed.

| MONDAY | TUESDAY | WEDNESDAY | THURSDAY | FRIDAY |
|---|---|---|---|---|
| **1 Cumulative Review** | **1 Cumulative Review** | **1 Cumulative Review** | **1 Cumulative Review** | **1 Cumulative Review** |
| Write letters, spellings, and syllables on index cards. Flash the cards and have students say the sounds. | **2 Dictation** Guide students to spell words with the new skill using supports such as sound boxes. | **2 Word Building** Use letter cards. | **2 Word Sort** Use word cards showing common spelling patterns. | **2 Word Ladder** Use words containing the target skill. |
| **2 Blend Words** Use the new skill. | **3 Decodable Text** Reread connected text to apply the skill and write a retelling or a list of facts learned. | **3 Decodable Text** Read a new connected text to apply the skill or reread a previous text and make a list of the words containing the target skill. | **3 Decodable Text** Listen to students read the text to you or a partner. | **3 Assess** Use cumulative decoding and spelling assessments. |
| **3 Decodable Text** Read connected text to apply the skill. | | | | |

*Based on your assessments of students' high-frequency word needs, select four to eight words each week to focus on. Use the Read, Spell, Write, Extend routine.

Level up the skill work. For example, if you are working with *r*-controlled vowels, provide sets of one-syllable practice words and then build to grade-level words containing the same skill. This "transition to longer words" work in each lesson will serve as a needed scaffold for students. Figure 14.1 provides an example. The "Check Foundational Skills" section has one-syllable words containing the target skill. The "Transition to Longer Words" section contains one-syllable words and related multisyllabic words that have an added word part (e.g., suffix or prefix). These words provide an easier scaffold to longer words. The "Challenge" section contains grade-level words. This section helps to level-up the lessons and provides a check for you in terms of which students are able or beginning to apply these previously taught skills to grade-level content.

Figure 14-1 • Transition to Longer Words

| | | | | | |
|---|---|---|---|---|---|
| **CHECK FOUNDATIONAL SKILLS** | | | | | |
| 1. cat | car | cart | pat | part | park |
| 2. bark | scar | star | start | spark | shark |
| 3. yard | yarn | barn | chart | smart | sharp |
| **TRANSITION TO LONGER WORDS** | | | | | |
| 4. hard | harder | hardest | large | larger | largest |
| 5. farm | farmer | start | starting | arm | armful |
| **CHALLENGE** | | | | | |
| 6. streetcar | backyard | postcard | ballpark | bookmark | landmark |
| 7. departing | restarting | recharge | lifeguard | harmful | guitar |
| **READING IN CONTEXT** | | | | | |
| 8. There's a big red barn on Farmer Bob's wheat farm. | | | | | |
| 9. Mark went to the market to get a large bag of apples. | | | | | |

## Additional Resources

Several websites offer additional resources and background information on early reading instruction. These include the following:

- www.fcrr.org (Florida Center for Reading Research)

- www.interdys.org (International Dyslexia Association)

- www.readingleague.org (The Reading League)

- www.readingrockets.org (Reading Rockets)

- www.righttoreadproject.com (Right to Read Project)

For a video explanation of how to use these routines for older students, go to https://www.youtube.com/watch?v=mdLIdfB-9pQM&t=32s (*Wiley Blevins Grades 3–5 Phonics Survival Guide*).

# Appendices: Assessments

## Reliable Checks of Phonics and Spelling Mastery Three Times a Year

*Photo Source:* iStock.com/FatCamera

Assessment of phonics skills must be done over an extended period of time, so that we can determine that students have achieved mastery. As I've highlighted in Chapter 4 entitled "Progress Monitoring" and throughout the chapters on routines, effective instruction and built-in repetition and review are baked into a strong scope and sequence. If any one skill is not worked on in subsequent weeks after its introduction, learning can decay. You can learn more about why and how to administer these assessments in Chapter 4.

In this appendix, you will find the following assessments. You can also download these from the companion website at **resources.corwin.com/differentiatingphonics.** online resources

### Appendix A: Comprehensive Phonics Surveys

#### Form 1: Quick Assessment for Placement

*Comprehensive Phonics Quick Survey: Nonsense-Word Reading*

*Comprehensive Phonics Assessment: Individual Scoring Sheet*

### Form 2: Diagnostic Assessment

*Comprehensive Phonics Survey—Diagnostic Assessment for Skills Analysis (Form 2a)*

*Comprehensive Phonics Survey—Diagnostic Assessment: Class Record Sheet (Form 2b)*

*Comprehensive Phonics Survey—Diagnostic Assessment for Skill Analysis: Error Analysis Sheet*

## Appendix B: Kindergarten and Grade 1 Quick Check: Beginning of Year

*Kindergarten and Early Grade 1 Phonics Quick Check*

## Appendix C: Comprehensive Spelling Surveys

### Form 1: Quick Assessment for Placement

*Comprehensive Spelling Survey—Quick Assessment*

*Comprehensive Spelling Survey—Quick: Individual Scoring Sheet*

### Form 2: Diagnostic Assessment for Skill Analysis

*Comprehensive Spelling Survey—Diagnostic Assessment*

*Comprehensive Spelling Survey—Diagnostic Assessment: Individual Scoring Sheet*

*Comprehensive Spelling Survey—Diagnostic Assessment: Error Analysis Sheet*

## Appendix D: Letter-Sound Assessment

## Appendix E: Letter-Name Assessment: Uppercase

## Appendix F: Letter-Name Assessment: Lowercase

## Appendix G: Fluency Check Examples

*Grade 1 Cumulative Phonics Mastery Check: Weekly Assessments*

## Appendix H: Cumulative Spelling Sentences—Examples

## Appendix I: Reading Observation Forms

*Kindergarten Reading Observation Form*

*Grade 1 Reading Observation Form*

*Grade 2 Reading Observation Form*

*Grade 3 Reading Observation Form*

## Appendix J: Phonics Skills Checklists for Writer's Notebooks

*Kindergarten Writer's Notebook Mastery Checklist*

*Grade 1 Writer's Notebook Mastery Checklist*

*Grade 2 Writer's Notebook Mastery Checklist*

*Grade 3 Writer's Notebook Mastery Checklist*

# Appendix A

## Comprehensive Phonics Surveys

These comprehensive phonics surveys offer options for administration and use:

### Form 1: Comprehensive Phonics Survey—Quick Assessment for Placement

This form consists of 50 nonsense words divided into five skill categories: Short Vowels, Consonant Blends and Digraphs, Long Vowels, Complex Vowels, and Word Study (Multisyllabic Words). The purpose of this form is to determine general skill category needs for each student.

### Form 2: Comprehensive Phonics Survey—Diagnostic Assessment for Skill Analysis

This form consists of 100 words divided into five skill categories: Short Vowels, Consonant Blends and Digraphs, Long Vowels, Complex Vowels, and Multisyllabic Words. The purpose of this form is to diagnose specific skill needs within each category for each student. For example, if students are placed in the short vowel skill category but, based on this assessment, they successfully read words with short *a* and short *o*, you can focus students' work on the remaining skills, thereby reducing the time spent in that skill set.

# FORM I: QUICK ASSESSMENT FOR PLACEMENT

**(© Wiley Blevins, 2011)**

## Preparation

1. Make a class supply of the *Comprehensive Phonics Quick Survey: Nonsense-Word Reading* and the *Comprehensive Phonics Assessment: Individual Scoring Sheet.*

2. Administer the assessment to each student in the class three times a year—at the beginning, middle, and end.

3. Gather and record all students' scores for each testing period to determine small-group differentiated instructional needs.

This assessment consists of 50 nonsense words to confirm students' decoding skills. Some students do well on real-word tests of phonics due to their wide sight-word knowledge yet struggle when applying those same decoding skills to new words. The nonsense word test accounts for this and assesses true decoding application. Administer this assessment as a follow-up to the real-word tests (cumulative phonics assessments), especially for students who do okay on these assessments but seem to struggle decoding while reading.

## Directions

1. Display the *Comprehensive Phonics Quick Survey: Nonsense-Word Reading.*

2. Have the student point to each word and read it aloud. Circle each correct response. Record the student's errors to use for error analysis (for example, *send* for *smend*). Record the number correct and note the speed in the boxes on the *Comprehensive Phonics Quick Survey: Individual Scoring Sheet.*

# Comprehensive Phonics Quick Survey: Nonsense-Word Reading

Name:                                                    Date:

| A. SHORT VOWELS | B. CONSONANT BLENDS AND DIGRAPHS | C. LONG VOWELS |
|---|---|---|
| 1. lat | 1. sheg | 1. sote |
| 2. ped | 2. chab | 2. mabe |
| 3. sib | 3. stot | 3. foap |
| 4. mog | 4. whid | 4. weam |
| 5. vun | 5. thuzz | 5. glay |
| 6. fim | 6. bruck | 6. shain |
| 7. hep | 7. cliss | 7. dright |
| 8. yot | 8. smend | 8. hupe |
| 9. rud | 9. thrist | 9. heest |
| 10. cag | 10. phum | 10. sny |

| D. COMPLEX VOWELS | E. WORD STUDY (MULTISYLLABIC WORDS) | |
|---|---|---|
| 1. doit | 1. rigfap | |
| 2. spoud | 2. churbit | |
| 3. clar | 3. napsate | |
| 4. foy | 4. reatloid | |
| 5. jern | 5. foutray | |
| 6. moof | 6. moku | |
| 7. lurst | 7. wolide | |
| 8. porth | 8. lofam | |
| 9. stook | 9. pagbo | |
| 10. flirch | 10. plizzles | |

# Comprehensive Phonics Quick Survey: Individual Scoring Sheet

Name: Date:

Circle correct responses. Record the child's incorrect responses on the lines.

| SHORT VOWELS | CONSONANT BLENDS AND DIGRAPHS | LONG VOWELS |
|---|---|---|
| 1. lat | 1. sheg | 1. sote |
| 2. ped | 2. chab | 2. mabe |
| 3. sib | 3. stot | 3. foap |
| 4. mog | 4. whid | 4. weam |
| 5. vun | 5. thuzz | 5. glay |
| 6. fim | 6. bruck | 6. shain |
| 7. hep | 7. cliss | 7. dright |
| 8. yot | 8. smend | 8. hupe |
| 9. rud | 9. thrist | 9. heest |
| 10. cag | 10. phum | 10. sny |

| | | |
|---|---|---|
| Number Correct: _____ | Number Correct: _____ | Number Correct: _____ |
| Speed: __ Slow/labored | Speed: __ Slow/labored | Speed: __ Slow/labored |
| __ Moderate | __ Moderate | __ Moderate |
| __ Fast | __ Fast | __ Fast |

| COMPLEX VOWELS | WORD STUDY (MULTISYLLABIC WORDS) |
|---|---|
| 1. doit _____ | 1. rigfap _____ |
| 2. spoud _____ | 2. churbit _____ |
| 3. clar _____ | 3. napsate _____ |
| 4. foy _____ | 4. reatloid _____ |
| 5. jern _____ | 5. foutray _____ |
| 6. moof _____ | 6. moku _____ |
| 7. lurst _____ | 7. wolide _____ |
| 8. porth _____ | 8. lofam _____ |
| 9. stook _____ | 9. pagbo _____ |
| 10. flirch _____ | 10. plizzles _____ |

Number Correct: _____
Speed: __ Slow/labored
      __ Moderate
      __ Fast

Number Correct: _____
Speed: __ Slow/labored
      __ Moderate
      __ Fast

## FORM 2: DIAGNOSTIC ASSESSMENT FOR SKILL ANALYSIS

**(© Wiley Blevins, 2023)**

### Preparation

Print a class supply of the *Comprehensive Phonics Survey— Diagnostic Assessment* and the *Comprehensive Phonics Survey— Diagnostic Assessment: Individual Scoring Sheet*. Also print a copy of the *Comprehensive Phonics Survey—Diagnostic Assessment: Class Record Sheet* (Form 2b).

### Administering the Assessment

Administer the *Comprehensive Phonics Survey—Diagnostic Assessment*, one child at a time, in the class three times a year—at the beginning, middle, and end.

1. Show the child the *Comprehensive Phonics Survey* (Form 2a). Explain to the child that he or she is to read each word. Point out that the words in the first column are nonsense, or made up, words. The words in the second column are real words.

2. Have the child point to each word and read it aloud. Circle each correct response. Record the child's errors on the *Comprehensive Phonics Survey—Diagnostic Assessment: Individual Scoring Sheet* to use for error analysis (for example, *send* for *smend*). Record the number correct and note the speed in the boxes for each part of the assessment.

### Scoring the Assessment

1. Count a word correct if the pronunciation is correct according to common sound-spelling relationships.

2. Total the number of words the child read correctly. Analyze the mispronounced words, looking for patterns that might give you information about the child's decoding strengths and weaknesses.

3. Focus future instruction on those sound-spelling relationship categories (e.g., short vowels, long vowels) in which the child made three or more errors.

4. Use the *Comprehensive Phonics Survey—Diagnostic Assessment: Class Record Sheet* (Form 2b) to record all children's scores for each testing period to determine small-group differentiated instructional needs.

# Comprehensive Phonics Survey—Diagnostic Assessment for Skill Analysis (Form 2a)

| A. SHORT VOWELS | | B. CONSONANT BLENDS AND DIGRAPHS | | C. LONG VOWELS | |
|---|---|---|---|---|---|
| *Nonsense Word* | *Real Word* | *Nonsense Word* | *Real Word* | *Nonsense Word* | *Real Word* |
| 1. lat | 11. zap | 1. sheg | 11. mesh | 1. sote | 11. dime |
| 2. ped | 12. den | 2. chab | 12. pinch | 2. mabe | 12. coal |
| 3. sib | 13. rim | 3. stot | 13. swell | 3. foap | 13. stow |
| 4. mog | 14. gob | 4. whid | 14. wham | 4. weam | 14. weak |
| 5. vun | 15. hut | 5. thuzz | 15. bath | 5. glay | 15. sway |
| 6. fim | 16. quill | 6. bruck | 16. drop | 6. shain | 16. chain |
| 7. hep | 17. wed | 7. cliss | 17. flick | 7. dright | 17. fright |
| 8. yot | 18. job | 8. smend | 18. snub | 8. hupe | 18. key |
| 9. rud | 19. cuff | 9. thrist | 19. split | 9. heest | 19. seep |
| 10. cag | 20. yak | 10. phum | 20. graph | 10. sny | 20. mild |

| D. COMPLEX VOWELS | | E. MULTISYLLABIC WORDS | |
|---|---|---|---|
| *Nonsense Word* | *Real Word* | *Nonsense Word* | *Real Word* |
| 1. doit | 11. join | 1. rigfap | 11. plastic |
| 2. spoud | 12. frown | 2. churbit | 12. barber |
| 3. clar | 13. harm | 3. napsate | 13. complete |
| 4. foy | 14. soy | 4. readloid | 14. explain |
| 5. jern | 15. perk | 5. foutray | 15. seaweed |
| 6. moof | 16. booth | 6. moku | 16. virus |
| 7. lurst | 17. nurse | 7. wolide | 17. stampede |
| 8. porth | 18. bore | 8. lofarm | 18. export |
| 9. stook | 19. wood | 9. pagbo | 19. mishap |
| 10. flirch | 20. dirt | 10. plizzles | 20. fiddle |

Name _____ Date _____

# Comprehensive Phonics Survey—Diagnostic Assessment: Class Record Sheet (Form 2b)

| A. SHORT VOWELS | | B. CONSONANT BLENDS AND DIGRAPHS | | C. LONG VOWELS | |
|---|---|---|---|---|---|
| *Nonsense Word* | *Real Word* | *Nonsense Word* | *Real Word* | *Nonsense Word* | *Real Word* |
| 1. lat _____ | 11. zap _____ | 1. sheg _____ | 11. mesh _____ | 1. sote _____ | 11. dime _____ |
| 2. ped _____ | 12. den _____ | 2. chab _____ | 12. pinch _____ | 2. mabe _____ | 12. coal _____ |
| 3. sib _____ | 13. rim _____ | 3. stot _____ | 13. swell _____ | 3. foap _____ | 13. stow _____ |
| 4. mog _____ | 14. gob _____ | 4. whid _____ | 14. wham _____ | 4. weam _____ | 14. weak _____ |
| 5. vun _____ | 15. hut _____ | 5. thuzz _____ | 15. bath _____ | 5. glay _____ | 15. sway _____ |
| 6. fim _____ | 16. quill _____ | 6. bruck _____ | 16. drop _____ | 6. shain _____ | 16. chain _____ |
| 7. hep _____ | 17. wed _____ | 7. cliss _____ | 17. flick _____ | 7. dright _____ | 17. fright _____ |
| 8. yot _____ | 18. job _____ | 8. smend _____ | 18. snub _____ | 8. hupe _____ | 18. key _____ |
| 9. rud _____ | 19. cuff _____ | 9. thrist _____ | 19. split _____ | 9. heest _____ | 19. seep _____ |
| 10. cag _____ | 20. yak _____ | 10. phum _____ | 20. graph _____ | 10. sny _____ | 20. mild _____ |

| D. COMPLEX VOWELS | | E. MULTISYLLABIC WORDS | |
|---|---|---|---|
| *Nonsense Word* | *Real Word* | *Nonsense Word* | *Real Word* |
| 1. doit _____ | 11. join _____ | 1. rigfap _____ | 11. plastic _____ |
| 2. spoud _____ | 12. frown _____ | 2. churbit _____ | 12. barber _____ |
| 3. clar _____ | 13. harm _____ | 3. napsate _____ | 13. complete _____ |
| 4. foy _____ | 14. soy _____ | 4. readloid _____ | 14. explain _____ |
| 5. jern _____ | 15. perk _____ | 5. foutray _____ | 15. seaweed _____ |
| 6. moof _____ | 16. booth _____ | 6. moku _____ | 16. virus _____ |
| 7. lurst _____ | 17. nurse _____ | 7. wolide _____ | 17. stampede _____ |
| 8. porth _____ | 18. bore _____ | 8. lofarm _____ | 18. export _____ |
| 9. stook _____ | 19. wood _____ | 9. pagbo _____ | 19. mishap _____ |
| 10. flirch _____ | 20. dirt _____ | 10. plizzles _____ | 20. fiddle _____ |

## Comprehensive Phonics Survey—Diagnostic Assessment for Skill Analysis: Error Analysis Sheet

**Check for accuracy of the pronunciations in \_\_color 2\_\_.**

| A. SHORT VOWELS | | B. CONSONANT BLENDS & DIGRAPHS | | C. LONG VOWELS | |
|---|---|---|---|---|---|
| *Nonsense Word* | *Real Word* | *Nonsense Word* | *Real Word* | *Nonsense Word* | *Real Word* |
| 1. lat | 11. zap | 1. sheg | 11. mesh | 1. sote | 11. dime |
| 2. ped | 12. den | 2. chab | 12. pinch | 2. mabe | 12. coal |
| 3. sib | 13. rim | 3. stot | 13. swell | 3. foap | 13. stow |
| 4. mog | 14. gob | 4. whid | 14. wham | 4. weam | 14. weak |
| 5. vun | 15. hut | 5. thuzz | 15. bath | 5. glay | 15. sway |
| 6. fim | 16. quill | 6. bruck | 16. drop | 6. shain | 16. chain |
| 7. hep | 17. wed | 7. cliss | 17. flick | 7. dright | 17. fright |
| 8. yot | 18. job | 8. smend | 18. snub | 8. hupe | 18. key |
| 9. rud | 19. cuff | 9. thrist | 19. split | 9. heest | 19. seep |
| 10. cag | 20. yak | 10. phum | 20. graph | 10. sny | 20. mild |

| D. COMPLEX VOWELS | | E. MULTISYLLABIC WORDS | |
|---|---|---|---|
| *Nonsense Word* | *Real Word* | *Nonsense Word* | *Real Word* |
| 1. doit | 11. join | 1. rigfap | 11. plastic |
| 2. spoud | 12. frown | 2. churbit | 12. barber |
| 3. clar | 13. harm | 3. napsate | 13. complete |
| 4. foy | 14. soy | 4. readloid | 14. explain |
| 5. jern | 15. perk | 5. foutray | 15. seaweed |
| 6. moof | 16. booth | 6. moku | 16. virus |
| 7. lurst | 17. nurse | 7. wolide | 17. stampede |
| 8. porth | 18. bore | 8. lofarm | 18. export |
| 9. stook | 19. wood | 9. pagbo | 19. mishap |
| 10. flirch | 20. dirt | 10. plizzles | 20. fiddle |

# Appendix B

## Kindergarten and Grade 1 Quick Check: Beginning of Year

### Kindergarten and Early Grade I Phonics Quick Check

**Student Name:**

**Directions:** Listen to the child read the list below. Mark one check in the first box if the word is read correctly (accuracy). Mark one check in the second box if it is read automatically (fluency).

| SHORT *a* | | | | SHORT *u* | | | |
|---|---|---|---|---|---|---|---|
| I | map | | | I3 | cup | | |
| 2 | rag | | | I4 | tug | | |
| 3 | sack | | | I5 | bus | | |
| 4 | jab | | | I6 | run | | |
| **SHORT *i*** | | | | **SHORT *e*** | | | |
| 5 | him | | | I7 | vet | | |
| 6 | zip | | | I8 | beg | | |
| 7 | kid | | | I9 | well | | |
| 8 | fin | | | 20 | yes | | |
| **SHORT *o*** | | | | **ADVANCED SKILLS** | | | |
| 9 | rod | | | 2I | gave | | |
| I0 | mp | | | 22 | life | | |
| II | got | | | 23 | hop | | |
| I2 | box | | | 24 | cute | | |

Number Correct (accuracy): _____

Number Automatic (fluency): _____

# Appendix C

## Comprehensive Spelling Surveys

Forms 1 and 2 of the *Comprehensive Spelling Survey* (© Wiley Blevins, 2023) offer options for administration and use.

### Form 1: Comprehensive Spelling Survey—Quick Assessment for Placement

This form consists of 40 words divided into eight skill categories: Short Vowels, Consonant Blends, Consonant Digraphs, Final/Silent *e*, Long Vowels, Complex Vowels, Word Study: Prefixes and Suffixes, Word Study: Multisyllabic Words. The purpose of this form is to determine general skill category needs for each student. For example, if students misspell more than two words in the short vowel skills category, then it is recommended that they begin with those skills if they also struggle reading those words as assessed by the *Comprehensive Phonics Survey—Diagnostic Assessment*.

### Form 2: Comprehensive Spelling Survey—Diagnostic Assessment for Skill Analysis

This form consists of 80 words divided into eight skill categories: Short Vowels, Consonant Blends, Consonant Digraphs, Final/Silent *e*, Long Vowels, Complex Vowels, Word Study: Prefixes and Suffixes, Word Study: Multisyllabic Words. The purpose of this form is to diagnose specific skill needs within each category for each student. For example, if students are placed in the Short Vowel skills set but, based on this assessment, they successfully spell words with short *a* and short *o*, you can focus students' work on the remaining skills, thereby reducing the time spent in that skills set.

## FORM I: COMPREHENSIVE SPELLING SURVEY

### Quick Assessment for Placement

(© **Wiley Blevins, 2023**)

## Preparation

1. Make a class supply of the *Comprehensive Spelling Survey—Quick Assessment: Individual Scoring Sheet.*

2. Administer the assessment to each child in the class three times a year—at the beginning, middle, and end. This assessment can be administered individually, in small groups, or with the whole class.

3. Gather and record all children's scores for each testing period to determine small-group differentiated instructional needs.

4. It is recommended that you administer the assessment over several days, covering only 2–3 skill categories each day.

## Administering the Assessment

This assessment consists of 40 words to confirm students' spelling skills. Some students do well reading words with taught phonics skill yet struggle spelling words using those same skills. Spelling generally lags behind reading development and requires more time and intensity in terms of instruction and practice. In addition, students might be at different places in their development and mastery of a phonics skills in decoding versus encoding.

1. Display the *Comprehensive Spelling Survey—Quick Assessment.*

2. Read each word aloud. Ask children to write the word on the *Comprehensive Spelling Survey—Quick Assessment: Individual Scoring Sheet.* Record the child's errors to use for error analysis. The specific errors in each category are more important than the overall score.

## Next Steps

If students misspell two or more of the target spellings in each section of the assessment, then instruction should begin in that skill set (e.g., short vowels).

# Comprehensive Spelling Survey—Quick Assessment

| A. SHORT VOWELS | B. CONSONANT BLENDS | C. CONSONANT DIGRAPHS |
|---|---|---|
| 1. zap | 1. glob | 1. thick |
| 2. peg | 2. drill | 2. chap |
| 3. bid | 3. stomp | 3. mesh |
| 4. fox | 4. crush | 4. whiz |
| 5. hum | 5. smell | 5. sung |

| D. FINAL/SILENT *e* | E. LONG VOWELS | F. COMPLEX VOWELS |
|---|---|---|
| 1. vote | 1. train | 1. boil |
| 2. grace | 2. soap | 2. sprout |
| 3. hive | 3. beam | 3. stark |
| 4. fuse | 4. stray | 4. dorm |
| 5. slope | 5. bright | 5. poof |

| G. WORD STUDY: PREFIXES AND SUFFIXES | H. WORD STUDY: MULTISYLLABIC WORDS |
|---|---|
| 1. unclean | 1. frantic |
| 2. recook | 2. recent |
| 3. turning | 3. invade |
| 4. baking | 4. oatmeal |
| 5. stopped | 5. barber |

Name _____  Date _____

# Comprehensive Spelling Survey—Quick Assessment: Individual Scoring Sheet

| A. SHORT VOWELS | B. CONSONANT BLENDS | C. CONSONANT DIGRAPHS |
|---|---|---|
| 1. | 1. | 1. |
| 2. | 2. | 2. |
| 3. | 3. | 3. |
| 4. | 4. | 4. |
| 5. | 5. | 5. |

| D. FINAL/SILENT e | E. LONG VOWELS | F. COMPLEX VOWELS |
|---|---|---|
| 1. | 1. | 1. |
| 2. | 2. | 2. |
| 3. | 3. | 3. |
| 4. | 4. | 4. |
| 5. | 5. | 5. |

| G. WORD STUDY: PREFIXES AND SUFFIXES | H. WORD STUDY: MULTISYLLABIC WORDS |
|---|---|
| 1. | 1. |
| 2. | 2. |
| 3. | 3. |
| 4. | 4. |
| 5. | 5. |

## FORM 2: COMPREHENSIVE SPELLING SURVEY

Diagnostic Assessment for Skill Analysis

**(© Wiley Blevins, 2023)**

### Preparation

1. Make a class supply of the *Comprehensive Spelling Survey—Diagnostic Assessment: Individual Scoring Sheet.*

2. Administer the assessment to each child in the class three times a year—at the beginning, middle, and end. This assessment can be administered individually, in small groups, or with the whole class.

3. Gather and record all children's scores for each testing period to determine small-group differentiated instructional needs.

4. It is recommended that you administer the assessment over several days, covering only one to two skill categories each day.

### Administering the Assessment

This assessment consists of 80 words to confirm students' spelling skills. Some students do well reading words with taught phonics skill yet struggle spelling words using those same skills. Spelling generally lags behind reading development and requires more time and intensity in terms of instruction and practice. In addition, students might be at different places in their development and mastery of a phonics skill in decoding versus encoding.

1. Display the *Comprehensive Spelling Survey—Diagnostic Assessment.*

2. Read each word aloud. Ask children to write the word on the *Comprehensive Spelling Survey—Diagnostic Assessment: Individual Scoring Sheet.* Record the child's errors to use for error analysis. The specific errors in each category are more important than the overall score.

3. Consult the *Error Analysis* sheet that follows. See the highlighted skill in each word that is the focus of the assessment. Take note of other spelling issues as well.

## Next Steps

If students misspell four or more of the target spellings in each section of the assessment, then instruction should begin in that skill set (e.g., short vowels).

# Comprehensive Spelling Survey—Diagnostic Assessment

| A. SHORT VOWELS | | B. CONSONANT BLENDS | | C. CONSONANT DIGRAPHS | |
|---|---|---|---|---|---|
| 1. zap | 6. vat | 1. glob | 6. clip | 1. thick | 6. moth |
| 2. peg | 7. yell | 2. drill | 7. brand | 2. chap | 7. patch |
| 3. bid | 8. win | 3. smell | 8. snug | 3. mesh | 8. shed |
| 4. fox | 9. job | 4. crush | 9. grass | 4. whiz | 9. quick |
| 5. hum | 10. cup | 5. stomp | 10. desk | 5. sung | 10. swing |

| D. FINAL/SILENT *e* | | E. LONG VOWELS | | F. COMPLEX VOWELS | |
|---|---|---|---|---|---|
| 1. vote | 6. robe | 1. train | 6. stray | 1. boil | 6. joy |
| 2. grace | 7. shade | 2. soap | 7. glow | 2. sprout | 7. gown |
| 3. hive | 8. lime | 3. beam | 8. deep | 3. stark | 8. turn |
| 4. fuse | 9. cube | 4. menu | 9. few | 4. dorm | 9. chirp |
| 5. these | 10. Steve | 5. bright | 10. sky | 5. poof | 10. brook |

| G. WORD STUDY: PREFIXES AND SUFFIXES | | H. WORD STUDY: MULTISYLLABIC WORDS | |
|---|---|---|---|
| 1. unclean | 6. precheck | 1. frantic | 6. basket |
| 2. recook | 7. dislike | 2. recent | 7. hotel |
| 3. turning | 8. stranded | 3. invade | 8. reptile |
| 4. baking | 9. fried | 4. oatmeal | 9. rainboots |
| 5. stopped | 10. trapping | 5. barber | 10. former |

Name _____ Date _____

# Comprehensive Spelling Survey—Diagnostic Assessment: Individual Scoring Sheet

| A. SHORT VOWELS | | B. CONSONANT BLENDS | | C. CONSONANT DIGRAPHS | |
|---|---|---|---|---|---|
| 1. | 6. | 1. | 6. | 1. | 6. |
| 2. | 7. | 2. | 7. | 2. | 7. |
| 3. | 8. | 3. | 8. | 3. | 8. |
| 4. | 9. | 4. | 9. | 4. | 9. |
| 5. | 10. | 5. | 10. | 5. | 10. |

| D. FINAL/SILENT e | | E. LONG VOWELS | | F. COMPLEX VOWELS | |
|---|---|---|---|---|---|
| 1. | 6. | 1. | 6. | 1. | 6. |
| 2. | 7. | 2. | 7. | 2. | 7. |
| 3. | 8. | 3. | 8. | 3. | 8. |
| 4. | 9. | 4. | 9. | 4. | 9. |
| 5. | 10. | 5. | 10. | 5. | 10. |

| G. WORD STUDY: PREFIXES AND SUFFIXES | | H. WORD STUDY: MULTISYLLABIC WORDS | |
|---|---|---|---|
| 1. | 6. | 1. | 6. |
| 2. | 7. | 2. | 7. |
| 3. | 8. | 3. | 8. |
| 4. | 9. | 4. | 9. |
| 5. | 10. | 5. | 10. |

# Comprehensive Spelling Survey—Diagnostic Assessment: Error Analysis Sheet

| A. SHORT VOWELS | | B. CONSONANT BLENDS | | C. CONSONANT DIGRAPHS | |
|---|---|---|---|---|---|
| I. zap | 6. vat | I. glob | 6. clip | I. thick | 6. moth |
| 2. peg | 7. yell | 2. drill | 7. brand | 2. chap | 7. patch |
| 3. bid | 8. win | 3. smell | 8. snug | 3. mesh | 8. shed |
| 4. fox | 9. job | 4. crush | 9. grass | 4. whiz | 9. quick |
| 5. hum | 10. cup | 5. stomp | 10. desk | 5. sung | 10. swing |

| D. FINAL/SILENT e | | E. LONG VOWELS | | F. COMPLEX VOWELS | |
|---|---|---|---|---|---|
| I. vote | 6. robe | I. train | 6. stray | I. boil | 6. joy |
| 2. grace | 7. shade | 2. soap | 7. glow | 2. sprout | 7. gown |
| 3. hive | 8. lime | 3. beam | 8. deep | 3. stark | 8. turn |
| 4. fuse | 9. cube | 4. menu | 9. few | 4. dorm | 9. chirp |
| 5. these | 10. Steve | 5. bright | 10. sky | 5. poof | 10. brook |

| G. WORD STUDY: PREFIXES AND SUFFIXES | | H. WORD STUDY: MULTISYLLABIC WORDS | |
|---|---|---|---|
| I. unclean | 6. precheck | I. frantic | 6. basket |
| 2. recook | 7. dislike | 2. recent | 7. hotel |
| 3. turning | 8. stranded | 3. invade | 8. reptile |
| 4. baking | 9. fried | 4. oatmeal | 9. rainboots |
| 5. stopped | 10. trapping | 5. barber | 10. former |

# Appendix D

## Letter-Sound Assessment

Name:                                          Date:

| | | ACCURACY | SPEED |
|------|------|----------|-------|
| 1. | c | | |
| 2. | a | | |
| 3. | b | | |
| 4. | t | | |
| 5. | p | | |
| 6. | s | | |
| 7. | k | | |
| 8. | o | | |
| 9. | j | | |
| 10. | z | | |
| 11. | f | | |
| 12. | d | | |
| 13. | m | | |

| | | ACCURACY | SPEED |
|---|---|---|---|
| 14. | v | | |
| 15. | e | | |
| 16. | g | | |
| 17. | l | | |
| 18. | h | | |
| 19. | n | | |
| 20. | r | | |
| 21. | q | | |
| 22. | i | | |
| 23. | w | | |
| 24. | x | | |
| 25. | u | | |
| 26. | y | | |

Accuracy _____ /26

Speed _____ /26

Letters Mastered _____

Focus Letters for Next
Instructional Cycle: _____

# Appendix E

## Letter-Name Assessment: Uppercase

Name:                                    Date:

| | UPPERCASE | ACCURACY | SPEED |
|------|-----------|----------|-------|
| 1. | O | | |
| 2. | B | | |
| 3. | A | | |
| 4. | C | | |
| 5. | X | | |
| 6. | P | | |
| 7. | S | | |
| 8. | E | | |
| 9. | H | | |
| 10. | T | | |
| 11. | W | | |
| 12. | M | | |
| 13. | R | | |

| | UPPERCASE | ACCURACY | SPEED |
|---|---|---|---|
| 14. | K | | |
| 15. | D | | |
| 16. | F | | |
| 17. | L | | |
| 18. | Y | | |
| 19. | Z | | |
| 20. | G | | |
| 21. | J | | |
| 22. | N | | |
| 23. | I | | |
| 24. | Q | | |
| 25. | U | | |
| 26. | V | | |

Accuracy _____ /26

Speed _____ /26

Letters Mastered _____

Focus Letters for Next
Instructional Cycle: _____

# Appendix F

## Letter-Name Assessment: Lowercase

Name:                                               Date:

|  | LOWERCASE | ACCURACY | SPEED |
|---|---|---|---|
| 1. | o | | |
| 2. | b | | |
| 3. | *a* | | |
| 4. | c | | |
| 5. | x | | |
| 6. | p | | |
| 7. | s | | |
| 8. | e | | |
| 9. | h | | |
| 10. | t | | |
| 11. | w | | |
| 12. | m | | |
| 13. | r | | |

| | LOWERCASE | ACCURACY | SPEED |
|---|---|---|---|
| 14. | k | | |
| 15. | d | | |
| 16. | f | | |
| 17. | l | | |
| 18. | y | | |
| 19. | z | | |
| 20. | g | | |
| 21. | j | | |
| 22. | n | | |
| 23. | i | | |
| 24. | q | | |
| 25. | u | | |
| 26. | v | | |

Accuracy _____ /26

Speed _____ /26

Letters Mastered _____

Focus Letters for Next
Instructional Cycle: _____

# Appendix G

## Fluency Check Examples

### GRADE 1 CUMULATIVE PHONICS MASTERY CHECK: WEEKLY ASSESSMENTS

## Assessment 1

| Week 1 | | | |
|---|---|---|---|
| 1 | at | | |
| 2 | map | | |
| 3 | had | | |
| 4 | rags | | |

**Number Accurate:** _____ / 4

**Number Automatic:** _____ / 4

## Assessment 3

| Week 3 | | | |
|---|---|---|---|
| 9 | mop | | |
| 10 | box | | |
| 11 | dot | | |
| 12 | log | | |
| Week 2 | | | |
| 5 | bit | | |

| 6 | lick | | |
|---|---|---|---|
| 7 | him | | |
| 8 | kits | | |
| **Week 1** <br> 1 | at | | |
| 2 | map | | |
| 3 | had | | |
| 4 | rags | | |

**Number Accurate:** _____ / 12

**Number Automatic:** _____ / 12

## Assessment 6

| **Week 6** <br> 21 | clip | | |
|---|---|---|---|
| 22 | flap | | |
| 23 | block | | |
| 24 | glad | | |
| **Week 5** <br> 17 | egg | | |
| 18 | pens | | |
| 19 | beg | | |
| 20 | let | | |

*(Continued)*

(Continued)

| | | | |
|---|---|---|---|
| **Week 4** 13 | hug | | |
| 14 | buns | | |
| 15 | fuzz | | |
| 16 | nut | | |
| **Week 3** 9 | mop | | |
| 10 | box | | |
| 11 | dot | | |
| 12 | log | | |
| **Week 2** 5 | bit | | |
| 6 | lick | | |
| 7 | him | | |
| 8 | kits | | |
| **Week 1** 1 | at | | |
| 2 | map | | |
| 3 | had | | |
| 4 | rags | | |

**Number Accurate:** _____ / 24

**Number Automatic:** _____ / 24

# Appendix H
## Cumulative Spelling Sentences—Examples

## Cumulative Spelling Sentences: Grade 1, Week 24

| SPELLING SENTENCES | SAMPLE WORDS FROM SKILLS ASSESSED |
|---|---|
| 1. My *house* is made of *wood*. | Target Skill, Week 24: *house, down, found* |
| 2. The *girl* ran *down* the street. | Target Skill, Week 23: *wood, books* |
| 3. I *found* a *few more books*. | Target Skill, Week 22: *more* |
| 4. It is *dark* at night. | Target Skill, Week 21: *girl* |
| | Target Skill, Week 20: *dark* |
| | Target Skill, Week 19: *few* |

*NOTE: You can increase the number of sentences and words to include for each skill based on how much students can write given the amount of time you have for the assessment.*

## Cumulative Spelling Sentences: Grade 3

| Week 7 | r-Controlled Vowels (/är/, /ôr/) | He will try to *score* another goal.<br>The wild dogs *barked* all night.<br>They will *explore* the *park* together.<br>The *farmer* will use his new *tractor*. |
|---|---|---|
| Week 8 | r-Controlled Vowels (er, ir, ur) | The *turtle* plopped into the *water*.<br>Two *teachers* have *birthdays* today.<br>The *color* of *her flowers* is *purple*.<br>The *girl* will start a new school. |
| Week 9 | Long oo and Short oo | It is *too* dark in her *bedroom*.<br>*Do you* have that *new shampoo*?<br>We *could* live in our *classroom*.<br>What is your favorite part of that *book*? |
| Week 10 | Diphthongs /ou/ and /oi/ | I have a loose tooth in my *mouth*.<br>The *cowboy* rode his horse into *town*.<br>The *mouse* chewed a hole in my shoe.<br>Is it hard to *join* that soccer team? |

# Appendix I

## Reading Observation Forms

## Kindergarten

**Student** _____ **Date** _____

Observe a student reading aloud. Use the Reading Behavior Look-Fors and Prompts to respond to student errors. Record your observations in the General Notes section.

| READING BEHAVIOR LOOK-FORS | PROMPTS |
|---|---|
| Student self-monitors and self-corrects using known letter-sound correspondences.<br><br>I    2    3 | *Run your finger under each letter as you say the sound. Blend the sounds to read the word.*<br><br>Point to and state any missed letter-sound, and then guide the student to blend the word again. |
| Student understands what is read.<br><br>I    2    3 | Fiction: *Tell me in your own words what the story is about so far.*<br><br>Informational: *Tell what you have learned about* _____ *so far.*<br><br>Ask questions periodically throughout the reading to check on the student's comprehension. Focus on both literal and higher-order questions. Have the student support answers using evidence from the text, such as reading the sentence that answers the question. |
| Student reads with appropriate grade-level phrasing and speed.<br><br>I    2    3 | *Read this sentence again. Make it sound like you are talking to me.*<br><br>*Look at this end mark. How does that change how you will read this sentence?*<br><br>Select sentences to model aspects of fluency, such as changes in intonation based on end punctuation. Model, and have students repeat. |

KEY: I = not observed   2 = developing   3 = observed

**General Notes**

## Kindergarten (continued): Focus on Skills

Note specific words the student struggled reading (both decodable words and irregular high-frequency words) and comment on overall fluency.

| DECODABLE WORDS | HIGH-FREQUENCY WORDS | FLUENCY |
|---|---|---|
|  |  |  |

Circle any phonics skills students struggled applying when decoding words.

Use this information to provide additional phonics instruction and practice during small groups.

| | | | | | |
|---|---|---|---|---|---|
| Short *a* | Consonants | m | s | t | |
| Short *i* | Consonants | p | n | c | |
| Short *o* | Consonants | f | d | h | |
| Short *e* | Consonants | r | b | l | k |
| Short *u* | Consonants | g | w | x | v |
| Final *e* | Consonants | j | q | y | z |

# Grade I Reading Observation Form

**Student** _____  **Date** _____

Observe a student reading aloud. Use the Reading Behavior Look-Fors and Prompts to respond to student errors. Record your observations in the General Notes section.

| READING BEHAVIOR LOOK-FORS | PROMPTS |
|---|---|
| Student self-monitors and self-corrects using known sound-spelling correspondences.<br><br>I    2    3 | *Run your finger under each letter or spelling as you say the sound. Blend the sounds together.*<br><br>Point to and state any missed letter-sound or sound-spelling, and then guide the student to blend the word again. |
| Student understands what is read.<br><br>I    2    3 | Fiction: *Tell me in your own words what the story is about so far.*<br><br>Informational: *Tell what you have learned about* _____ *so far.*<br><br>Ask questions periodically throughout the reading to check on the student's comprehension. Focus on both literal and higher-order questions. Have the student support answers using evidence from the text, such as by reading the sentence that answers the question. |
| Student reads with appropriate grade-level phrasing and speed.<br><br>I    2    3 | *Read this sentence again. Make it sound like you are talking to me.*<br><br>*Look at the punctuation and end mark. How does that change how you will read this sentence?*<br><br>Select sentences to model aspects of fluency, such as proper phrasing or chunking and changes in intonation based on end punctuation. Model and have the student repeat. |

KEY: I = not observed   2 = developing   3 = observed

**General Notes**

## Grade 1 Reading Observation Form (continued): Focus on Skills

Note specific words the student struggled reading (both decodable words and irregular high-frequency words) and comment on overall fluency.

| DECODABLE WORDS | HIGH-FREQUENCY WORDS | FLUENCY |
|---|---|---|
|  |  |  |

Circle any phonics skills the student struggled applying when decoding words.

Use this information to provide additional phonics instruction and practice during small groups.

| | |
|---|---|
| Short Vowels    *a*   *e*   *i*   *o*   *u* | Long Vowels    *a*   *e*   *i*   *o*   *u* |
| *l*-blends | r-Controlled Vowels   *ar*   *er/ir/ur*   *or* |
| *s*-blends | Short and Long *oo* |
| *r*-blends | Diphthongs *ou/ow*   *oi/oy* |
| Digraphs   *sh*   *th*   *ch/tch*   *wh*   *ng/nk* | Complex Vowel /ô/ (*au, aw, al*) |
| Final *e* | r-Controlled Vowels *are/air/ear* |

# Grade 2 Reading Observation Form

**Student** _____  **Date** _____

Observe the student reading aloud. Use the Reading Behavior Look-Fors and Prompts to respond to student errors. Record your observations in the General Notes section.

| READING BEHAVIOR LOOK-FORS | PROMPTS |
|---|---|
| Student self-monitors and self-corrects using known sound-spelling correspondences and knowledge of syllables.<br><br>1    2    3 | *Use what you know about syllables to chunk and pronounce each word part. Blend the sounds (word parts) together to read the word.*<br><br>Reinforce the steps in the "Reading Big Words Strategy." Model using the steps with words the student struggles to decode. |
| Student understands what is read.<br><br>1    2    3<br><br>Self-Monitoring: Have the student point out places in the text that were difficult and explain what actions helped resolve comprehension or decoding issues. *What part was hard to read? What did you do to help you understand?* | Fiction: *Tell me in your own words what the story is about so far.*<br><br>Informational: *Tell what you have learned about _____ so far.*<br><br>Ask questions periodically throughout the reading to check on the student's comprehension. Focus on both literal and higher-order questions. Have the student support answers using evidence from the text, such as reading the sentence that answers the question. |
| Student reads with appropriate grade-level phrasing and speed.<br><br>1    2    3 | *Read this dialogue again. Make it sound like the character is talking.*<br><br>*Look at the punctuation and end mark. How does that change how you will read this sentence?*<br><br>Select sentences to model aspects of fluency, such as proper phrasing or chunking and intonation. Model and have the student repeat. |

**KEY:** 1 = not observed   2 = developing   3 = observed

**General Notes**

# Grade 2 Reading Observation Form (continued): Focus on Skills

Note specific words the student struggled to read (both decodable words and irregular high-frequency words) and comment on overall fluency.

| DECODABLE WORDS | HIGH-FREQUENCY WORDS | FLUENCY |
| --- | --- | --- |
| | | |

Circle any phonics or word study skills the student struggled applying when decoding words.

Use this information to provide additional phonics instruction and practice during small groups.

| | |
| --- | --- |
| Short Vowels   a   e   i   o   u | r-Controlled Vowels<br><br>ar  er/ir/ur  or |
| Long Vowels   a   e   i   o   u | Short and Long oo |
| Final e | Diphthongs ou/ow    oi/oy |
| l-blend, s-blends, r-blends | Complex Vowel /ô/ (au, aw, al) |
| Digraphs sh  th  ch/tch  wh  ng/nk | Syllable Types<br><br>Closed          Open<br>Final e         Vowel Team<br>r-Controlled    Consonant + le |
| Inflectional Endings (and other suffixes) | Prefixes |

# Grade 3 Reading Observation Form

**Student** _____  **Date** _____

Observe the student reading aloud. Use the Reading Behavior Look-Fors and Prompts to respond to student errors. Record your observations in the General Notes section.

| READING BEHAVIOR LOOK-FORS | PROMPTS |
|---|---|
| Student self-monitors and self-corrects using known sound-spelling correspondences and knowledge of syllables.<br><br>I      2      3 | *Use what you know about syllables to chunk and pronounce each word part. Blend the sounds (word parts) together to read the word.*<br><br>Reinforce the steps in the "Reading Big Words Strategy." Model using the steps with words the student struggles to decode. |
| Student understands what is read.<br><br>I      2      3<br><br>Self-Monitoring: Have the student point out places in the text that were difficult and explain what actions helped resolve comprehension or decoding issues. | Fiction: *Tell me in your own words what the story is about so far.*<br><br>Informational: *Tell what you have learned about _____ so far.*<br><br>Ask questions periodically throughout the reading to check on the student's comprehension. Focus on both literal and higher-order questions. Have the student support answers using evidence from the text, such as reading the sentence that answers the question. |
| Student reads with appropriate grade-level phrasing and speed.<br><br>I      2      3 | *Read this dialogue again. Make it sound like the character is talking.*<br><br>*Look at the punctuation and end mark. How does that change how you will read this sentence?*<br><br>Select sentences to model aspects of fluency, such as proper phrasing or chunking and intonation. Model and have students repeat. |

**KEY:** I = not observed   2 = developing   3 = observed

**General Notes**

# Grade 3 Reading Observation Form (continued): Focus on Skills

Note specific words the student struggled to read (both decodable words and irregular high-frequency words) and comment on overall fluency.

| DECODABLE WORDS | HIGH-FREQUENCY WORDS | FLUENCY |
|---|---|---|
| | | |

Circle any phonics or word study skills the student struggled to apply when decoding words.

Use this information to provide additional phonics instruction and practice during small groups.

| | |
|---|---|
| Short Vowels     a     e     i     o     u | r-Controlled Vowels<br><br>ar          er/ir/ur          or |
| Long Vowels     a     e     i     o     u | Short and Long oo |
| Final e | Diphthongs ou/ow          oi/oy |
| Inflectional Endings (and other suffixes) | Complex Vowel /ô/ (au, aw, al) |
| Prefixes | Syllable Types<br><br>Closed                    Open<br><br>Final e                    Vowel Team<br><br>r-Controlled          Consonant + le |
| Homophones and Homographs | Compound Words and Contractions |

# Appendix J

## Phonics Skills Checklists for Writer's Notebooks

### Kindergarten Writer's Notebook Mastery Checklist

| SKILL | MASTERY | EXAMPLES | SKILL | MASTERY | EXAMPLES |
|-------|---------|----------|-------|---------|----------|
| Mm | | | Bb | | |
| Short *a* | | | Ll | | |
| Ss | | | Kk | | |
| Tt | | | Short *e* | | |
| Pp | | | Gg | | |
| Nn | | | Ww | | |
| Short *i* | | | Xx | | |
| Cc | | | Vv | | |
| Ff | | | Short *u* | | |
| Dd | | | Jj | | |
| Hh | | | Qu | | |
| Short *o* | | | Yy | | |
| Rr | | | Zz | | |

# Grade 1 Writer's Notebook Mastery Checklist

| SKILL | MASTERY | EXAMPLES | SKILL | MASTERY | EXAMPLES |
|---|---|---|---|---|---|
| Short *a* | | | Long *e* (*ee, ea*) | | |
| Short *i* | | | Long *o* (*oa, ow*) | | |
| Short *o* | | | Long *i* (*y, igh*) | | |
| Short *u* | | | Long *u* (*u, ew, ue*) | | |
| Short *e* | | | *r*-Controlled *ar* | | |
| *l*-blends | | | *r*-Controlled *er, ir, ur* | | |
| *s*-blends | | | *r*-Controlled *or, ore, oar* | | |
| *r*-blends | | | Short *oo* (*book*); Long *oo* (*oo, ou, ew, ue, u_e*) (*room*) | | |
| Digraph *sh*; Digraph *th* (both sounds) | | | Diphthong /ou/ (*ou, ow*) | | |
| Digraph *ch, tch*; Digraph *wh* | | | Diphthong /oi/ (*oi, oy*) | | |
| Digraph *ng* (also cover *nk*) | | | Complex Vowel /â/ [*au, aw, a(lk), a(lt), a(ll)*] | | |
| Final *e* (*a_e, i_e*) | | | *r*-Controlled *are, air, ear* | | |
| Final *e* (*o_e, u_e, e_e*) | | | Long *i* and *o* [*i(ld), i(nd), o(ld)*] | | |
| Single Letter Long Vowels *e, i, o* | | | Long *i* and *o* (*ie, oe*) | | |
| Long *a* (*ai, ay*) | | | Long *e* (*y, ey, ie, ei*) | | |

# Grade 2 Writer's Notebook Mastery Checklist

| SKILL | MASTERY | EXAMPLES | SKILL | MASTERY | EXAMPLES |
|---|---|---|---|---|---|
| Short Vowels | | | r-Controlled ar | | |
| l-blend, r-blends, s-blends | | | r-Controlled er, ir, ur | | |
| Final Blends | | | r-Controlled or, ore, oar | | |
| Final e (a_e, i_e, o_e, e_e, u_e) | | | r-Controlled are, air, ear | | |
| Digraph sh | | | Short oo (oo); Long oo (oo, ou, ew, ue, u_e) | | |
| Digraph ch, tch | | | Diphthong /ou/ (ou, ow) | | |
| Digraph th | | | Diphthong /oi/ (oi, oy) | | |
| Digraph wh | | | Complex Vowel /â/ [au, aw, a(lk), a(lt), a(ll)] | | |
| Digraph ph | | | MULTISYLLABIC WORDS | | |
| Digraph ng (also cover nk) | | | Open Syllables | | |
| Long a | | | Closed Syllables | | |
| Long e | | | Consonant + le Syllables | | |
| Long i | | | Vowel Team Syllables | | |
| Long o | | | r-Controlled Vowel Syllables | | |
| Long u | | | Final e Syllables | | |

# Grade 3 Writer's Notebook Mastery Checklist

| SKILL | MASTERY | EXAMPLES | SKILL | MASTERY | EXAMPLES |
|---|---|---|---|---|---|
| Short Vowels | | | Closed Syllable | | |
| Long *a* | | | Open Syllables | | |
| Long *o* | | | Final Stable Syllables | | |
| Long *e* | | | Vowel Team Syllables | | |
| Long *i* | | | *r*-Controlled Vowel Syllables | | |
| Long *u* | | | Final e Syllables | | |
| *r*-Controlled Vowel *ar* | | | Inflectional Endings (*-ed, -ing*) With Spelling Changes | | |
| *r*-Controlled Vowel *or, oar, ore* | | | Irregular Plurals | | |
| *r*-Controlled Vowel *er, ir, ur* | | | Prefixes | | |
| Short *oo* and Long *oo* | | | Suffixes | | |
| Diphthong /*ou*/ (*ou, ow*) | | | Homophones and Homographs | | |
| Diphthong /*oi*/ (*oi, oy*) | | | Compound Words | | |
| Complex Vowel /â/ [*au, aw, a*(*lk*), *a*(*lt*), *a*(*ll*)] | | | Contractions | | |

# References and Further Reading

Adams, M. J. (1990). *Beginning to read: Thinking and learning about print.* Massachusetts Institute of Technology.

Anderson, R. C., Hiebert, E. H., Scott, J. A., & Wilkinson, I. A. G. (1985). *Becoming a nation of readers: The report of the commission on reading.* Center for the Study of Reading and National Academy of Education.

Bear, D. R., Templeton, S., Invernizzi, M., & Johnston, F. (2019). *Words their way: Word study for phonics, vocabulary, and spelling instruction* (7th ed.). Pearson.

Beck, I., & Beck, M. E. (2013). *Making sense of phonics: The hows and whys* (2nd ed.). Guilford Press.

Blevins, W. (1997). *Phonemic awareness activities for early reading success.* Scholastic.

Blevins, W. (2000) *A research study on the effects of using decodable texts with systematic phonics instruction.* Sadlier School Professional Development Series. https://www.weare-teachers.com/wp-content/uploads/Using-Decodable-Texts_eBook.pdf

Blevins, W. (2001). *Building fluency: Lessons and strategies for reading success.* Scholastic.

Blevins, W. (2011a). *Teaching phonics: A flexible, systematic approach to building early reading skills.* Scholastic.

Blevins, W. (2011b). *Teaching the alphabet: A flexible, systematic approach to building early phonics skills.* Scholastic.

Blevins, W. (2011c). *Week-by-week phonics and word study activities for the intermediate grades.* Scholastic.

Blevins, W. (2016). *A fresh look at phonics: Common causes of failure and 7 ingredients for success.* Corwin.

Blevins, W. (2017). *Teaching phonics and word study in the intermediate grades* (2nd ed.). Scholastic.

Blevins, W. (2019). *Meeting the challenges of early literacy phonics instruction.* Literacy leadership brief No. 9452. International Literacy Association.

Blevins, W. (2020a). *Choosing and using decodable texts: Practical tips and strategies for enhancing phonics instruction.* Scholastic.

Blevins, W. (2020b). *Meaningful phonics and word study: Lesson fix ups for impactful teaching.* Benchmark Education.

Blevins, W. (2023a). *Phonics from A to Z: A practical guide* (4th ed.). Scholastic.

Blevins, W. (2023b) *Teaching phonics and word study in the intermediate grades* (3rd ed.). Scholastic.

Brady, S. (2021, October 28). *Current knowledge about instruction in letter knowledge, phoneme awareness, and handwriting: What to teach, when to start, and why to integrate.* Learning Ally [web posting]. https://learningally.org/Portals/6/Docs/white-papers/Current-Knowledge-About-Instruction_Brady.pdf

Brown, K. J., Patrick, K. C., Fields, M. K., & Craig, G. T. (2021). Phonological awareness materials in Utah kindergartens: A case study in the science of reading. *Reading Research Quarterly, 56*(S1), S249–S272.

Carroll, J. B., Davies, P., & Richman, B. (1971). *Word frequency book.* Houghton Mifflin.

Cheatham, J. P., & Allor, J. H. (2012). The influence of decodability in early reading text on reading achievement: A review of the evidence. *Reading and Writing: An Interdisciplinary Journal, 25*(9), 2223–2246.

Chu, M., & Chen, S. (2014). Comparison of the effects of two phonics training programs on L2 word reading. *Psychological Reports, 114*(1), 272–291. https://doi.org/10.2466/28.10.pr0.114k17w0

Clemens, N., Solari, E., Kearns, D. M., Fien, H., Nelson, N. J., Stelega, M., Burns, M., Martin, K. St., & Heoft, F. (2021, December

14). *They say you can do phonemic aware-ness instruction "in the dark," but should you? A critical evaluation of the trend toward advanced phonemic awareness training.* Reading Rockets [Research Report]. https://www.readingrockets .org/resources/resource-library/they-say-you-can-do-phonemic-awareness-instruction-dark-should-you

Duke, N. K., & Cartwright, K. B. (2021). The science of reading progresses: Communicating advances beyond the simple view of reading. *Reading Research Quarterly, 56*(S1), S25–S44.

Ehri, L. C. (1992). Reconceptualizing the development of sight word reading and its relationship to recoding. In P. Gough, L. Ehri, & R. Treiman (Eds.), *Reading acquisition* (pp. 107–143). Erlbaum.

Ehri, L. C. (1996). Phases of development in learning to read words. In J. Oakhill & R. Beard (Eds.), *Reading development and the teaching of reading: A psycholog-ical perspective* (pp. 79–108). Blackwell Publishers.

Frey, R. C. (2012). *Rethinking the role of decodable texts in early literacy instruc-tion* (UMI No. 3593795) [Doctoral dis-sertation, University of California, Berkeley]. ProQuest Dissertations Publishing. https://www.proquest.com/ docview/1441347886

Fry, E. B., Kress, E., & Fountoukidis, D. L. (1993). *The new reading teacher's book of lists.* Prentice-Hall.

Gonzalez-Frey, S. M., & Ehri, L. C. (2021). Connected phonation is more effective than segmented phonation for teaching beginning readers to decode unfamiliar words. *Scientific Studies of Reading, 25*(3), 272–285. https://doi.org/10.1080/1088 8438.2020.1776290

Gough, P. B., & Tunmer, W. E. (1986). Decoding, reading, and reading disabil-ity. *Remedial and Special Education, 7*(1), 6–10.

Gough, P. B., Hoover, W. A., & Peterson, C. L. (1996). Some observations on a sim-ple view of reading. In C. Cornoldi & J. Oakhill (Eds.), *Reading comprehension*

*difficulties: Processes and intervention* (pp. 1–13). Erlbaum.

Gough, P. B., & Walsh, M. A. (1991). Chinese, Phoenicians, and the orthographic cipher of English. In S. A. Brady & D. P. Shankweiler (Eds.), *Phonological process in literacy: A tribute to Isabelle Y. Liberman* (pp. 199–209). Erlbaum.

Haddock, M. (1978). Teaching blending in beginning reading instruction is import-ant. *The Reading Teacher, 31*(6), 654–658.

Hasbrouck, J., & Tindal, G. (2017). *An update to compiled ORF norms* (Technical Report No. 1702). Behavioral Research and Teaching, University of Oregon.

International Dyslexia Association. (2022, June). *Building phoneme awareness: Know what matters*[Factsheet].https://surreyschoolsone .ca/cms-data/depot/depot/IDA-phoneme-awareness-fact-sheet-2022.pdf

Jenkins, J. R., Peyton, J. A., Sanders, E. A., & Vadasy, P. F. (2004). Effects of read-ing decodable texts in supplemental first-grade tutoring. *Scientific Studies of Reading, 8*(1), 53–85, https://doi .org/10.1207/s1532799xssr0801_4

Johns, J. L. (1980). First graders' concepts about print. *Reading Research Quarterly, 15*(4), 529–549.

Juel, C., & Roper-Schneider, D. (1985). The influence of basal readers on first-grade reading. *Reading Research Quarterly, 20*(2), 134–152.

Leitch, T. (2023). *Decodable readers versus lev-eled texts* [Master's thesis, Minnesota State University, Moorhead]. *Dissertations, Theses, and Projects.* 800. https://red .mnstate.edu/thesis/800

Lovett, M. W. (1987). A developmental approach to reading disability: Accuracy and speed criteria of normal and defi-cient reading skill. *Child Development, 58*(1), 234–260.

Mesmer, H. A. E. (2005). Text decodability and the first-grade reader. *Reading & Writing Quarterly, 21*(1), 61–86.

Moats, L. C. (1995). *Spelling: Development, disabilities, and instruction.* York Press.

Moats, L. C. (2000). *Speech to print.* Paul Brookes Publishing Co., Inc.

Pearson, P. D., & Gallagher, M. C. (1983). The instruction of reading comprehension. *Contemporary Educational Psychology, 8*(3), 317–344. https://doi.org/10.1016/0361-476X(83)90019-X

Pugh, A., Kearns, D. M., & Hiebert, E. H. (2023), Text types and their relation to efficacy in beginning reading interventions. *Reading Research Quarterly* https://doi.org/10.1002/rrq.513

Rasinski, T. V. (2005). *Daily word ladders.* Scholastic.

Resnick, L. B., & Beck, J. L. (1976). Designing instruction in reading: Interaction of theory and practice. In J. T. Guthrie (Ed.), *Aspects of reading acquisition* (pp. 180–204). Johns Hopkins University Press.

Rinsland, H. D. (1945). *A basic vocabulary of elementary school children.* Macmillan.

Rosenshine, B., & Stevens, R. (1984). Classroom instruction in reading. In P. D. Pearson, R. Barr, M. L. Kamil, & P. Mosenthal (Eds.), *Handbook of reading research* (pp. 745–798). Longman.

Sakiey, E., & Martin, J. (1980). *Primary level graphemic syllable lists with pronunciation variations.* Paper presented at the meeting of the College Reading Association, Baltimore, October.

Scarborough, H. S. (2001). Connecting early language and literacy to later reading (dis)abilities: Evidence, theory, and practice. In S. Neuman & D. Dickinson (Eds.), *Handbook for research in early literacy* (pp. 97–110). Guilford Press.

Schwartz, S. (2020). Decodable books: Boring, useful, or both? *Education week, 39*(26), 1–15.

Sedita, J. (2022). *The writing rope: A framework for explicit writing instruction in all subjects.* Brookes Publishing.

Shanahan, T. (2021, November 13). *RIP to advanced phonemic awareness.* Shanahan on Literacy web posting. https://www.shanahanonliteracy.com/blog/rip-to-advanced-phonemic-awareness

Treiman, R., & Baron, J. (1981). Segmental analysis ability: Development and relation to reading ability. In G. E. MacKinnon & T. G. Waller (Eds.), *Reading research: Advances in theory and practice* (Vol. 3, pp. 159–198). Academic Press.

Wong, M. (2015, May 29). Brain wave study shows how different teaching methods affect reading development. *Medical Xpress.* medicalxpress.com/news/2015-05-brain-methods-affect.html

Yoncheva, Y. N., Wise, J., & McCandliss, B. (2015). Hemispheric specialization for visual words is shaped by attention to sublexical units during initial learning. *Brain and Language, 145–146,* 23–33.

# Index

# Because...

## ALL TEACHERS ARE LEADERS

### AFRIKA AFENI MILLS

This guide explores why racial identity work is crucial, especially for White-identifying students and teachers, and guides educators to provide opportunities for antiracist learning.

### ALLISON SKERRETT, PETER SMAGORINSKY

Engage students in critical thinking, literacy activities, and inquiry using the personal and social issues of pressing importance to today's students.

### MARIA WALTHER

This resource offers a scaffolding for moving from teacher-led demonstration of read alouds to student-led discovery of literacy skills—across the bridge of shared reading.

### VERA AHIYYA

Spark courageous conversations with children about race, identity, and social justice using read alouds as an entry point.

**To order your copies, visit corwin.com/literacy**

At Corwin Literacy we have put together a collection of just-in-time, classroom-tested, practical resources from trusted experts that allow you to quickly find the information you need when you need it.

**DOUGLAS FISHER, NANCY FREY, DIANE LAPP**

Like an animated encyclopedia, this book delivers the latest evidence-based practices in 13 interactive modules that will transform your instruction and reenergize your career.

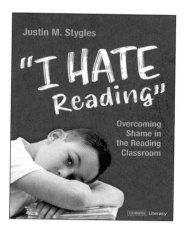

**JUSTIN M. STYGLES**

Learn how to build relationships so shame-bound readers trust enough to risk enough to grow.

**GRETCHEN BERNABEI, JAYNE HOVER**

Use these lessons and concrete text structures designed to help students write self-generated commentary in response to reading.

**CHRISTINA NOSEK, MELANIE MEEHAN, MATTHEW JOHNSON, MATTHEW R. KAY, DAVE STUART JR.**

This series offers actionable answers to your most pressing questions about teaching reading, writing, and ELA.

**A Sage Company**